Lecture Notes in Computer Science   9971

Commenced Publication in 1973
Founding and Former Series Editors:
Gerhard Goos, Juris Hartmanis, and Jan van Leeuwen

More information about this series at http://www.springer.com/series/7408

Sandrine Blazy · Marsha Chechik (Eds.)

Verified Software

Theories, Tools, and Experiments

8th International Conference, VSTTE 2016
Toronto, ON, Canada, July 17–18, 2016
Revised Selected Papers

Springer

Editors
Sandrine Blazy
IRISA, University of Rennes 1
Rennes
France

Marsha Chechik
Department of Computer Science
University of Toronto
Toronto, ON
Canada

ISSN 0302-9743   ISSN 1611-3349 (electronic)
Lecture Notes in Computer Science
ISBN 978-3-319-48868-4   ISBN 978-3-319-48869-1 (eBook)
DOI 10.1007/978-3-319-48869-1

Library of Congress Control Number: 2016956493

LNCS Sublibrary: SL2 – Programming and Software Engineering

Printed on acid-free paper

This Springer imprint is published by Springer Nature
The registered company is Springer International Publishing AG
The registered company address is: Gewerbestrasse 11, 6330 Cham, Switzerland

Preface

This volume contains the papers presented at the 8th International Conference on Verified Software: Theories, Tool and Experiments (VSTTE), which was held in Toronto, Canada, during July 17–18, 2016, co-located with the 28th International Conference on Computer-Aided Verification. The final version of the papers was prepared by the authors after the event took place, which permitted them to take feedback received at the meeting into account. VSTTE originated from the Verified Software Initiative (VSI), which is an international initiative directed at the scientific challenges of large-scale software verification. The inaugural VSTTE conference was held at ETH Zurich in October 2005, and was followed by VSTTE 2008 in Toronto, VSTTE 2010 in Edinburgh, VSTTE 2012 in Philadelphia, VSTTE 2013 in Menlo Park, VSTTE 2014 in Vienna, and VSTTE 2015 in San Francisco. The goal of the VSTTE conference is to advance the state of the art through the interaction of theory development, tool evolution, and experimental validation.

The call for papers for VSTTE 2016 solicited submissions describing large-scale verification efforts that involve collaboration, theory unification, tool integration, and formalized domain knowledge. We were especially interested in papers describing novel experiments and case studies evaluating verification techniques and technologies. We welcomed papers describing education, requirements modeling, specification languages, specification/verification, formal calculi, software design methods, automatic code generation, refinement methodologies, compositional analysis, verification tools (e.g., static analysis, dynamic analysis, model checking, theorem proving), tool integration, benchmarks, challenge problems, and integrated verification environments. We received 21 submissions. Each submission was reviewed by at least three members of the Program Committee. The committee decided to accept 12 papers for presentation at the conference. The program also included six invited talks, given by Zachary Tatlock (Washington), Mark Lawford (McMaster), Kristin Yvonne Rozier (Iowa State), Michael Tautschnig (Amazon), and Oksana Tkachuk (NASA Ames). The volume includes abstracts or full-paper versions of some of these talks.

We would like to thank the invited speakers and all submitting authors for their contribution to the program. We are very grateful to our general chair, Temesghen Kahsai, for his tremendous help with organizing this event. We also thank Azadeh Farzan (CAV PC co-chair) and Zak Kinsaid (CAV Workshops chair) for logistical support, and to Natarajan Shankar for his vision for this year's VSTTE and other events in this series. Last but definitely not least, we thank the external reviewers and the Program Committee for their reviews and their help in selecting the papers that appear in this volume. This volume was generated with the help of EasyChair.

September 2016   Marsha Chechik
                                                                                  Sandrine Blazy

Organization

Program Committee

June Andronick	NICTA and UNSW, Australia
Frédéric Besson	Inria, France
Nikolaj Bjørner	Microsoft Research, USA
Sandrine Blazy	IRISA, France
Marsha Chechik	University of Toronto, Canada
Ernie Cohen	Amazon, USA
Deepak D'Souza	Indian Institute of Science, Bangalore, India
Jean-Christophe Filliatre	CNRS, France
Vijay Ganesh	University of Waterloo, Canada
Arie Gurfinkel	Software Engineering Institute, Carnegie Mellon University, USA
William Harris	Georgia Institute of Technology, USA
Temesghen Kahsai	NASA Ames/CMU, USA
Vladimir Klebanov	Karlsruhe Institute of Technology, Germany
Rustan Leino	Microsoft Research, USA
Tiziana Margaria	Lero, Ireland
David Naumann	Stevens Institute of Technology, USA
Nadia Polikarpova	MIT CSAIL, USA
Kristin Yvonne Rozier	University of Cincinnati, USA
Natarajan Shankar	SRI International, USA
Natasha Sharygina	University of Lugano, Switzerland
Richard Trefler	University of Waterloo, Canada
Michael Whalen	University of Minnesota, USA
Naijun Zhan	Institute of Software, Chinese Academy of Sciences, China

Additional Reviewers

Alt, Leonardo	Hyvärinen, Antti
Berzish, Murphy	Kuraj, Ivan
Bormer, Thorsten	Marescotti, Matteo
Chen, Mingshuai	Tiwari, Ashish
Fedyukovich, Grigory	Zhang, Wenhui
Graham-Lengrand, Stephane	Zheng, Yunhui
Guelev, Dimitar	Zulkoski, Ed

Abstracts Short Papers

Advanced Development of Certified OS Kernels

Zhong Shao

Yale University, New Haven, USA

Abstract. Operating System (OS) kernels form the backbone of all system software. They can have a significant impact on the resilience, extensibility, and security of today's computing hosts. We present a new compositional approach [3] for building certifiably secure and reliable OS kernels. Because the very purpose of an OS kernel is to build layers of abstraction over hardware resources, we insist on uncovering and specifying these layers formally, and then verifying each kernel module at its proper abstraction level. To support reasoning about user-level programs and linking with other certified kernel extensions, we prove a strong contextual refinement property for every kernel function, which states that the implementation of each such function will behave like its specification under any kernel/user (or host/guest) context. To demonstrate the effectiveness of our new approach, we have successfully implemented and specified a practical OS kernel and verified its (contextual) functional correctness property in the Coq proof assistant. We show how to extend our base kernel with new features such as virtualization [3], interrupts and device drivers [1], and end-to-end information flow security [2], and how to quickly adapt existing verified layers to build new certified kernels for different domains.

This research is based on work supported in part by NSF grants 1065451, 1319671, and 1521523 and DARPA grants FA8750-12-2-0293 and FA8750-15-C-0082. Any opinions, findings, and conclusions contained in this document are those of the authors and do not reflect the views of these agencies.

References

1. Chen, H., Wu, X., Shao, Z., Lockerman, J., Gu, R.: Toward compositional verification of interruptible OS kernels and device drivers. In: PLDI 2016: 2016 ACM SIGPLAN Conference on Programming Language Design and Implementation, pp. 431–447(2016)
2. Costanzo, D., Shao, Z., Gu, R.: End-to-end verification of information-flow security for C and assembly programs. In: PLDI 2016: 2016 ACM SIGPLAN Conference on Programming Language Design and Implementation, pp. 648–664 (2016)
3. Gu, R., Koenig, J., Ramananandro, T., Shao, Z., Wu, X., Weng, S-C., Zhang, H., Guo. Y.: Deep specifications and certified abstraction layers. In: POPL 2015: Proceedings of the 42nd Annual ACM SIGPLAN-SIGACT Symposium on Principles of Programming languages, pp. 595–608 (2015)

Automating Software Analysis at Large Scale

Michael Tautschnig

Queen Mary University of London, London, UK
Amazon Web Services, Ashburn, USA

Abstract. Software model checking tools promise to deliver genuine traces to errors, and sometimes even proofs of their absence. As static analysers, they do not require concrete execution of programs, which may be even more beneficial when targeting new platforms. Academic research focusses on improving scalability, yet largely disregards practical technical challenges to make tools cope with real-world code.

At Amazon, both scalability requirements as well as real-world constraints apply. Our prior work analysing more than 25,000 software packages in the Debian/GNU Linux distribution containing more than 400 million lines of C code not only led to more than 700 public bug reports, but also provided a solid preparation for the challenges at Amazon.

RACE to Build Highly Concurrent and Distributed Systems

Oksana Tkachuk

NASA Ames Research Center, Moffett, USA
oksana.tkachuk@nasa.gov

Abstract. Instantiating, running, and monitoring highly concurrent and distributed systems presents many challenges. Such systems are prone to: concurrency-related issues (races, deadlocks), communication problems (dropped connections), functional issues (unhandled messages), and scalability (the size of the system grows with the number of communicating components).

This talk will present solutions to the above problems implemented in RACE: Runtime for Airspace Concept Evaluation, designed and developed at NASA Ames Research Center. RACE is a framework for instantiating and running highly concurrent and distributed systems. RACE employs actor programming model, as implemented in the Akka framework. Akka actors communicate through asynchronous messages, do not share state, and process their own messages sequentially. RACE is implemented in the Scala programming language, which improves type safety compared to other JVM languages. RACE includes many building blocks needed to create distributed systems, including actors for exporting, importing, translating, archiving, replaying, and visualizing data.

RACE is being evaluated in the context of building and running simulations for National Airspace System (NAS) at NASA. For example, RACE can be used to get flight and weather data from various FAA servers, process, and visualize it in the NASA's World Wind viewer. However, RACE is an open source, highly-configurable and extensible platform, which makes it suitable for a wide range of applications. RACE source code is available at https://github.com/NASARace/race. More information can be found on the RACE web site at http://nasarace.github.io/race.

Contents

Stupid Tool Tricks for Smart Model Based Design

Mark Lawford(⊠)

McMaster Centre for Software Certification, McMaster University,
Hamilton, ON L8S 4K1, Canada
lawford@mcmaster.ca

Abstract. Formal methods tools can be used to detect and prevent errors so researchers assume that industry will use them. We are often frustrated when we see industrial projects where tools could have been used to detect or prevent errors in the final product. Researchers often fail to realize that there is a significant gap between aa potentially useful tool and its use in a standards compliant, commercially viable, development process. In this talk I take a look at seemingly mundane industrial requirements - qualification (certification) of tools for use in standards compliant development process for general safety (IEC 61508), Automotive (ISO 26262) and Avionics (DO-178C), Model Based Design coding guidelines compliance, standards compliance documentation generation and integration with existing industry partner development processes. For each of these topics I show how "stupid tool tricks" can be used to not only increase adoption of academic methods and tools, but also lead to interesting research questions with industry relevant results.

Keywords: Simulink · Model-based design · Tool qualification · Software tools

1 Introduction

The title of this talk is based upon the former television host David Letterman's popular "Stupid Pet tricks" segment from the Late Show where people brought out their pets to perform various tricks. In introducing the segment during the November 15, 2013 show, Letterman described the segment as follows:

> Now please, the pets are not stupid. The people who taught them the tricks are not stupid. It's just that it's a colloquialism for ... "Oh! Isn't that cute!"

In the remainder of the paper I will briefly describe joint work with colleagues and students from industrial research projects that form the basis of the "Stupid Tool Tricks" I refer to in the title. In order to avoid confusion about my opinion of the excellent people I get to work with and the high quality work they produce, let me rephrase Letterman's description:

© Springer International Publishing AG 2016
S. Blazy and M. Chechik (Eds.): VSTTE 2016, LNCS 9971, pp. 1–7, 2016.
DOI: 10.1007/978-3-319-48869-1_1

Now please, the tools are not stupid. The people who programmed the tool tricks are not stupid. It's just that it's a colloquialism for ... "Oh! Isn't that useful!"

Recently embedded software development has turned to Model Based Design (MBD) with code generation from models created with tools like Matlab/Simulink. In recent talks John Knight has declared that "Coding is over!", basically saying that it doesn't matter what language you teach anymore. Java, Python, C, C# are irrelevant. What matters is models. Engineers will create models and generate the code. Or to think of it another way, "Coding is dead! Long live encoding! (of models ... in MATLAB/Simulink)". As a result managers might think that we do not need software engineers any more. While domain engineers may create the models, companies will still need the Software Engineers to help manage the models and abstractions.

A recurring theme at VSTTE is moving the focus up the levels of abstraction to a more productive layer closer to the engineering problem. For example, automotive controls engineers will provide insight into how to model and design control systems using the controls oriented models of Matlab/Simulink, but with the pace of development, diverse product lines and absolute need for dependable software and systems will require appropriate software engineering methods and concepts to be applied. From precise requirements to design for change, software engineering principles will need to be applied to the models. A problem currently facing many industries is that the majority of engineers developing the models are not taught Software Engineering fundamentals such as those pioneered by Parnas [4]. With the move to Model Based Development, coding is mostly over. Software Engineering is *definitely* not over.

It is clear that many industries need help in dealing with Model Based Development of software. So why is the industry not using researchers tools, theories and methods that are promoted at conferences and workshops like VSTTE? In the remainder we provide some possible answers to this question.

2   What Is Tool Qualification? (and Why Should I Care About It?)

In a nutshell? Tool qualification comes down to insure that the tool is fit for use in the intended development context. Researchers should care about it because it is one of the biggest hurdles to getting their tools and theories used.

Figure 1 represents at the top level what is the main hazard that is of the utmost concern for most standards regarding tool use - the tool fails to detect an error or inserts an error. A rudimentary interpretation of the *DO-330 Software Tool Qualification Considerations* supplement to the DO-178B/C standard that is applied to civilian aviation software provides the second level possible causes that can lead to this hazard. The diagram then provides some detail of the third level of what could lead to the tool not being properly installed that then results in the tool failing to detect an error or inserting an error. For the purposes of

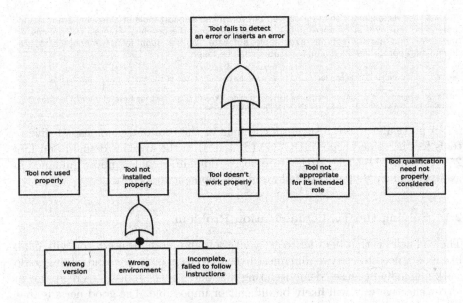

Fig. 1. Representation of tool hazard analysis implicit in DO-330

brevity we have not provided the complete third level expansion. Other standards such as IEC 61508 and ISO 26262 have similar reasoning behind their need for tool qualification before the tools are used in the development of a critical system.

The successful use of the PVS theorem prover to perform software verification of the Darlington Nuclear Reactor Shutdown Systems software has been documented in [6] and a description of how consideration of the entire development process was important to that success can be found in [7]. One of the key insights is that while the use of a formal methods tool like PVS provided increased confidence and considerable benefits, the final development process accepted by the regulator required all of the proofs done in PVS to be performed manually too in order to mitigate any potential failures of PVS and the supporting tool chain used in the design verification of Darlington. Tools are great, but they do not buy you as much as you think if they can be a single point of failure. At the time of the Darlington Redesign Project the regulator wanted to mitigate a failure of PVS with a known method, manual proof. It was a reasonable requirement at the time, but it limited the benefits of the formal methods tools.

In the intervening years since the Darlington Redesign Project was completed, standards have evolved to provide better guidance to engineers wishing to use software tools. For example, the Latest version of IEC-61508-3 now provides better guidance here:

7.4.4.5 An assessment shall be carried out for offline support tools in classes T2 and T3 to determine the level of reliance placed on the tools, and the potential failure mechanisms of the tools that may affect the executable software. Where such failure mechanisms are identified, appropriate mitigation measures shall be taken.

NOTE 1   Software HAZOP is one technique to analyse the consequences of potential software tool failures.

NOTE 2   Examples of mitigation measures include: avoiding known bugs, restricted use of the tool functionality, checking the tool output, use of diverse tools for the same purpose.

In particular, Note 2 suggests checking of the tool output or use of diverse tools for the same purpose. DO-330 (S. 4.4(e)) in the avionics domain and ISO 26262 (clause 11.4.1.1) in the automotive domain provide similar guidance in avoidance of single points of failure in development tool chains.

2.1   Solving the Tool Qualification Problem

The bad news is that in order to get your tools and methods used, you will, in all likelihood, need to use two different (diverse) tools in order to avoid having to do work manually because "demonstrating soundness of the tools" to a regulator in a cost effective way will likely be difficult or impossible. The good news is that it is not as hard as you might think to knock the tool qualification requirements down a level by doing the same thing with 2 or more tools. Intermediate Domain Specific Languages (DSLs) can be used to generate code for multiple theorem provers, SMT solvers, or model checkers, often providing more than one way to get the same result. This technique has the additional benefit that it can help avoid vendor lock-in for verification tools.

In developing tools and methods, researchers need to consider this tool qualification problem if they want industry to use their work. In developing the Tabular Expression Toolbox for Matlab Simulink [2] this was the main impetus behind having the completeness and disjointness conditions checkable by both PVS and an SMT solver. This could then be used as part of an argument to the regulator the checks for domain coverage and determinism of the specification would not need to be manual checked. This brings us to

Stupid Tool Trick #1

Do everything twice in two different ways.

3   Integrating with the Development Process and Documentation

Recent industrial research projects have given us access to a large number of industrial Matlab/Simulink models that are used for code generation. In an effort to understand those models, we began examining the explicit dataflow due to model input/output ports and implicit data flow due to (scoped) data stores and goto/from blocks in Simulink [1]. This led to the development of tools for Matlab/Simulink that help with model comprehension and refactoring for improved software qualities such as model comprehension, testability, modularity [3].

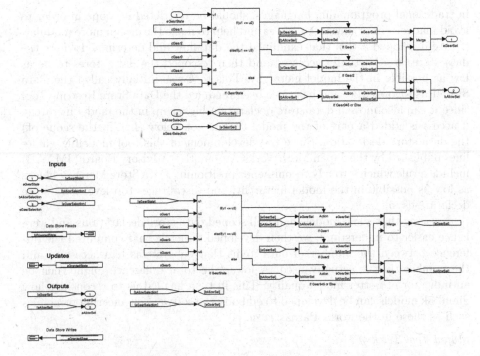

Fig. 2. Original Simulink model (top) and with "signature" (bottom)

One tool in particular, the signature tool, made all of the dataflow explicit by modifying the models to create explicit ports for all of the dataflow, explicit and implicit, on the left side of the model (see Fig. 2). One could think of this as the equivalent of a function prototype in a C header file. The industry partner did not want to modify the layout of their models because of potential code generation impacts so the tool was initially rejected, but later found use as a test harness generator when we demonstrated significant improvements in test coverage, with reduced testing effort, when the signature was used to help make dataflow explicit to commercial test case generation tools.

Stupid Tool Trick #2

Consider alternative uses of a tool. These might be more useful than your original purpose.

4 Coding Guideline Compliance and Research

During our examination of implicit dataflow in Simulink models we noted that many of the models developed by domain experts tended to have the majority of their data store declarations at the top level of the model hierarchy. This is equivalent to programming with global variables. Data stores, like variables in traditional programming languages, should be restricted in scope in order to avoid inadvertent or unwanted access and help to make the design more modular.

We developed a tool that examined the dataflow and determined where the data stores were actually accessed and then rescoped the data stores to be as low as possible in the model hierarchy. This tool was initially called the Data Store Push-Down Tool and has since been renamed the Data Store Rescope Tool since it can also move a data store declaration higher up in the model hierarchy if access is added a part of the model that is not below (i.e., in the scope of) the data store declaration. Since the development of this tool modeling guidelines published by the Japan MathWorks Automotive Advisory Board (JMAAB) include a rule which strongly recommends positioning Data Store Memory blocks as low as possible in the model hierarchy, and discourages top level data store declarations [5].

Noticing that some models had well scoped data store declarations and were hence easier to understand, we then developed a metric that computed the difference between the number of data items that subsystems had access to and the number that it actually used. A lower the total difference might then be an indicator of better model quality. This in turn has led us to reconsider how Simulink models can be developed to embody the software engineering principles such as those in the works Parnas *et al.* [4].

Stupid Tool Trick #3

If a tool is useful, ask yourself why is it useful. This might lead to interesting research ideas.

5   Conclusion

By working with our industrial partners we were motivated to discover simple "stupid" tool tricks that improved the applicability of research tools, helping to improve software engineering methods for Model Based Design and led to interesting research problems that had industrial relevance. The reader is encouraged to examine their own research tooling efforts in the context of industrial development to see if similar stupid tool tricks can lead to improved industry uptake of research results.

Acknowledgments. The author would like to acknowledge the work of all of the researchers and students in the McMaster Centre for Software Certification (McSCert). This work would not have been possible without the support of our industry partners.

References

1. Bender, M., Laurin, K., Lawford, M., Pantelic, V., Korobkine, A., Ong, J., Mackenzie, B., Bialy, M., Postma, S.: Signature required: making Simulink data flow and interfaces explicit. In: Science of Computer Programming, Part 1, vol. 113, pp. 29–50 (2015). Model Driven Development (Selected & extended papers from MODELSWARD 2014)

2. Eles, C., Lawford, M.: A tabular expression toolbox for Matlab/Simulink. In: Bobaru, M., Havelund, K., Holzmann, G.J., Joshi, R. (eds.) NFM 2011. LNCS, vol. 6617, pp. 494–499. Springer, Heidelberg (2011). doi:10.1007/978-3-642-20398-5_38

3. Pantelic, V., Postma, S., Lawford, M., Korobkine, A., Mackenzie, B., Ong, J., Bender, M.: A toolset for Simulink: improving software engineering practices in development with Simulink. In: 3rd International Conference on Model-Driven Engineering and Software Development (MODELSWARD), pp. 50–61. IEEE, February 2015

4. Parnas, D.L.: Software design. In: Hoffman, D.M., Weiss, D.M. (eds.) Software Fundamentals: Collected Papers by David L. Parnas, pp. 137–142. Addison-Wesley (2011)

5. The MathWorks. Japan MathWorks Automotive Advisory Board (JMAAB): Control Algorithm Modeling Guidelines Using MATLAB, Simulink, and Stateflow, Version 4.01, March 2015. www.mathworks.com/solutions/automotive/standards/maab.html. Accessed Feb 2016

6. Wassyng, A., Lawford, M.: Lessons learned from a successful implementation of formal methods in an industrial project. In: Araki, K., Gnesi, S., Mandrioli, D. (eds.) FME 2003. LNCS, vol. 2805, pp. 133–153. Springer, Heidelberg (2003). doi:10.1007/978-3-540-45236-2_9

7. Wassyng, A., Lawford, M.: Software tools for safety-critical software development. Int. J. Softw. Tools Technol. Transf. (STTT) 8(4–5), 337–354 (2006)

Specification: The Biggest Bottleneck in Formal Methods and Autonomy

Kristin Yvonne Rozier[✉]

Iowa State University, Ames, IA, USA
kyrozier@iastate.edu

Abstract. Advancement of AI-enhanced control in autonomous systems stands on the shoulders of formal methods, which make possible the rigorous safety analysis autonomous systems require. An aircraft cannot operate autonomously unless it has design-time reasoning to ensure correct operation of the autopilot and runtime reasoning to ensure system health management, or the ability to detect and respond to off-nominal situations. Formal methods are highly dependent on the specifications over which they reason; there is no escaping the "garbage in, garbage out" reality. Specification is difficult, unglamorous, and arguably the biggest bottleneck facing verification and validation of aerospace, and other, autonomous systems.

This VSTTE invited talk and paper examines the outlook for the practice of formal specification, and highlights the on-going challenges of specification, from design-time to runtime system health management. We exemplify these challenges for specifications in Linear Temporal Logic (LTL) though the focus is not limited to that specification language. We pose challenge questions for specification that will shape both the future of formal methods, and our ability to more automatically verify and validate autonomous systems of greater variety and scale. We call for further research into LTL Genesis.

1 Introduction

Formal methods have now scaled to the point of enabling rigorous safety analysis of full-scale, real-life systems, and none too soon, as such capabilities are required for developing the autonomous systems of the future. This is because autonomy requires systems to be reactive and concurrent [36], operating in real-time and in an open environment. Formal methods have been recognized as a critical, and often expected, design-time component for autonomous and life-critical systems, such as aircraft and spacecraft. FAA standards including DO-178-B [46] DO-178-C [48], and DO-254 [47] incorporate formal specification, validation, and verification. For one example, NASA's Lunar Atmosphere Dust Environment Explorer (LADEE) mission was a resounding success. LADEE used model-based development starting with specification of the requirements; refinement of these specifications via analysis against system models; automatic generation of software

Thanks to NASA's Autonomy Operating System (AOS) Project and NSF CAREER Award CNS-1552934 for supporting this work.

S. Blazy and M. Chechik (Eds.): VSTTE 2016, LNCS 9971, pp. 8–26, 2016.
DOI: 10.1007/978-3-319-48869-1_2

from verified models; and a variety of verification techniques including formal methods, static analysis, formal inspection, and code coverage applied early and often throughout the system design lifecycle [22]. We have influenced the design of an automated air traffic control system via model checking analysis [55–57]. We have also used formal methods to help NASA assess the Functional Allocation question: in the early design stage, when there are thousands of options for allocating essential system functions, how can we formally analyze the space of many possible deigns to determine which are the most safe [16,37]?

In addition to design-time analysis, autonomous systems in particular critically depend on formal runtime reasoning, for runtime verification that unanticipated events do not violate their specifications, and to ensure system health management, or the ability to detect and respond to off-nominal situations that could not be verified at design time. NASA's Copilot language and compiler generates runtime monitors for distributed, hard real-time systems, including pitot tube subsystems and MAVLink (Micro Air Vehicle Link); these verified systems have flown in the Edge 540 aircraft [38]. Our own Realizable, Responsive, Unobtrusive Unit (R2U2) [18,41,49–51] utilizes formal specifications to generate runtime observers integrated with Bayesian reasoning to provide runtime system health management for Unmanned Aerial Systems (UAS) such as NASA's Swift and DragonEye UAS.

All of these formal methods, from design time to runtime, require formal specifications. A *formal methodology*, as defined by Manna and Pnueli in their seminal text on reactive and concurrent systems [36], consists of a specification language and a repertoire of proof methods by which the correctness of a proposed system, relative to the specification, can be formally verified. By this definition, a formal methodology provides two components central to autonomy: (1) the ability to make early, precise decisions, e.g. between multiple possible designs, about major system functions; (2) the ability to remove ambiguities from the system's expected behavior, from design-time behavioral descriptions to runtime behavioral monitors. For clarity through the remainder of the paper, we will distinguish the formal specification, or the description of the behavioral requirement that most often appears in the form of a formula (which we will call φ), from the system model that instead specifies how the system works (M). The verification question is then the question of whether (or not) these two things match; both are necessary inputs to a proof method.

Figure 1 shows one such example of a formal methodology. In this case, the formal specification is given as a set of Linear Temporal Logic (LTL) formulas; the system model is a description of system operation in a formal semantics we call M. A set of *validation specifications* is written simultaneously with the system model M; specification debugging increases confidence in the correctness of this set, and model checking against M serves to validate M. A set of *verification specifications*, which first pass specification debugging, are model-checked against M to verify that the early design satisfies its requirements. These specifications can then be carried throughout the system development process, e.g., used for test-case generation or simulation, and all the way to runtime verification of the final

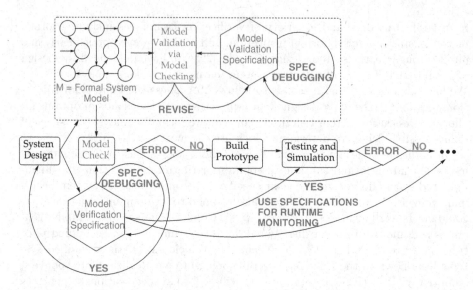

Fig. 1. A goal system design process (based on LTL model checking) where specifications are first debugged, then utilized for early system design validation, used in design verification, and carried through the system development process to runtime [56].

system implementation. This goal system design process, using Linear Temporal Logic (LTL) as the specification language and model checking as a proof method appeared in [56], where it was used successfully during the design time of a coordination protocol for an automated air traffic control system. Formal methods, including model checking, are highly dependent on the specifications over which they reason; not only are specifications required for analysis, but there is no escaping the "garbage in, garbage out" reality.

Figure 2 zooms in on the inputs to this process. The bottom line for formal methods is that the inputs to formal analysis are the biggest challenge. In [56], over 100 person-hours were required to create the inputs, which dwarfs the less than 10 hours of total runtime required to complete model checking analysis. In the follow-on study of a more complex version of the system with a large space of possible designs, over 1000 person-hours were required to generate the inputs that resulted in the 1620 model-checking instances (model-specification-set pairs) whose automated verification then averaged approximately 5 minutes per pair [16]. (Validation and

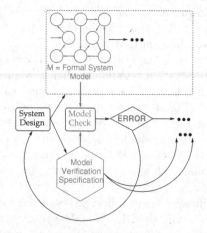

Fig. 2. Bottom line: **inputs** to formal analysis are the **biggest** challenge.

further analysis, e.g., using fault trees, took several hours per pair but still far less time than specification; total time for input generation of all automated analysis including validation, verification, and fault tree analysis totaled over 2000 person-hours [17].)

When it comes to formal system modeling, there is some hope in the form of *synthesis*. Recall that in model checking, we check whether $M \models \varphi$, e.g., does the system model satisfy its specification? *LTL Synthesis* is predicated on the fact that designing M is hard and expensive; re-designing M when $M \nvDash \varphi$ is also hard and expensive [52]. Starting from LTL formula φ synthesis designs M such that $M \models \varphi$, which simplifies verification, eliminates the problem of re-designing M, and, for algorithmic derivations, eliminates the burden of design entirely [52]. While synthesis as a technique does not yet enjoy the same level of tool support or scalability as verification techniques such as model checking, the field is well on the way to being able to greatly improve the bottleneck of the system model as input to the formal verification process. However, synthesis shares with model checking the requirement of a formal specification: the input formula φ. So, while synthesis is a worthwhile goal with the potential to eventually solve half of the inputs bottleneck, what we really need is **LTL Genesis**!

The remainder of this paper is organized as follows. Section 2 asks where we will get specifications from, while Sect. 3 examines how we will examine their quality. Section 4 asks how do we best use specifications, including introducing new ideas for specification patterns. Section 5 asks how should we organize specifications to enable these uses and examines the merits of strategies for accomplishing this. Section 6 concludes and gives an outlook for a future of well-specified autonomous systems.

2   Specification Origins

Specifications are required for all applications of formal methods, yet extracting specifications for real-life safety critical systems often proves to be a huge bottleneck or even an insurmountable hurdle to the application of formal methods in practice. This is the state for safety-critical systems today and as these systems grow more complex, more pervasive, and more powerful in the future, there is not a clear path even for maintaining the bleak status quo [3, 4].

At NASA in particular, extracting specifications needed for any formal analysis is a huge challenge [4,5,16,37,55,56]. Some critical systems are designed without ever having what this community would consider to be a formal set of requirements. Some design processes don't formally define requirements until the testing phase, far too late to use them for design or design-time analysis, or other key periods in the system development life-cycle where formal methods are applicable. Even for critical systems where specifications are defined early in the system development life-cycle, they often mix many different objectives, mixing many different levels of detail and describing things like how the system is defined, how the system should behave, legal-speak on why the system satisfies rules, and more – sometimes all in the same sentence! As safety-critical systems

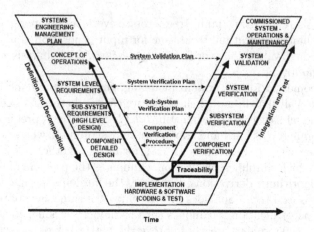

Fig. 3. An illustration of the outdated V Systems Engineering Model from [27].

become increasingly complex and the budgetary and other constraints tighten, where can we look in the future to hope to extract the specifications we need for formal analysis?

Even outside of the formal methods community, systems engineering processes are adapting to the fact that the old standard V model of systems engineering (shown in Fig. 3) is outdated and does not capture the steps necessary for the design of today's complex, possibly autonomous, systems [27]. This realization comes from the need to define, and debug, requirements first, modify them throughout the system design lifecycle with each new phase of development, and perform verification at every stage of system design, not just at the end. AFRL has documented the unreasonable cost associated with the V model [21,25,26]. While an estimated 70 % of faults are introduced in the early design phases on the left of the V, all but 3.5 % are found in the later stages of system integration and testing (on the right of the V), where they are increasingly costly to fix. The estimated nominal cost for fault removal is 300-1000x for faults found in the final "Acceptance" or "Operation" phase versus the early design phases [25,26]. The emerging realization that we need to define precise specifications that can be automatically analyzed from the earliest stages of system design has given rise to many different methods for deriving specifications, e.g., in LTL.

Though none of these have emerged as industrial standards, several specification extraction strategies remain under study as active areas for further research.

Human Authorship: Train system designers to write formal specifications first and have them author their own LTL, or pair designers with formal methods team to write specifications.

- Advantages include potential for accuracy and improved design-level reasoning; disadvantages include high learning curves and lack of automation.

Natural Language Processing (NLP): Extract formal specifications from English Operational Concepts, encoding them in LTL for automated analysis. Notable tools include ARSENAL [20] and VARED [5]. NLP is highly input-dependent: it is difficult to handle unstated assumptions, implied/arbitrary functions, slang, mixed abstraction levels, and other inconsistencies. There is a question whether structured English is advantageous over natural language.

– Advantages include the high level of automation and low learning curve required; disadvantages include that is it hard to measure correctness, completeness, and closeness to the designers intentions.

Specification Mining: Extract behaviors from existing systems. Can combine with test-case generation to explore system behavior [13].

– Advantages include automation; disadvantages include the need for a code specification as input.

Static Analysis: Map all paths of a program.

– Advantages include automation; disadvantages include that it is hard to differentiate normal usage from exceptions; also some essential specifications, like function postconditions, can be difficult to extract [54].

Learning/Dynamic Invariants: Analyze actual executions; observe use-cases.

– Advantages include that checking observed variable values against a library of fixed invariant patterns can automatically generate valuable specifications. Disadvantages include that specifications might refer to internal details or be irrelevant; observations are too limited and are heavily dependent on the set of observed executions [54].

Specification Wizard: Semi-automated exploration of system facets, guided by human input.

– Disadvantages include that similar ideas similar were tried previously and failed to catch on widely; advantages include that today's complex autonomous systems demand a more standardized system design process that may provide a better platform to build upon. With the widespread use of COTS components that could be added to an online database and the recent advances in specification extraction from LTL patterns and component parameters, there is a new opportunity for a wizard.

Notably, Zeller asked: can we have specifications for free [54]? Can we combine specification mining, test-case generation, static analysis, and dynamic invariants to extract specifications automatically? The specifications would be automatically mined from code, so that specification validation would equate to software defect detection. While this is a promising strategy for software runtime verification, fundamentally this process still requires code as an input. (In a sense, the code is now the specification; so we have not solved the specification genesis problem.) This strategy does not solve the specification problem for early design time, where code has not yet been written, or for cyber-physical systems that combine code with other components. The problem of requiring input code can be mitigated by using specifications extracted from the last version of a system for creating new designs. However, there remain challenges with specialization of the previous code, levels of abstraction, and relevance to the new system. Other challenges include scalability, efficiency, and expressiveness of extracting specifications for free. Still, Zeller's idea is highly intriguing!

3   Specification Quality

How can we know when we're "done" extracting specifications or have some idea of how well we've done? As critical systems continue to grow in complexity, how will we measure the completeness, coverage, or general quality of a specification or a set of specifications? We asked these questions in a panel at NFM2014 [4], yet in large degree they remain open areas for future research.

The emerging area of *specification debugging* [24,30], also called *sanity checking*, has made notable progress in automated analysis of specification quality, chiefly in four areas. We briefly discuss each, with respect to LTL specifications specifically.

Satisfiability. For LTL, satisfiability checking reduces to model checking against a *universal model*, or a model that accepts all possible valuations of the variables at all states [43]. Formally, if we let φ be a specification over the set $Prop$ of propositions then a system model M is *universal* if it contains all possible traces over $Prop$: $L_\omega(M) = (2^{Prop})^\omega$. A model checker negates φ and checks for emptiness of the combined model for $\neg\varphi$ and M. Then φ is satisfiable by any counterexample returned by model checking against M: $M \not\models \neg\varphi$ iff φ is satisfiable. If there is no counterexample, then φ is not satisfiable. In [43,44] we advocate for a sanity check of checking φ, $\neg\varphi$, and the conjunction of all specifications describing the same system for satisfiability before using them in system design and verification.

Stated another way, let φ describe a "good" requirement that the system must uphold. Then $\neg\varphi$ describes a "bad" behavior that the system must never display. The model checker takes as input φ, then negates it, combines it with the input model, and checks if the resulting combined automaton is empty, outputting a counterexample if not. Model checking φ against a universal model will show whether or not $\neg\varphi$ is satisfiable. A counterexample returned by the model checker in this case is a satisfying assignment to the formula. If $\neg\varphi$ is not satisfiable, then the model checking search of its combination with the universal model will not return a counterexample because no satisfying assignment exists. The reverse situation is also a problem. If φ is not satisfiable, then $\neg\varphi$ is a tautology. So, in a normal model checking run, we would model check $\neg\varphi$ against a system model, the model checker would negate φ to get $\neg\varphi$, and return a counterexample, which we are expecting to indicate that there is something wrong with the system model. However, since $\neg\phi$ is a tautology, no matter how we change the system model, we will always get some counterexample.

In [44], we conducted an extensive experimental evaluation of LTL satisfiability checking via model checking, concluding that using symbolic model checking for this task is vastly superior to explicit-state model checking in terms of both correctness and performance. (Symbolic tools always returned the correct SAT/UNSAT result; this was not true for any of the explicit tools available at the time, perhaps due to the difficulty of implementing their algorithms.) In [45] we designed a portfolio approach consisting of 30 new encodings for LTL satisfiability via symbolic model checking that performed up to exponentially faster than was previously possible. In [33, 34], the explicit approach was improved, circumventing explicit-state model checking and solving the LTL satisfiability problem directly using techniques borrowed from propositional SAT solving. Today, the (freely available) tools PANDA [45] and Aalta [34], represent the state of the art in symbolic (via the nuXmv model checker) and explicit LTL satisfiability checking, respectively.

Vacuity. Sanity checks in industry include many types of simple, often ad hoc, tests such as checking for duplicate conflicting variable assignments or enabling conditions that are never enabled [32]. *Vacuity checking* can help detect errors in specifications by checking whether a subformula of a specification does not affect the satisfaction of the specification in the system model [31]. A common example is checking for implications like $\Box(p \rightarrow \Diamond q)$ where p can never be enabled. *Inherent vacuity checking* is a set of sanity checks that can be applied to a set of temporal properties, even before a model of the system has been developed, but many possible errors cannot be detected by inherent vacuity checking [15]. This capability is available in some proprietary industrial tools [7], and VaqUoT provides a front-end checker for nuXmv, but it only handles the subset of LTL that can be encoded as CTL [19]. VARED [5] integrates an updated algorithm for vacuity checking [23] into an end-to-end toolchain for requirements analysis.

Realizability. Realizability checking provides another, stronger sanity check for a set of temporal properties in LTL by testing whether there is an open system that satisfies all the properties in the set [40], but such a test is very computationally expensive: 2ExpTime-Complete. However, notable progress on the problem is underway. RATSY [8] checks realizability of the class of Generalized Reactivity(1) (GR(1) [39]) specifications via an interactive game with the specifier. Acacia+ [9] also solves LTL realizability problems encoded as safety games. Another approach to realizability checking [35] builds upon RATSY using a template-based specification mining approach to identify situations of an under-constrained environment or an over-constrained system. This approach is complimented by work on detecting unrealizability due to overly-strong system guarantees or overly restricted signals [29]. An algorithm for finding minimal cores of unrealizability of GR(1) specifications is implemented in nuXmv [12]. All of these address the tricky space of checking specifications that are satisfiable but unrealizable because there is no implementation that can produce outputs that satisfy the specification given all possible inputs that can be generated by the environment. Realizability is inherently tied to synthesis: the LTL synthesis problem seeks to produce a model such that φ is realizable.

Coverage. Coverage is a complicated sanity check because significant research has been contributed just to a set of definitions; measuring coverage for each such definition is a separate research question. Informally, coverage asks whether a set of LTL specifications considers all of the behaviors of the system; behaviors may be defined in various ways with respect to states or paths through an execution graph/automaton required for a specification to pass, the set of system variables, model checking analysis, checks for incomplete or redundant sub-models, etc. In a sense, coverage is complimentary to vacuity checking in that it asks whether there are parts of the system that are not relevant for the verification process to proceed. Coverage checking for LTL can be integrated into model checking [11]. Algorithms for automatically checking LTL coverage and completeness have been successfully used in industry for sanity checking, e.g., the requirements for an airplane control system [6].

4 Specification Usage

How should formal specifications (both those we are given and those we must extract) fit into the design life-cycle for different kinds of critical systems? How can we indoctrinate formal specifications into diverse teams of system designers without hitting barriers to adoption such as huge costs in terms of time and learning curves? What should our roadmap look like for a future full of well-specified (formally analyzable) critical systems?

Figure 4 shows the updated waterfall model for system design that has supplanted the former V model of Fig. 3. The need to define specifications early and carry them through all stages of system design has given rise to many different specification use strategies. All present interesting challenges for future research.

Property-Based Design: system design centers around specifications

– Challenge: defining a foundation of specifications early

Synthesis: generate M such that $M \models \varphi$

– Challenge: how can we synthesize a *cyber-physical* system M?

Specification-Based Testing: use specifications in test-case generation

– Challenge: how can we carry specifications through different levels of abstraction?

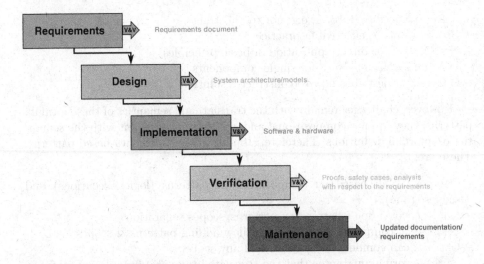

Fig. 4. The current waterfall model for system engineering incorporates the specifications (aka system requirements) throughout all phases of system design.

From Design- to Run-Time: carry specifications through the design cycle

– Challenge: how do we define a specification design lifecycle?

Maintenance: using specifications in system up-keep

– Challenge: what do best practices for maintenance of specifications look like?

4.1 Specification Patterns

Since the early days of temporal logic specifications, we have been concerned with dividing them into classes like Safety/Liveness/Guarantee/Obligation, Fairness/Justice/Compassion, or Safety/Response/Reactivity [36]. While these classes have proven useful in specializing algorithms for automated analysis, they are still too coarse and tied to syntax for practical use; there is a need for more functional and hierarchical specification.

Dwyer et al. [14] answered with definitions of specification formula patterns that have many practically useful properties. Formula patterns are organized in a hierarchy based on semantics and leverage experience with design and coding patterns to enable system designers to more efficiently generate specifications. This *specification pattern system* captures recurring solutions and allows specifiers to generalize across domain-specific problems. It encourages re-use by better enabling practitioners to identify the same patterns across systems and makes transparent the means by which requirements are satisfied.

Formula patterns each have a *name*, *intent*, *logic* (language), *scope* (time interval), and *relationship* to other patterns. Each pattern is characterized by the following traits:

- Solves a Specific Problem, e.g. not too abstract
- Proven Concept effective in practice
- Not Obvious or direct application of basic principles
- Describes Relationships, not single components
- Generative, describes how to construct a solution

However, challenges remain with the translational semantics of these formula patterns: they are not compositional and are often inconsistent with the semantics of informal definitions. Therefore, [10] introduced automata-based patterns. These are:

- Compositional: based on compositions of patterns (logic executions) and scopes (time)
- Homogeneous: don't flatten key patterns/scopes separation
- Extensible: compositional semantics allow adding patterns & scopes
- Generic: can combine any pattern and any scope
- Faithful: formal guarantee that the translated temporal formula is faithful to the intended natural semantics

While automata-based patterns correct some inconsistencies in the previous formula patterns, they present other challenges: it is often more natural for practitioners to think of specifications in terms of time lines (temporal logic) than automata, and automata patterns pose a challenge for many of the sanity checks from Sect. 3. Design-time formula patterns and automata patterns still do not answer the pressing question: what about *runtime specifications* for *autonomous systems*?

4.2   R2U2: Runtime Specification Patterns in the Field

Work on specification patterns focuses mostly on *design time*, which is impactful for applications such as model checking. But in today's complex, cyber-physical, and/or autonomous systems, exhaustive verification is not achievable for all subsystems; in practice, more specifications are used for applications such as runtime verification. Formula patterns are not compositional, which can be a challenge for runtime evaluation. Automata patterns are not decomposable and are more complex to sanity check, e.g., because it is easier to check satisfiability and realizability on a formula than an automaton. Yet it is vital to sanity check runtime specifications.

Therefore, we ask the question: what about *functional patterns*?[1] Are there different patterns for specification functions, e.g., between design time and runtime? In our experience with runtime verification in the field [18,41,49–51], we have observed the following five functional patterns.

---

[1] Note that the term *functional patterns* has been used in a different context: describing Requirements Specification Language (RSL) patterns for system state changes in response to external stimuli [2].

Ranges. Sensors have well-defined operating ranges: both ranges of the values they can report and ranges of operation. For example, a laser altimeter has a ceiling; above this altitude its readings should not be trusted. For each sensor, we check its operating ranges and the bounds on correct values it can return.

Rates. For each sensor stream on a system, there are rate constraints. We must check that value changes fall within realistic bounds, both for the sensitivity and tolerances of the individual sensor and for the physics of the system. For example, if a sensor indicates that an aircraft is falling faster than gravity, clearly there is something wrong with that sensor!

Relationships. There are predictable relationships between multiple sensors; we need to compare temporal outputs from related or redundant sensors for correctness. For example, the readings from all three altimeters should be consistent, modulo sensor noise. Pitching up and increasing power to the engines should result in a rise in altitude shortly afterward.

Control Sequences. A sequence of events will predictably happen following a command to take off, land, or carry out a procedure like a waypoint visit, with check-able milestones along the way A command to take off requires an ordered set of actions such as turning on the engines, taxiing, increasing altitude above ground level, and reaching a prescribed altitude. A command to land involves a series of actions in a precise order, such as an initial decrease in altitude, deploying of landing gear, and approaching the appropriate runway.

Consistency Checks. Do all components have the same view of system state/environment? We consider both intra- and inter-component properties. For example, the rate of noise from a sensor should not suddenly increase. The flight computer and autopilot should always agree on which waypoint the UAS is currently visiting.

In industrial systems, LTL is often not the exclusive specification language. While languages and constructs for specification vary widely and are often tailored

---

R2U2 specification format:

1. **TL Observers**: Efficient temporal reasoning
   (a) Asynchronous: output $\langle t, \{0,1\} \rangle$
   (b) Synchronous: output $\langle t, \{0,1,?\} \rangle$
   - Logics: MTL, pt-MTL, Mission-time LTL
   - Variables: Booleans (from system bus), sensor filter outputs
2. **Bayes Nets**: Efficient decision making
   - Variables: outputs of TL observers, sensor filters, Booleans
   - Output: most-likely status + probability

Fig. 5. R2U2 system health management framework in a nutshell [41,50].

to specific applications, one general trend is the propensity for expanding upon LTL or combining it with other specification constructs. An example of this is the specification format we use for R2U2, the Realizable, Responsive, Unobtrusive Unit for runtime system health management. Figure 5 summarizes R2U2 specifications, which combine two encodings for each linear-time temporal logic formula, which may be in one of several variants of LTL, with efficient (non-dynamic) Bayes Nets to provide diagnostic decision-making capabilities. Specifications analyzed via R2U2 are exclusively checked during runtime and do not follow previously defined patterns for formulas or automata because those describe design-time specifications consisting exclusively of temporal logic formulas.

We need to expand specification patterns to runtime! How do we expand patterns to reason about specifications in the field?

Health Nodes / Failure Modes	
H_FG	**Magnetometer sensor**
H_FC_RxUR	Receiver underrun
H_FC_RxOVR	Receiver overrun
H_FG_TxOVR	**Transmitter overrun in sensor**
H_FG_TxErr	Transmitter error in in sensor

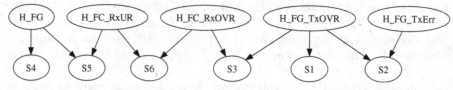

Fig. 6. The possible failures a Fluxgate Magnetometer can suffer can be diagnosed by a Bayes Net with a health node corresponding to each type of failure. These nodes take as input the valuations from six temporal logic runtime observers; many failures require inputs from multiple temporal observers in order to make an accurate diagnosis [18].

As an example, Fig. 6 displays a pictorial representation of a set of specifications for determining if a fault has occurred in the fluxgate magnetometer during runtime. From the manual, we know that there are five possible faults that can occur. We can write six temporal logic specifications that we encode as runtime observers outputting statuses S1, ..., S6. The outputs from these runtime observers are inputs to five Bayesian health nodes, one for determining whether it is probabilistically likely that each possible fault has occurred. A health node may hierarchically depend on the output from more than one runtime sensor node and the runtime observers may supply temporal information to multiple health nodes.

Cyber-physical, autonomous systems often utilize hierarchical, multi-formalism specifications; see, e.g., [53]. In R2U2, we combine specifications in a way that is hierarchically structured, compositional, and cross-language. *How do we organize R2U2 specifications?*

5   Specification Organization

How should we organize specifications? How do we store specifications in an accessible way that allows for automated analysis including verification? How do we best enable re-use from design time to runtime to the design of future systems? How do we pair English and formal specifications in an understandable way? How do we preserve the hierarchical structure, compositionality, and relationships between specifications in our practical, organizational structure? Can we do all of this in a performable way?

Scenario definition languages such as the Aviation Scenario Definition Language (ASDL) [28] establish structured specification standards over domain-specific vocabulary for verification, execution, simulation, sharing, comparing, and re-using scenario specifications. This approach provides transparency to system designers via model-to-text translation, and graphical modeling environments. ASDL is an Eclipse modeling framework suited to defining scenario models for simulation, but we still need an efficient way to store and codify specifications. Most significantly, there is the question of M vs φ: how do we distinguish functions of the system model from design- and runtime specifications so that we can analyze specifications automatically and use them throughout the system lifecycle?

One can turn to an *all-in-one tool suite such as Matlab/Simulink*, but since these tools were not designed for specification organization, this solution tends to be kludgy and not scalable. Considering the often long life of specifications, which follow a system throughout its entire lifecycle, the lack of backwards-compatibility in successive tool versions presents a significant negative.

SQL databases are routinely used for longterm, scalable information storage. However, the relationships between specifications are inherently non-tabular; fitting them into this schema requires flattening the database, and accessing them requires extensive JOINs, making this solution non-performable.

None of these strategies solve the organization problem. We have hit an era of *Big Data of Specifications*. If we follow recommended practices for system design, then specifications are everywhere! So, how do we organize specifications for each subsystem, subcomponent, and level of abstraction? How do we mine specifications for data, patterns, statistical analysis, and coverage? How do we search specifications? How do we sort specifications? How do we integrate specification languages for different purposes? How do we make specifications available for reuse?

5.1   A Property Graph Database Approach to Specification Organization with Neo4j

We can represent R2U2 specifications using a *property graph*.

Definition 1. [42] *A property graph* $G = (V, E, \lambda, \mu)$ *is a directed, edge-labeled, attributed multi-graph where* V *is a set of nodes,* E *is a multiset of directed edges,* $\lambda : E \to \Sigma$ *is an edge labeling function assigning a label from the alphabet* Σ *to* *each edge, and* $\mu : (V \cup E) \times K \to S$ *is a property assignment function over the sets* K *of property keys and* S *of property values.*

Organizing big data requires a database that can store and enable efficient access to large specification sets, so we use a *property graph database*. Neo4j[2] is a publicly available, performable, NoSQL graph database implemented in Java and Scala that efficiently implements the property graph model to allow, e.g., constant-time traversals for relationships in the graph. A property graph database stores Nodes (graph data records), and Relationships (directional connect nodes), with Properties (named data values of type string, number, Boolean, or array), on both Nodes and Relationships.

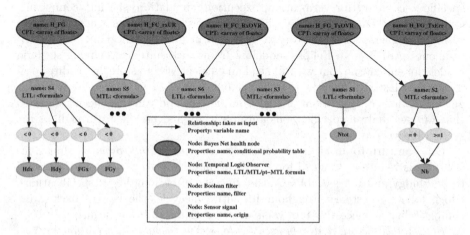

Fig. 7. A property graph database storage scheme for the Fluxgate Magnetometer failure specifications of Fig. 6 with additional details from the case study in [18].

Figure 7 re-draws Fig. 6 with the Neo4j database schema we are currently investigating for R2U2 specifications. We have four types of Nodes: Bayes Net health nodes that contain conditional probability tables, Temporal Logic Observer nodes that store logic formulas, Boolean filter nodes that filter direct sensor signals, and Sensor signal nodes that designate which system signals we are reasoning about. All relationships pictured are of type "takes as input" and are labeled with the name of the variable whose value is set by the given input. Note that nodes can mix properties, so we can define our Temporal Logic Observer nodes to have one type of formula, either LTL, MTL, or pt-MTL.

6   Conclusions and Outlook

Going forward, as a community, we need to continuously re-assess our answer to the question "Where are we now?" with regards to specifications. For the foreseeable future, specifications remain arguably the biggest bottleneck in formal

---

[2] https://neo4j.com.

methods and autonomy. While there are several promising research thrusts in specification debugging, updated system design processes that encourage specification extraction, and specification patterns, we still do not have a clear path forward, particularly in the context of cyber-physical, autonomous systems. The questions posed by this paper of where we will get specifications from, how should we measure their quality, how should we best use them, and how should we organize them, continue to drive future research directions.

In future work, we plan to devise formal definitions of the functional specification patterns introduced here. There are many experimental evaluations in the pipeline, including use of functional specification patterns and technical analysis and performance evaluation of a new Neo4j specification organization scheme for R2U2 specifications. We also plan to advance capabilities for specification debugging, particularly satisfiability checking, and methods for efficiently reasoning about specifications in new logics now appearing in industrial settings, such as MTL [1].

Acknowledgments. Thanks to the VSTTE chairs Sandrine Blazy, Marsha Chechik, and Temesghen Kahsai for inviting this paper, which is the expansion of an invited talk delivered July 18, 2016. Thanks to Julia Badger for instigating the framing of the specification bottleneck as a series of questions for our NFM2014 panel. Thanks to André Platzer for encouraging me to update and expand on these challenges; a shorter, preliminary version of this talk appeared at the NSF Workshop on "Cyber-Physical System (CPS) Verification & Validation Industrial Challenges & Foundations (I&F): CPS and AI Safety" in May, 2016. (http://www.ls.cs.cmu.edu/CPSVVIF-2016/index.html.) Thanks to Arie Gurfinkel, Eric Rozier, and Johann Schumann for technical discussions on earlier drafts of this paper. Information on our recent work can be found at: http://laboratory.temporallogic.org.

References

1. Alur, R., Henzinger, T.A.: Real-time logics: complexity and expressiveness. In: LICS, pp. 390–401. IEEE (1990)
2. Backes, J.D., Whalen, M.W., Gacek, A., Komp, J.: On implementing real-time specification patterns using observers. In: Rayadurgam, S., Tkachuk, O. (eds.) NFM 2016. LNCS, vol. 9690, pp. 19–33. Springer, Heidelberg (2016). doi:10.1007/978-3-319-40648-0_2
3. Badger, J., Rozier, K.Y. (eds.): NFM 2014. LNCS, vol. 8430. Springer, Heidelberg (2014)
4. Badger, J., Rozier, K.Y.: Panel: future directions of specifications for formal methods. In: Badger, J., Rozier, K.Y. (eds.) NFM. LNCS, vol. 8430, pp. XX-XXI. Springer, May 2014
5. Badger, J., Throop, D., Claunch, C.: Vared: verification and analysis of requirements and early designs. In: Requirements Engineering, pp. 325–326. IEEE (2014)
6. Barnat, J., Bauch, P., Beneš, N., Brim, L., Beran, J., Kratochvíla, T.: Analysing sanity of requirements for avionics systems. Formal Aspects Comput. **28**(1), 45–63 (2016)
7. Beer, I., Ben-David, S., Eisner, C., Rodeh, Y.: Efficient detection of vacuity in ACTL formulas. Formal Methods Syst. Des. **18**(2), 141–162 (2001)

8. Bloem, R., Cimatti, A., Greimel, K., Hofferek, G., Könighofer, R., Roveri, M., Schuppan, V., Seeber, R.: RATSY – a new requirements analysis tool with synthesis. In: Touili, T., Cook, B., Jackson, P. (eds.) CAV 2010. LNCS, vol. 6174, pp. 425–429. Springer, Heidelberg (2010). doi:10.1007/978-3-642-14295-6_37

9. Bohy, A., Bruyère, V., Filiot, E., Jin, N., Raskin, J.-F.: Acacia+, a tool for LTL synthesis. In: Madhusudan, P., Seshia, S.A. (eds.) CAV 2012. LNCS, vol. 7358, pp. 652–657. Springer, Heidelberg (2012). doi:10.1007/978-3-642-31424-7_45

10. Castillos, K.C., Dadeau, F., Julliand, J., Kanso, B., Taha, S.: A compositional automata-based semantics for property patterns. In: Johnsen, E.B., Petre, L. (eds.) IFM 2013. LNCS, vol. 7940, pp. 316–330. Springer, Heidelberg (2013). doi:10.1007/978-3-642-38613-8_22

11. Chockler, H., Kupferman, O., Kurshan, R.P., Vardi, M.Y.: A practical approach to coverage in model checking. In: Berry, G., Comon, H., Finkel, A. (eds.) CAV 2001. LNCS, vol. 2102, pp. 66–78. Springer, Heidelberg (2001). doi:10.1007/3-540-44585-4_7

12. Cimatti, A., Roveri, M., Schuppan, V., Tchaltsev, A.: Diagnostic information for realizability. In: Logozzo, F., Peled, D.A., Zuck, L.D. (eds.) VMCAI 2008. LNCS, vol. 4905, pp. 52–67. Springer, Heidelberg (2008). doi:10.1007/978-3-540-78163-9_9

13. Dallmeier, V., Knopp, N., Mallon, C., Hack, S., Zeller, A.: Generating test cases for specification mining. In: ISSTA, pp. 85–96. ACM (2010)

14. Dwyer, M.B., Avrunin, G.S., Corbett, J.C.: Property specification patterns for finite-state verification. In: FMSP, pp. 7–15. ACM (1998)

15. Fisman, D., Kupferman, O., Sheinvald-Faragy, S., Vardi, M.Y.: A framework for inherent vacuity. In: Chockler, H., Hu, A.J. (eds.) HVC 2008. LNCS, vol. 5394, pp. 7–22. Springer, Heidelberg (2009). doi:10.1007/978-3-642-01702-5_7

16. Gario, M., Cimatti, A., Mattarei, C., Tonetta, S., Rozier, K.Y.: Model checking at scale: automated air traffic control design space exploration. In: Chaudhuri, S., Farzan, A. (eds.) CAV 2016. LNCS, vol. 9780, pp. 3–22. Springer, Heidelberg (2016). doi:10.1007/978-3-319-41540-6_1

17. Gario, M., Cimatti, A., Mattarei, C., Tonetta, S., Rozier, K.Y.: Model checking at scale: automated air traffic control design space exploration. Presentation: https://es-static.fbk.eu/projects/nasa-aac/download/CAV2016_presentation.pdf#21 (2016-07-22)

18. Geist, J., Rozier, K.Y., Schumann, J.: Runtime observer pairs and Bayesian Network reasoners on-board FPGAs: flight-certifiable system health management for embedded systems. In: Bonakdarpour, B., Smolka, S.A. (eds.) RV 2014. LNCS, vol. 8734, pp. 215–230. Springer, Heidelberg (2014). doi:10.1007/978-3-319-11164-3_18

19. Gheorghiu, M., Gurfinkel, A., Chechik, M.: VaqUoT: a tool for vacuity detection. In: Posters & Research Tools Track, FM 2006 (2006)

20. Ghosh, S., Shankar, N., Lincoln, P., Elenius, D., Li, W., Steiener, W.: Automatic Requirements Specification Extraction from Natural Language (ARSENAL). Technical report, DTIC Document (2014)

21. Gross, K.H., Fifarek, A.W., Hoffman, J.A.: Incremental formal methods based design approach demonstrated on a coupled tanks control system. In: HASE, pp. 181–188. IEEE (2016)

22. Gundy-Burlet, K.: Validation and verification of LADEE models and software. In: 51st AIAA Aerospace Sciences Meeting Including the New Horizons Forum and Aerospace Exposition (2013)

23. Gurfinkel, A., Chechik, M.: Robust vacuity for branching temporal logic. ACM Trans. Comput. Logic (TOCL) 13(1), 1 (2012)

24. Heitmeyer, C., Jeffords, R., Labaw, B.: Automated consistency checking of requirements specifications. ACM Trans. Softw. Eng. Methodol. **5**(3), 231–261 (1996)
25. Hoffman, J.A.: Utilizing assume guarantee contracts to construct verifiable simulink model blocks. S5 (2015). http://mys5.org/Proceedings/2015/Day_1/2015-S5-Day1_1255_Hoffman.pdf
26. Hoffman, J.A.: V&V of Autonomy: UxV Challenge Problem (UCP). S5 (2016). http://mys5.org/Proceedings/2016/Day_3/2016-S5-Day3_0805_Hoffman.pdf
27. Jackson, C.: Face it: The engineering V is outdated (2014). https://www.linkedin.com/pulse/20140721140340-5687591-face-it-the-engineering-v-is-outdated
28. Jafer, S., Chhaya, B., Durak, U., Gerlach, T.: Formal scenario definition language for aviation: aircraft landing case study. In: AIAA MST (2016)
29. Könighofer, R., Hofferek, G., Bloem, R.: Debugging unrealizable specifications with model-based diagnosis. In: Barner, S., Harris, I., Kroening, D., Raz, O. (eds.) HVC 2010. LNCS, vol. 6504, pp. 29–45. Springer, Heidelberg (2011). doi:10.1007/978-3-642-19583-9_8
30. Kupferman, O.: Sanity checks in formal verification. In: Baier, C., Hermanns, H. (eds.) CONCUR 2006. LNCS, vol. 4137, pp. 37–51. Springer, Heidelberg (2006). doi:10.1007/11817949_3
31. Kupferman, O., Vardi, M.: Vacuity detection in temporal model checking. J. Softw. Tools Technol. Transf. (STTT) **4**(2), 224–233 (2003)
32. Kurshan, R.: FormalCheck User's Manual. Cadence Design, Inc. (1998)
33. Li, J., Zhang, L., Pu, G., Vardi, M.Y., He, J.: LTL satisfiability checking revisited. In: TIME, pp. 91–98. IEEE (2013)
34. Li, J., Zhu, S., Pu, G., Vardi, M.Y.: SAT-based explicit LTL reasoning. In: Piterman, N. (ed.) HVC 2015. LNCS, vol. 9434, pp. 209–224. Springer, Heidelberg (2015). doi:10.1007/978-3-319-26287-1_13
35. Li, W., Dworkin, L., Seshia, S.A.: Mining assumptions for synthesis. In: MEMOCODE, pp. 43–50. IEEE (2011)
36. Manna, Z., Pnueli, A.: The Temporal Logic of Reactive and Concurrent Systems: Specification. Springer Science & Business Media, New York (2012)
37. Mattarei, C., Cimatti, A., Gario, M., Tonetta, S., Rozier, K.Y.: Comparing different functional allocations in automated air traffic control design. In: FMCAD. IEEE/ACM (2015)
38. Pike, L., Wegmann, N., Niller, S., Goodloe, A.: Copilot: monitoring embedded systems. Innov. Syst. Softw. Eng. **9**(4), 235–255 (2013)
39. Piterman, N., Pnueli, A., Sa'ar, Y.: Synthesis of reactive(1) designs. In: Emerson, E.A., Namjoshi, K.S. (eds.) VMCAI 2006. LNCS, vol. 3855, pp. 364–380. Springer, Heidelberg (2005). doi:10.1007/11609773_24
40. Pnueli, A., Rosner, R.: On the synthesis of a reactive module. In: POPL, pp. 179–190 (1989)
41. Reinbacher, T., Rozier, K.Y., Schumann, J.: Temporal-logic based runtime observer pairs for system health management of real-time systems. In: Ábrahám, E., Havelund, K. (eds.) TACAS 2014. LNCS, vol. 8413, pp. 357–372. Springer, Heidelberg (2014). doi:10.1007/978-3-642-54862-8_24
42. Rodriguez, M.A., Neubauer, P.: The graph traversal pattern. arXiv preprint arXiv:1004.1001 (2010)
43. Rozier, K.Y., Vardi, M.Y.: LTL satisfiability checking. In: Bošnački, D., Edelkamp, S. (eds.) SPIN 2007. LNCS, vol. 4595, pp. 149–167. Springer, Heidelberg (2007). doi:10.1007/978-3-540-73370-6_11
44. Rozier, K., Vardi, M.: LTL satisfiability checking. Int. J. Softw. Tools Technol. Transf. (STTT) **12**(2), 123–137 (2010)

45. Rozier, K.Y., Vardi, M.Y.: A multi-encoding approach for LTL symbolic satisfiability checking. In: Butler, M., Schulte, W. (eds.) FM 2011. LNCS, vol. 6664, pp. 417–431. Springer, Heidelberg (2011). doi:10.1007/978-3-642-21437-0_31

46. RTCA: DO-178B: Software Considerations in Airborne Systems and Equipment Certification (1992). http://www.rtca.org

47. RTCA: DO-254: Design assurance guidance for airborne electronic hardware, April 2000

48. RTCA: DO-178C/ED-12C: Software considerations in airborne systems and equipment certification (2012). http://www.rtca.org

49. Schumann, J., Moosbrugger, P., Rozier, K.Y.: R2U2: monitoring and diagnosis of security threats for unmanned aerial systems. In: Bartocci, E., Majumdar, R. (eds.) RV 2015. LNCS, vol. 9333, pp. 233–249. Springer, Heidelberg (2015). doi:10.1007/978-3-319-23820-3_15

50. Schumann, J., Moosbrugger, P., Rozier, K.Y.: Runtime analysis with R2U2: a tool exhibition report. In: Falcone, Y., Sánchez, C. (eds.) RV 2016. LNCS, vol. 10012, pp. 504–509. Springer, Heidelberg (2016). doi:10.1007/978-3-319-46982-9_35

51. Schumann, J., Rozier, K.Y., Reinbacher, T., Mengshoel, O.J., Mbaya, T., Ippolito, C.: Towards real-time, on-board, hardware-supported sensor and software health management for Unmanned Aerial Systems. IJPHM **6**(1), 1–27 (2015)

52. Vardi, M.Y.: From verification to synthesis. In: Shankar, N., Woodcock, J. (eds.) VSTTE 2008. LNCS, vol. 5295, pp. 2–2. Springer, Heidelberg (2008). doi:10.1007/978-3-540-87873-5_2

53. Whalen, M.W., Rayadurgam, S., Ghassabani, E., Murugesan, A., Sokolsky, O., Heimdahl, M.P., Lee, I.: Hierarchical multi-formalism proofs of cyber-physical systems. In: MEMOCODE, pp. 90–95. IEEE (2015)

54. Zeller, A.: Specifications for free. In: Bobaru, M., Havelund, K., Holzmann, G.J., Joshi, R. (eds.) NFM 2011. LNCS, vol. 6617, pp. 2–12. Springer, Heidelberg (2011). doi:10.1007/978-3-642-20398-5_2

55. Zhao, Y., Rozier, K.Y.: Formal specification and verification of a coordination protocol for an automated air traffic control system. In: AVoCS. Electronic Communications of the EASST, vol. 53 (2012)

56. Zhao, Y., Rozier, K.Y.: Formal specification and verification of a coordination protocol for an automated air traffic control system. SCP J. **96**(3), 337–353 (2014)

57. Zhao, Y., Rozier, K.Y.: Probabilistic model checking for comparative analysis of automated air traffic control systems. In: ICCAD, pp. 690–695. IEEE/ACM (2014)

Order Reduction for Multi-core Interruptible Operating Systems

Jonas Oberhauser[(⊠)]

Saarland University, Saarbrücken, Germany
`jonas@wjpserver.cs.uni-saarland.de`

Abstract. If one wishes to verify a program in high-level semantics, one has to deal with the fact that the compiled code is run on an architecture very different from the one the program was verified in. For example, one unit of execution in the high-level language can be compiled to a block consisting of multiple units of execution in the target architecture. Order reduction is then the property that this block can indeed be considered to be executed in a single step, i.e., that the behavior of the program remains unchanged. Order reduction is dependent on certain properties of the compiled code, e.g., that there is at most one linearization point in each block. Conditions under which order reduction is possible have been studied in depth for user programs, but not for operating systems. Interruptible operating systems are particularly exciting because inter processor interrupts can interrupt an operating system thread while it has not yet completed a block of execution. In this paper, we show an order reduction theorem for interruptible operating systems. Unlike most order reduction theorems, all properties of the compiled code necessary for order reduction can be verified on the order-reduced program. Thus, one can verify high-level programs completely in the high-level semantics, including the property that the behavior of the program is unchanged when executed on a low-level machine. Furthermore, we make no assumptions about user code. We use a simple ownership annotation which can be deduced mechanically and thus be used to find data races in programs. The order reduction theorem presented here is strong in the sense that multiple memory accesses can be part of a single block, as long as at most one of them is racing.

1 Introduction

Programming in high-level languages is more efficient than programming in assembly. The same is true for verifying the programs. However, programs are not executed in their high-level semantics; they are executed in a low-level refinement of their high-level semantics. This refinement adds additional computations, like weak memory behaviors [SFC92, Obe16b] or more chaotic interleavings. That these chaotic interleavings can always be sorted and cleaned up in such a way that the behavior of the program is unchanged and corresponds to a behavior of the original, high-level program is known as order reduction. This is obviously

© Springer International Publishing AG 2016
S. Blazy and M. Chechik (Eds.): VSTTE 2016, LNCS 9971, pp. 27–45, 2016.
DOI: 10.1007/978-3-319-48869-1_3

not always the case, an example being the well known parallel increment

$$i\text{++} \parallel i\text{++},$$

which in an order-reduced computation must increment twice, but once refined becomes

$$t = i.load(); \ i.store(t+1) \parallel t = i.load(); \ i.store(t+1),$$

which might increment only once.

It is trivial to assume properties of all computations, e.g., left- or right-commutativity of steps, to show that all computations correspond to an order-reduced computation [Lip75]. The disadvantage of this is that the properties can not be verified on the high-level program, requiring a compilation and expensive and tedious analysis of the compiled code in the refined semantics of the target machine. Instead, one can assume (possibly stronger) properties only on the order-reduced computations, and show that these properties are strong enough to be transferred to arbitrary interleavings [SC06, Bau14]. In this setting, order reduction can be made dependent only on properties of the high-level program, and thus tools like VCC [CDH+09] can be used to pervasively verify programs. One typical way to achieve this is with dynamic ownership of addresses, where each unit of execution may access at most one of the variables which are shared between multiple threads (in the above program, i is accessed twice by both threads in a single unit of execution).

The situation becomes more dire when one wants to verify interruptible operating systems, where additional interleavings are not only created between cores, but also inside of a core, namely when external interrupts can occur in the middle of a compiled statement of the operating system. In this case, one has to reorder steps of the interrupted thread with the interrupt handler on the same core, which is using the same processor registers. This utterly breaks commutativity (and thus all classical techniques such as partial order reduction); in fact, since the steps of the interrupted thread are disabled while the interrupt handler is running, those steps have to be reordered across the complete handler, which can consist of multiple blocks of execution. We have found a set of conditions, which, if satisfied in all order-reduced computations, are sufficient for order-reduction in such a setting.

It is easy to come up with such rules in a high-level view:

Linearizability. At most one access to a shared variable (or register) per block
Transparency. The interrupt handlers restore the configuration of the interrupted thread when they return control to them
Independence. Interrupt handlers do not use the register content of interrupted threads and therefore are independent of the precise configuration in which the interrupt occurred

Sadly, the high-level picture here turns out to be quite useless, because formalizations of these rules tend to be *wrong*[1]. As the saying goes, the devil is in

---

[1] As an example, the conditions in Pentchev's PhD thesis [Pen16] can not be satisfied by any multi-core program.

the details. In this paper, we lay out several of the key challenges and give a more in-depth solution to these challenges. For lack of space and for the sake of readability, we defer the mathematical formalisms to the PhD thesis of the author [Obe16a], and focus on the key insights, using more readable pseudo-formalism where appropriate.

As a machine model we consider sequentially consistent[2] multi-core processors with operating system support and inter processor interrupts, triggered by memory-mapped programmable interrupt controllers. Our model supports interlocked memory operations such as fetch-and-add. It does not support memory management units that are active while kernel code is running. We also do not assume single-cycle fetch-and-execute, but our theorem can be easily used to prove that single-cycle fetch-and-execute is simulated by the machine in the absence of *concurrent* code modification[3].

We add to this model an ownership discipline (Sect. 7) and explain how it can be used to mimic ownership states known from the literature, one of which is slightly too weak to be used in order reduction. We also quickly hint at how ownership can be mechanically deduced from execution histories and thus used to detect (low-level) data races (Sect. 9.1). The central new idea is to keep track of registers and memory cells that contain data of interrupted threads, in particular the register and interrupted thread that the data is taken from (Sect. 8). On an exception return, that data has to be restored *independently* of its value, and it may not be used for the computation of certain key functions, such as the set of accessed addresses, whether a given point is a linearization point or an access to a shared variable, etc.

We briefly discuss the theorem in Sect. 4, and its proof in Sect. 9.

2   Architecture

In this section we introduce some notation, the model of the machine, and its semantics.

We consider a processor with a set of cores P. Each core $i \in P$ has its own processor registers and interrupt controller. The set of addresses $\mathcal{A}$ is partitioned into

Processor Registers. $A_{PR,i}$ such as an instruction buffer, program counters, general purpose registers, special purpose registers, and the translation lookaside buffer. We assume for each processor a binary register that distinguishes between interruptible mode (where hardware interrupt requests will trigger a jump to the interrupt service routine, *jisr*) and non-interruptible mode (where

---

[2] For some architectures, such as TSO, it is possible to apply a reduction theorem that first reduces to a sequentially consistent machine, and then apply the theorem in this paper, to obtain a sequentially consistent C level.

[3] Well-synchronized code modification in general is necessary (e.g., for page fault handlers). It is also difficult, and not supported by any other order reduction theorem to the best of our knowledge.

hardware interrupt requests are stored in the APIC until a) cleared or b) the processor returns to interruptible mode)

$$Int_i \in A_{PR,i}.$$

Interrupt Controller Registers. $A_{IC,i}$ such as interrupt request registers (IRR)[4], which act as an inbox for interrupts, and the interrupt command register (ICR), which is used to send interrupts to other processors.
Main Memory. A_M which is a sequentially consistent memory component.

Our non-deterministic machine has an operational semantics that uses an oracle input to distinguish between processor steps and interrupt controller steps, and allows further distinctions (e.g., in case a translation look-aside buffer has multiple matching translations, it can non-deterministically choose one of the translations). A configuration c is a map from addresses to their values, and a computation is a finite labeled sequence of configurations, where the labels are oracle inputs and each configuration is obtained by applying the operational transition function δ on previous configuration and the previous label (which is one of the oracle inputs)

$$c^{t+1} = \delta(c^t, x^t).$$

In our pseudo-formalization, we will often drop t and $t+1$ and use f and f' for f^t or f^{t+1}. When an oracle input x signals a step of processor i, we write that the *current processor* is processor i

$$cp = i.$$

3   Programming Language

For the examples in this paper, we use C-like pseudo code with mostly obvious semantics, but with the following caveats.

Variables t and u are always thread-local, i.e., each thread has a local copy, while other variables are always global (but not necessarily shared). The double pipe || means parallel execution. An *interleaving point* is denoted by a semicolon ; and separates atomic units of execution in both the high-level and low-level language, while a comma , separates atomic units of execution only in the low-level language. In other words, a thread may only be scheduled out at a ; in the high-level machine, but also at a , in the low-level semantics. Therefore, the parallel increment of above could be written as

```
t = i.load(), i.store(t+1); || t = i.load(), i.store(t+1);,
```

making clear the atomicity of the load and increment in the high-level language and the lack of this atomicity in the low-level language.

---

[4] Real architectures also have in-service registers, which prevent low-priority interrupts from overtaking high-priority interrupts. Those registers have no effect on the proof.

We use operations `x.load()` and `x.store(v)` to mark accesses to shared variables, and a special construct for interlocked compare-exchange

$$y = x.cxg(cmp \rightarrow data),$$

which changes x to `data` if it equals to `cmp` and leaves it unchanged otherwise, loading into y the old value of x in either case.

Additionally, threads can access their own interruptability via `IC.int`.

To define the interrupt handler, we use a triangle ▷ (read as "on interrupt"). We leave context store and restore usually implicit, as in the following example

$$x.store(1); \ t = x.load(); \ \triangleright \ x = 0;.$$

We write down computations as a table, read from top to bottom, where each column corresponds to a thread and each row to one step in the computation, as in

```
t = i.load(),
                    t = i.load(),
                    i.store(t+1);
i.store(t+1);
```

In this form, a high-level computation stays in the same column until a ; is reached, and thus the above must be a computation in the low-level machine.

4   Correctness Statement

Our theorem says that if all order-reduced computations of a program have an ownership annotation that is safe, each low-level computation can be rearranged into an order-reduced computation, changing only the value of dirty data and data owned by threads that were not at an interleaving point. Let D be the set of threads which are not at an interleaving point at the end of computation (sequence) s. Our result can then be written formally as

Theorem 1

$$(\forall s.Reduced(s) \rightarrow \exists o.safe(s, o)) \rightarrow \forall s.\exists r \equiv_{D(s)} s.Reduced(r).$$

The equivalence relation $\equiv_D$ does not preserve dirty data and locally writable data of threads in D. The ownership annotation o is a sequence of ownership states, where the ownership of a thread may only change at a linearization point of that thread. Due to the existential quantification, one does not have to actually decide the ownership change at the linearization point; threads can "look into the future", i.e., how the computation will go on, to decide which ownership to acquire. This turns out to be extremely useful for mechanically deducing the existence of an ownership annotation (cf. Sect. 9.1), and is the main reason we keep ownership implicit in our programming language. For more information about ownership, see Sect. 7.

This theorem begs the question which types of properties are being reduced. One answer is that given a global invariant I and thread local invariants $I_{i,n}$, one can obtain that in the low-level computation the global invariant always holds and the thread local invariants hold while the thread is at an interleaving point if, assuming the global invariant and the local invariant of the current thread at the beginning of a block, one can always assert the global invariant and the local invariant of the current thread at the end of that block. Here, the global invariant is a predicate over (a) the set of shared addresses, (b) the dirtiness of these addresses, and (c) the value of the clean addresses, and the thread local invariant is a predicate over (a) the set of addresses owned by that thread and not write-owned by another thread, (b) the dirtiness of these addresses, and (c) the value of the clean addresses.

It makes sense to add an additional safety criterion to ownership safety, which is that there may be no ownership conflict, i.e., a read-owned or write-owned address which is write-owned by another thread. It is easy to show that this criterion is equivalent to the original criterion. The advantage of this restriction is that the precondition of the local invariant — that the address not be write-owned by another thread — becomes trivially satisfied, thus removing the need to consider ownership of other threads for the local invariant.

5   Interrupt Levels and Threads

Whenever a thread is interrupted, a thread is created for the interrupt handler. The interrupted thread is scheduled out and the interrupting thread is scheduled in. This creates a stack of threads, where only the top thread is currently executing on the core, and all lower threads are sleeping. The *interrupt level* is the depth of this stack, and an interrupt level of zero corresponds to the user. We do not allow thread migration, and an interrupt handler has to return to the next lower interrupted thread. Therefore we can uniquely identify a thread by its associated core i and its interrupt level n as the tuple i, n, and *operating system threads* have an interrupt level highter than zero

$$OST = \{\, i, n \mid n > 0 \,\}.$$

The top-level thread is the thread with the highest interrupt level

$$top(i) = i, il(i).$$

Each step has a *current thread*, which normally is either the top-level thread of the processor making the step, or the interrupt controller making the step. The only exemption to this rule are *jisr* steps[5], during which we already count

---

[5] In the scope of this theorem, a *jisr* step in operating system mode only includes hardware interrupts. Software interrupts in operating system mode, e.g., when using a system call, do not increase the interrupt level or create a new thread and are most certainly not guaranteed to occur at an interleaving point, although they may technically cause a jump to the interrupt service routine.

the top-level thread as interrupted, and thus the current thread is the thread one level above the top-level thread on the current processor

$$jisr \rightarrow ct = top(cp) + 1.$$

When a thread returns, it has to restore the configuration (i.e., processor registers) of the next lower thread. However, this is not actually possible on all architectures. Certain special purpose registers are usually used by the hardware to restore the others during exception return (*eret*), e.g., an exception program counter register that restores the program counter. These registers themselves can not be restored. We therefore distinguish between retrievable and irretrievable registers

$$A_{R,i} \uplus A_{I,i} = A_{PR,i}.$$

On jisr, we put the current value of these registers on top of a (processor-local) stack that we call *register stack*

$$jisr \rightarrow rs'(ct - 1) = c\big|_{A_{R,cp}}.$$

One may now wish to define transparency as "on eret, all retrievable registers are restored", but this is incorrect. To show why this is the case, consider a program where only one of the interleaving points is in interruptible mode. If we would use a condition like the above, it would be safe (but not correct) to always restore the configuration at that interleaving point.

```
IC.int = 1; x++, IC.int = 0;  ▷ restore before x++;
```

Note that the only order-reduced computation in which the interrupt handler occurs is the following one:

```
IC.int = 1;
▷ restore before x++;
x++,
IC.int = 0;
```

In this computation, restoring before x++ is what we might call "accidentally" correct. The following low-level computation, in which x is incremented twice, makes the problem apparent

```
IC.int = 1;
x++,
▷ restore before x++;
x++,
IC.int = 0;
```

We will need to introduce additional technology (in Sect. 8) before we can give an acceptable, complete solution.

6 Shared Steps

In order to count the number of accesses to shared variables in our theorem, we require that programmers mark those accesses. This is not an additional burden on the programmer, as languages such as[6] C and C++ (atomic accesses), D (`shared`), Java (`volatile`), etc., already have keywords or operators for this, and provide little (Java) or no (C, C++) guarantees on the behavior of a program where the markings are incomplete[7]. The decision has to be made before reading from memory, even in case of an interlocked operation with a conditional write where only the write step accesses a shared variable.

In addition to memory accesses marked by the programmer, we consider as shared all jisr steps and all exception return steps

$$sh \equiv jisr \vee eret \vee marked.$$

These shared steps are the linearization points in our theorem. Already in our theorem for finite computations, we require that after a thread has reached a linearization point, it can always reach a linearization point in a finite number of steps, i.e., when we have committed to an action, we can also complete it. Consider the following problematic program

```
x.store(1), while(1);  ||  t = x.cxg(1 → 2);
```

with the following problematic computation

$$\left. \begin{array}{l} \texttt{x.store(1),} \\ \\ \texttt{t = x.cxg(1 → 2);} \end{array} \right\|$$

This computation can not be order-reduced; neither instruction can be dropped or moved, because that would change the value of x, but we can also not insert steps to reach an interleaving point for the thread on the left hand side. A notable coincidence is that at least in the C and C++ languages, side effect-free, non-terminating loops already have undefined behavior (cf. [Boe]); whereas the rationale there is to allow for certain compiler optimizations, here it has more fundamental reasons.

7 Ownership Annotation

Rather than having a fixed classification of variables as shared or local (e.g., Java), the programmer can decide at each memory access whether the accessed variables are shared or not; in other words, it is possible to think of the access as being shared or local, rather than the variable. The access has to be shared in case it is racing, i.e., there is a *concurrent* access to the same object, and at

---

[6] Languages which do not have such a feature usually disallow shared state altogether, e.g., Erlang or Go.

[7] Indubitably for weak memory and optimizations, but also for order reduction.

least one of them is attempting to modify the object. A naive way to formalize this simply looks at steps t and $t+1$ (cf. [Obe16b]). This does not work for an order reduction theorem, as the following example shows.

$$t = 0, \ x = t, \ t = 1; \ \| \ u = x;$$

Recall that we only check our conditions in order reduced schedules, i.e., one of the following two.

$$\begin{array}{l} t = 0, \\ x = t, \\ t = 1; \end{array} \Big\| \begin{array}{l} \\ \\ u = x; \end{array}$$

Or, when the thread on the right hand side makes the first step,

$$\begin{array}{l} \\ \\ t = 0, \\ x = t, \\ t = 1; \end{array} \Big\| \begin{array}{l} u = x; \\ \\ \end{array}$$

The obvious data race does not manifest in either of these two computations, and the naive formalization is not sound. Instead, we use dynamic ownership to distinguish between shared and local accesses. We have for each thread read-owned and write-owned addresses. Intuitively, a thread can locally (i.e., non-shared) access what it owns, and can only access what nobody else owns. The only exception to this rule are read-owned addresses, which can be read by other threads.

We define the set of all ownership sets by

$$\mathcal{O} = \{ \, (r, w) \mid r, w \subseteq A_M \, \}.$$

We keep track of these addresses in a function

$$o(i, n) \in \mathcal{O}.$$

Users do not have ownership, and so we hardcode

$$o(i, 0) = (\emptyset, \emptyset).$$

Ownership may only change during a shared step, and only of the current thread

$$sh \wedge i, n = ct \vee o'(i, n) = o(i, n).$$

It is now clear why the above program is unsafe: both threads would need to own x at some point, but due to the lack of shared steps, the thread that makes the first access to x can not give away the ownership before the second thread accesses x, causing an ownership violation.

However, this ownership does not identify all accesses to shared variables, because some processor registers are shared between the interrupt handler and the interrupted thread. One important example is the interruptible mode register, which is obviously used during the jisr step — which belongs to the interrupt handler — to determine that the interrupt occurred in the first place. We therefore consider a subset of *local processor registers*

$$A_{LPR,i} \subseteq A_{PR,i}.$$

The interruptible mode register is not local

$$Int_i \notin A_{LPR,i}.$$

Let *read* and *written* be the set of addresses read and written in the step. A step is *ownership-safe* if all of the following four conditions are met:

– A local step only reads read-owned data and local and retrievable processor registers:

$$\neg sh \to read \subseteq \mathcal{O}(ct).r \cup A_{LPR,i} \cup A_{R,i}.$$

– A local step only writes to write-owned data and local processor registers:

$$\neg sh \to written \subseteq c.\mathcal{O}(ct(c,x)).w \cup A_{LPR,i}.$$

– Write-owned data is read only by the owner:

$$read \cap \mathcal{O}(i,n).w \neq \emptyset \to ct = i,n.$$

– Owned data is written to only by the owner:

$$written \cap (\mathcal{O}(i,n).w \cup \mathcal{O}(i,n).r) \neq \emptyset \to ct = i,n.$$

7.1 Mimicking Address-Based Ownership

In the literature [Bau14, Pen16, CL98] ownership is usually defined as address-based, i.e., by assigning to each address a state. We describe quickly how typical states can be simulated in our model.

Read-Only: A read-only address is one that can not be written to and may thus be accessed (or fetched) locally. In our model this is the case for addresses which are read-owned by all threads that wish to access it. Note that this change is necessary to obtain dynamic read-only addresses, which is useful, e.g., for readers-writer locks or swapping in code pages of the kernel; in our model, an address ceases to be read-only only when all threads agree that it is writable and relinquish read-ownership. For address-based ownership, one thread may change the ownership of an address without the permission of other threads, which is not sound with respect to order reduction. Consider the following readers-writer lock x which protects y, but due to the illusion of atomicity it seems sound to read from y one more time after releasing x.

```
x.store(IDLE), ‖t = x.cxg(IDLE → LOCKED),
  t = y;        ‖if (t = IDLE)
               ‖   y = 1;
```

In an order reduced computation, y will always be executed before the assignment to it, but this is clearly not true in the low-level machine, so the program is not order-reducible. If y is read-only at the beginning, the second thread can change y to locally owned if it can acquire the lock, and the program would be safe (but incorrect)[8].

Another work-around is permission-based read-only, where each thread that wants to access the address needs a permission; only when all permissions have been released can the ownership state be changed. This is similar to fractional permissions or permissions counting in separation logic (e.g., [HLMS13]), or to VCC's claims.

Shared: A shared address can be accessed by any thread, but only by using shared accesses. All addresses in our model are shared unless they are owned.

Owned-Shared: An owned-shared address can be locally read and shared written to by one thread and shared read by other threads. This is the same as having the address read-owned by that thread and not owned by any other thread.

Locally Owned: A locally owned address can be locally accessed by a single thread. This is the same as obtaining both read- and write-ownership of that address.

7.2   Ownership Transfer on Interrupt

Note that an interrupt handler knows that the interrupted thread is not running. It is therefore tempting to allow the interrupt handler to acquire the ownership of the interrupted thread. This is false, as the following example shows.

$$t = x, \ u = x; \quad \triangleright \quad x = 1;$$

In any order-reduced computation, the values of t and u will always be equal, but this is clearly not the case if an interrupt is received in the middle of the block. If we would allow the handler to "steal" the ownership of x, the program would be safe (but incorrect), so this is not allowed.

The opposite, that the interrupt handler can not make use of the fact that the interrupted thread is not running except for using the same registers, is also not true. While the handler can not "steal" ownership, it can use the absence of races by acquiring the ownership of variables which would be otherwise shared, as in the following correct example:

$$t = x.\text{load}(); \ u = x.\text{load}(); \quad \triangleright \quad x = 1, \ x = 2;$$

Both in the high-level and the low-level machine, neither t nor u will ever equal 1.

---

[8] At the time of writing, an implementation bug in VCC allows this program to be verified.

8   Dirty Data

Recall now the independence condition, i.e., that the handler should not use data belonging to the interrupted thread. In order to restore the thread configuration on eret - and in order to store it after jisr - the interrupt handler most certainly will use the register content of the registers of the interrupted thread. Therefore, one can not claim that the registers are not used, only that in some sense the general shape of the execution is independent of the concrete values. This is somewhat hard to make precise.

Note that shared registers only change at linearization points. Therefore the exact position of the interrupt in the block does not matter (only whether it occurs before or after the linearization point), so using these is actually absolutely fine. For local registers, we introduce a concept we call *dirtiness*, i.e., at the beginning of a jisr we flag all local registers of the interrupted thread as dirty. As dirty data is being used, e.g., while storing the context, it makes dirty everything that it comes into contact with. Note that a step may have outputs that depend on the dirty data (such as the target memory cell) and other outputs which do not (such as the program counter, which is simply incremented independently of the data), and one has to distinguish between these. We do this by defining *computational inputs of a function*, which are all sets of addresses that stabilize the output of that function, i.e., all configurations that agree on a computational input of f also agree on the value of f

$$cin[f](c) = \left\{\, A \subseteq \mathcal{A} \mid \forall c'.c\big|_A = c'\big|_A \rightarrow f(c) = f(c') \,\right\}.$$

Independence. The following functions (and a few others) always have a clean computational input

$$jisr, eret, read, written, sh$$

However, simply having a flag for each address is not enough. Firstly, recall our issue with the transparency condition, where simply restoring the register contents does not work. We keep track not only of the set of registers that contain dirty data, but also the source register and source thread to which the data belongs, with a function

$$d(a) \in \{\, \bot, \square \,\} \cup \bigcup_i (A_{R,i} \cap A_{LPR,i}) \times \{\, i \,\} \times \mathbb{N},$$

with the following meaning

$d(a) = \bot$: The address is clean.

$d(a) = \square$: The address is dirty, but will not need to be restored (e.g., because it didn't come from a retrievable register or the thread has been restored). We call this state generically dirty.

$d(a) = (b, i, n)$: The address contains the data of retrievable register $b \in A_{R,i}$ of interrupted thread i, n.

Secondly, note that if we would simply make all local registers dirty on a jisr, we would destroy the previous information about what was dirty and what was not. Therefore we use a *dirt stack* analogous to the register stack

$$jisr \rightarrow ds'(ct - 1) = d\big|_{A_{R,i}}.$$

We use a somewhat technical construction to keep track of dirtiness. In a nutshell, we first figure out the current dirtiness d^* (with a special case for jisr), then we figure out what the new dirtiness would be if the step was a normal step with *dout*, and finally we look at whether we have an eret, in which case we restore the dirtiness using ds, or we have a normal step, in which case we use *dout*. More formally, we choose

$$d^*(a) = \begin{cases} (a, ct - 1) & jisr \wedge a \in A_{LPR,cp} \cap A_{R,cp} \\ d(a) & \text{o.w.,} \end{cases}$$

and then choose *dout* as follows.

If the new value of a can be computed using only clean data, it should become clean

$$dout(a) = \bot.$$

If the new value of a depends on exactly one dirty address $din(a)$, we propagate that dirtiness

$$dout(a) = d^*(din(a)).$$

If a can not be computed using clean data, but also there is no clear origin, we default to generically dirty

$$dout(a) = \Box.$$

A retrievable register is correctly restored during eret if it is local and we restore it to itself, or if it is shared and we restore the previous dirtiness

$$correctr(a) \equiv eret \wedge a \in A_{R,cp} \wedge dout(a) = \begin{cases} ds(ct - 1, a) & a \in A_{R,cp} \setminus A_{LPR,cp} \\ (a, ct - 1) & \text{o.w.} \end{cases}$$

An address becomes stale if it is not correctly restored, but would contain dirty data of the restored thread (e.g., the process control block typically becomes stale during eret)

$$stale(a) \equiv eret \wedge dout(a) = (\_, ct - 1) \wedge \neg correctr(a).$$

Finally, we make the stale copies of a dirty address generically dirty and restore the previous dirtiness of correctly restored addresses during eret, and simply use the normal output in case of a normal step

$$d'(a) = \begin{cases} \Box & stale(a) \\ ds(ct - 1, a) & correctr(a) \\ dout(a) & \text{o.w.} \end{cases}$$

We can now formulate a transparency criterion for dirtiness.

Transparency (Dirty). The dirtiness of retrievable registers is correctly restored on eret

$$eret \wedge a \in A_{R,cp} \rightarrow correctr(a).$$

This says nothing about the data yet, so we add the following two conditions for shared registers, and for local registers, respectively.

Transparency (Shared). Shared retrievable registers are restored on eret

$$eret \rightarrow c'\big|_{A_{R,cp} \setminus A_{LPR,cp}} = rs(ct - 1).$$

Tracking. Retrievable, local data is always tracked correctly[9]

$$din(a) \neq \bot \rightarrow \forall v.\delta(c[din(a): = v], x)(a) = v.$$

Dirtiness still has one problem, which is that for the interrupted thread, things become dirty only at interleaving points. Consider the following example, where t is a local, irretrievable register which becomes stale during eret

```
t = 1, IC.int = 1, x = t;   ▷ ...
```

The access to t seems safe because t is a local processor register and it does not appear to be dirty in any order-reduced computation. In reality, it may have been destroyed by an interrupt that occurred right after enabling the interrupts, and the program is not correct. Such accesses have to be forbidden.

Finally, one may never use dirty data to activate devices, in particular, the interrupt controller. It appears to be fine to *store* dirty data in devices, e.g., a hard disk, but we do not have a theorem (let alone proof) that handles such cases.

9   Proof Sketch

On a high level, the proof of this theorem is as follows. We consider first incomplete block computations, which are computations where a thread is only scheduled *in* at an interleaving point (but, unlike in order-reduced computations, can be scheduled out or interrupted at any time). We go now through such a computation and, after each block that has not reached an interleaving point, either drop the block completely (if it has not reached a linearization point) or complete it (if it has reached a linearization point, in which case by assumption

---

[9]

$$c[a: = v](b) = \begin{cases} v & a = b \\ b & \text{o.w.} \end{cases}$$

there is a finite number of steps that bring it to an interleaving point). Since we never change the number or order of shared steps, we do not change ownership, interrupt levels, the IRR, the interruptibility, etc., of any of the threads. Furthermore, we only change the value of owned addresses and local processor registers. Only the latter are ever accessed by another thread (due to ownership), and then only in case of a jisr step - but during jisr, all local processor registers become dirty. Therefore, any changes in data used by a thread not in $D(s)$ will be correctly flagged as dirty, and therefore not used for the computation of any of the functions that matter (independence).

Therefore we have the claim when s is an incomplete block computation. For the case where s is not an incomplete block computation, we show that it can be reordered to an equivalent incomplete block computation. The proof is a simple proof by induction over the length of s, very similar to that in Baumann's PhD thesis [Bau14]: in the inductive step from s to $s \circ x$, we consider the incomplete block computation $r \equiv_{D(s)} s$ given by the induction hypothesis. As in Baumann's proof, in case x is a local step or belongs to a new block, we simply put it into its place and the proof is easy. Otherwise, we reorder the incomplete block that x belongs to as far to the right as possible[10]. Note that since x is shared and there is at most one shared access per block, that block must consist only of local steps. Unlike in Baumann's theorem, either reordering may include moving the block or step across multiple interrupt handlers on the same core, but this is not a big problem as it really corresponds to either

- first dropping an incomplete, local block, which is a technique we have already used in the completion proof above and then inserting the local steps behind the interrupt handler
- inserting a local step before an interrupt handler, and showing that the step has the same effect before and after the handler, which follows from the tracking and transparency results

A detailed version of the proof is available alongside the mathematical formalization in the upcoming PhD thesis of the author.

9.1 Deducing Ownership Mechanically

The existence of an ownership o for each order reduced computation can be checked mechanically in multiple ways. We construct a witness ownership o as follows. We go through the computation from right to left, and for each thread record all addresses accessed locally. When we reach an shared step, we acquire exactly those addresses.

Checking whether o is safe is easy, as one only has to go through the enhanced computation and check every single step. There are two cases.

Ownership o is safe: We have found a safe ownership.

---

[10] Baumann's proof has a small gap here. Baumann simply assumes the existence of a computation with such a shape, without proving that it can be obtained through this reordering.

Ownership o is unsafe: In this case we have to show that no other ownership is safe. Note that by definition, o is the minimal ownership that satisfies the requirement that local accesses only access owned addresses, thus any safe ownership must subsume o. Since o is not safe, there is a violation of the requirement that owned addresses are not accessed by other threads. But that requirement is also violated by any ownership that subsumes o. Consequently there is no safe ownership.

One can thus use the results of the paper to check whether an annotation of shared accesses and interleaving points is safe without having to give ownership annotations. Most programming languages (e.g., C11) only annotate shared accesses and interleaving points (the latter by the compiler), and it is unrealistic to ask programmers to add an ownership annotation to their program. The method is also complete resp. our model. If o is not safe, there clearly is a data race in our model, as one can reorder the local access next to the violating access of another thread. If there is a safe ownership, the computation — but not necessarily the program — is data race free (i.e., this interleaving of shared accesses can not cause a data race).

The disadvantage of this method is that the computation needs to be known in advance. If this is not the case, one instead records for each thread an upper and a lower bound for the ownership that the thread *could have* acquired at its most recent shared step. The lower bound is increased by each local step of that thread (since the thread should have acquired those addresses), and the upper bound is decreased by each step (shared or local) of another thread. An ownership exists exactly while the lower bound of each thread is subsumed by its upper bound.

10   Conclusion, Related and Future Work

We have shown, using only assumptions on the operating system in order reduced computations and realistic assumptions on the architecture, that for interruptible operating systems arbitrary interleavings can be reordered into order reduced computations. Thus many properties such as the shared annotation only have to be verified on order-reduced computations, decreasing state space in model checkers and burden on verifiers, as well as allowing verification work to be done completely in the semantics of high-level languages. Our method also acts as a complete data race detector in execution histories, and can be employed by model checkers to find data races in programs, again checking only order-reduced computations. Our theorem has many applications, e.g., for proving the theoretical compilability of a given high-level (system programming) language; for verifying (system) software with a more abstract interleaving model than that provided by the hardware; for proving the correctness of pipelined multi-core processors, in particular if memory accesses are involved in multiple pipeline stages; etc.

For user level programs, there has been considerable work in theorems of a similar type, most notably by Stoller and Cohen [SC06] and the PhD thesis of Baumann [Bau14] who used no assumptions on arbitrary interleavings. All results in the literature to the best of our knowledge use ownership models which can not be used to model dynamic read-only addresses, i.e., the set of read-only addresses is static and fixed at compile time, which can not be used to check page fault handlers and readers-writer locks. Furthermore, Baumann's model can not be used to model interrupt controllers, and in particular, reordering of an interrupted thread with its interrupt handler. Baumann's work was extended independently of this work to cover interrupt controllers in the PhD thesis of Pentchev [Pen16], which however has several crucial shortcomings. Most notably it has an unsatisfiable condition related to their version of the independence condition (they require that the context be stored in a dedicated data structure before registers are used, but at least one of the registers needs to be used for computing the base address of that data structure), only covers a single level of interrupts, and requires that each shared access immediately reaches an interleaving point (rather than eventually). The latter is due to the fact that they do not have a unified theorem for order reduction, but instead apply Baumann's theorem first (where interrupt handler and interrupted thread share ownership, linearization points, and interleaving points), after which they show that the interrupt handler itself can also be reordered with the interrupted threads. Nevertheless, parts of the proof show similarities to our proof. In order to verify a fully interruptible operating system, we introduced the interrupt stack, dirty data, and the irretrievable registers, all of which to the best of our knowledge are novel ideas. We are not aware of any other work on the topic of order reduction for operating systems, let alone interruptible operating systems.

On the other hand, there has been work on verifying interruptible and preemptive kernels, e.g., by Feng et al. [FSDG08], which gives a very elegant program logic for verifying single-core preemptive operating systems without shared state on an x86 level. We on the other hand give a theorem for verifying multi-core operating systems with shared state and low-level concurrency on a C (or even higher) level. The central idea of the Feng paper is to do an ownership transfer when entering (or leaving) interruptible mode. Since the interruptible mode register is shared, this is also possible in our theorem; in some sense, our theorem is a generalization of Feng's theorem, if one restricts the set of processors to a singleton and prevents shared accesses except to shared processor registers.

There are several venues of improvement and several rewarding open questions related to our work. The first are guard conditions, which in real architectures prevent ill-formed computations (e.g., extending a translation which does not exist). Guard conditions are useful because one does not have to show safety for ill-formed computations. The second are MMUs which are active while kernel code is running. MMUs are difficult because they behave both like a different processor - non-deterministic entities that make steps independent of the program counter - and like a part of the processor, interacting directly via the processor registers (such as the translation look-aside buffer or the page table origin register). In many real-world kernels, some parts of the kernel are running in translated mode, in which case the MMU may actually race the thread. Furthermore, even if the kernel is not running in translated mode, a pipelined processor may switch to kernel mode while a set-access or set-dirty-bit operation of the MMU has been started. Such memory operations can usually not be aborted easily, and therefore the MMU may continue to make such steps even in kernel mode. In either case, our theorem is not equipped to deal with MMUs that run concurrently with kernel code (on which we want to apply the order-reduction). We conjecture that they can be dealt with using monotonicity of the translation look-aside buffer (as in Cohen Kovalev Chen [CCK14]), and specific constraints on TLB operations such as flushing only occurring at the end of a block. Thirdly, it may be necessary to swap out pages that contain dirty data (at least in a pageable kernel), in which case dirty data is moved into a device such as a disk. Our theorem does not tackle this problem, and although it should be easy to give an extension to the theorem on a case-by-case basis, a generic theorem that handles dirty data in storage devices sounds interesting and useful. Fourthly, it has been brought to our attention that for real-time kernels, it may be useful to return to any interrupt handler (e.g., one from another core), or even switch to another interrupt handler voluntarily. Such an extension may require some serious technical work, but would allow higher priority threads from other processors to overtake the current low-priority interrupt easily. Finally, a delicate theorem like the one presented in this paper would benefit greatly from a mechanization of the proof.

References

[Bau14] Baumann, C.: Ownership-based order reduction and simulation in shared-memory concurrent computer systems. Ph.D. thesis, Saarland University (2014)

[Boe] Boehm, H.: N1528: why undefined behavior for infinite loops? http://www.open-std.org/jtc1/sc22/wg14/www/docs/n1528.htm

[CCK14] Chen, G., Cohen, E., Kovalev, M.: Store buffer reduction with MMUs. In: Giannakopoulou, D., Kroening, D. (eds.) VSTTE 2014. LNCS, vol. 8471, pp. 117–132. Springer, Heidelberg (2014). doi:10.1007/978-3-319-12154-3_8

[CDH+09] Cohen, E., Dahlweid, M., Hillebrand, M., Leinenbach, D., Moskal, M., Santen, T., Schulte, W., Tobies, S.: VCC: a practical system for verifying concurrent C. In: Berghofer, S., Nipkow, T., Urban, C., Wenzel, M. (eds.) TPHOLs 2009. LNCS, vol. 5674, pp. 23–42. Springer, Heidelberg (2009). doi:10.1007/978-3-642-03359-9_2

[CL98] Cohen, E., Lamport, L.: Reduction in TLA. In: Sangiorgi, D., Simone, R. (eds.) CONCUR 1998. LNCS, vol. 1466, pp. 317–331. Springer, Heidelberg (1998). doi:10.1007/BFb0055631

[FSDG08] Feng, X., Shao, Z., Dong, Y., Guo, Y.: Certifying low-level programs with hardware interrupts and preemptive threads. In: ACM SIGPLAN Notices, vol. 43, pp. 170–182. ACM (2008)

[HLMS13] Heule, S., Leino, K.R.M., Müller, P., Summers, A.J.: Abstract read permissions: fractional permissions without the fractions. In: Giacobazzi, R., Berdine, J., Mastroeni, I. (eds.) VMCAI 2013. LNCS, vol. 7737, pp. 315–334. Springer, Heidelberg (2013). doi:10.1007/978-3-642-35873-9_20

[Lip75] Lipton, R.J.: Reduction: a method of proving properties of parallel programs. Commun. ACM **18**(12), 717–721 (1975)

[Obe16a] Oberhauser, J.: Justifying the Semantics of High-Level Languages. Ph.D. thesis, Saarland University, unpublished thesis (2016)

[Obe16b] Oberhauser, J.: A simpler reduction theorem for x86-TSO. In: Gurfinkel, A., Seshia, S.A. (eds.) VSTTE 2015. LNCS, vol. 9593, pp. 142–164. Springer, Heidelberg (2016). doi:10.1007/978-3-319-29613-5_9

[Pen16] Pentchev, H.: Sound Semantics of a High-Level Language with Interprocessor Interrupts. Ph.D. thesis, Saarland University (2016)

[SC06] Stoller, S.D., Cohen, E.: Optimistic synchronization-based state-space reduction. Form. Methods Syst. Des. **28**(3), 263–289 (2006)

[SFC92] Sindhu, P.S., Frailong, J.-M., Cekleov, M.: Formal specification of memory models. In: Dubois, M., Thakkar, S. (eds.) Scalable Shared Memory Multiprocessors, pp. 25–41. Springer, US (1992). doi:10.1007/978-1-4615-3604-8_2

Producing All Ideals of a Forest, Formally (Verification Pearl)

Jean-Christophe Filliâtre[1,2] and Mário Pereira[1,2(✉)]

[1] Lab. de Recherche en Informatique, Univ. Paris-Sud, CNRS, 91405 Orsay, France
mpereira@lri.fr
[2] INRIA Saclay – Île-de-France, 91893 Orsay, France

Abstract. In this paper we present the first formal proof of an implementation of Koda and Ruskey's algorithm, an algorithm for generating all ideals of a forest poset as a Gray code. One contribution of this work is to exhibit the invariants of this algorithm, which proved to be challenging. We implemented, specified, and proved this algorithm using the Why3 tool. This allowed us to employ a combination of several automated theorem provers to discharge most of the verification conditions, and the Coq proof assistant for the remaining two.

1 Introduction

Given a forest, we consider the problem of coloring its nodes in black and white, such that a white node only has white descendants. Consider for instance this forest:

It has exactly 15 colorings, which are the following:

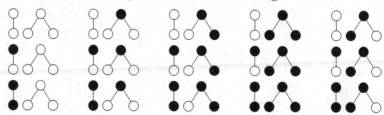

Koda and Ruskey proposed a very nice algorithm [4] to generate all these colorings.[1] This is a Gray code algorithm, which only changes the color of one node to move from one coloring to the next one. If we read the figure above in a zig-zag way, we can notice that any coloring is indeed obtained from the previous one by changing the color of exactly one node.

This research was partly supported by the Portuguese Foundation for Sciences and Technology (grant FCT-SFRH/BD/99432/2014) and by the French National Research Organization (project VOCAL ANR-15-CE25-008).
[1] Such a coloring has a mathematical interpretation as an ideal of a forest poset.

S. Blazy and M. Chechik (Eds.): VSTTE 2016, LNCS 9971, pp. 46–55, 2016.
DOI: 10.1007/978-3-319-48869-1_4

There are many ways to implement Koda-Ruskey's algorithm. Koda and Ruskey themselves give two implementations in their paper. Filliâtre and Pottier propose several implementations based on higher-order functions and their defunctionalization [1]. Knuth has two implementations in C, including one using coroutines [3]. In particular, Knuth makes the following comment:

[...] I think it's a worthwhile challenge for people who study the science of computer programming to verify that these two implementations both define the same sequence of bitstrings.

Before trying to verify Knuth's intricate C code, a reasonable first step is to work out the invariants of Koda-Ruskey's algorithm on a simpler implementation. This is what we do in this paper, using the Why3 system. To our knowledge, this is the first formal proof of this algorithm.

This paper is organized as follows. Section 2 describes our implementation in Why3. Then Sect. 3 goes over the formal specification. Finally, Sect. 4 details the most interesting parts of the proof. The Why3 source code and its proof can be found at http://toccata.lri.fr/gallery/koda_ruskey.en.html.

2   Implementation

Our implementation of Koda-Ruskey's algorithm is given in Fig. 1. The syntax of Why3 is close to that of OCaml, and we explain it whenever necessary. The algebraic datatype of forests is declared on lines 1–3. A forest is either empty (constructor E) or composed of an integer node together with two forests, namely the forest of its children nodes and its sibling forest (constructor N). One can notice that the type forest is isomorphic to a list of pairs of nodes and forests.

The type of colors is introduced on line 4. The entry point is function main (lines 24–25). It takes an array bits as argument, to hold the coloring, and a forest f0. It then calls a recursive function enum, which implements the core of the algorithm.

Function enum operates over a stack of forests, using the predefined type list of Why3 (with constructors Nil and Cons). On entry, function enum inspects the stack. It will never be empty (line 9). If the stack is reduced to a single empty forest, we have just discovered a new coloring. We are free to do whatever we want with the contents of array bits (line 10), such as printing it, storing it, etc. If the stack starts with an empty forest, we skip it (line 11). Otherwise, the top of the stack contains a non-empty tree, with a root node i, a children forest f1, and a sibling forest f2 (line 12). If node i is white (line 13), we first enumerate the colorings of f2 together with the remaining st' of the stack (line 14), then we blacken node i (line 15), and finally we enumerate the colorings of f1, interleaving them with the colorings of f2 and st'. If node i is black (line 17), the process is reversed. First, we enumerate the colorings of f1 (line 18), so that all nodes of f1 are white again at the end. Then we whiten node i (line 19). Finally, we enumerate the colorings of f2 (line 20).

```
1   type forest =
2     | E
3     | N int forest forest
4
5   type color = White | Black
6
7   let rec enum (bits: array color) (st: list forest) =
8     match st with
9     | Nil → absurd
10    | Cons E Nil → ... (* visit array bits *) ...
11    | Cons E st' → enum bits st'
12    | Cons (N i f1 f2) st' →
13        if bits[i] = White then begin
14          enum bits (Cons f2 st');
15          bits[i] ← Black;
16          enum bits (Cons f1 (Cons f2 st'))
17        end else begin
18          enum bits (Cons f1 (Cons f2 st'));
19          bits[i] ← White;
20          enum bits (Cons f2 st')
21        end
22    end
23
24  let main (bits: array color) (f0: forest) =
25    enum bits (Cons f0 Nil)
```

Fig. 1. An implementation of Koda-Ruskey's algorithm.

3 Specification

In this section we give function main a specification. The specification of function enum is considered being part of the proof and thus only described in the next section. The first requirement over function main is to have array bits large enough to hold all the nodes of the forest. So we start by defining the number of elements in a forest:

```
function size_forest (f: forest) : int = match f with
  | E → 0
  | N _ f1 f2 → 1 + size_forest f1 + size_forest f2
  end
```

In Why3, the function keyword introduces a logical function, *i.e.*, a function with no side-effects and whose termination is checked automatically, and that one can use in a specification context. We use size_forest to introduce the first precondition of function main:

```
let main (bits: array color) (f0: forest)
  requires { size_forest f0 = length bits } ...
```

To execute correctly, the program also requires the forest to have nodes numbered with distinct integers that are also valid indexes in array `bits`. These conditions are expressed, respectively, by predicates `no_repeated_forest` and `between_range_forest`, as follows:

```
predicate no_repeated_forest (f: forest) = match f with
| E → true
| N i f1 f2 →
    no_repeated_forest f1 && no_repeated_forest f2 &&
    not (mem_forest i f1) && not (mem_forest i f2) &&
    disjoint f1 f2
end
```

```
predicate between_range_forest (i j: int) (f: forest) =
  forall n. mem_forest n f → i ≤ n < j
```

where `mem_forest` expresses that an element belongs to a forest:

```
predicate mem_forest (n: int) (f: forest) = match f with
| E → false
| N i f1 f2 → i = n || mem_forest n f1 || mem_forest n f2
end
```

and `disjoint` indicates that two trees have disjoint sets of nodes:

```
predicate disjoint (f1 f2: forest) =
  forall x. mem_forest x f1 → mem_forest x f2 → false
```

To write more succinct specifications in the following, we combine predicates `between_range_forest` and `no_repeated_forest` into a single predicate `valid_nums_forest`, which is added to the precondition of `main`.

```
predicate valid_nums_forest (f: forest) (n: int) =
  between_range_forest 0 n f && no_repeated_forest f
```

```
let main (bits: array color) (f0: forest)
  requires { valid_nums_forest f0 (size_forest f0) } ...
```

We now turn to the part of the specification related to the enumeration of colorings. A coloring is a map from nodes, which are integers, to values of type `color`:

```
type coloring = map int color
```

At the beginning of the algorithm, all nodes of the forest must be colored white. We introduce a predicate `white_forest` to say so.

```
predicate white_forest (f: forest) (c: coloring) = match f with
| E → true
| N i f1 f2 → c[i] = White && white_forest f1 c && white_forest f2 c
end
```

This predicate traverses the forest and checks that for each node `i`, its color `c[i]` is `White`. As for functions, termination of recursive predicates is automatically also checked. We can now use this predicate in the precondition of `main`:

```
let main (bits: array color) (f0: forest)
  requires { white_forest f0 bits.elts } ...
```

Here `bits.elts` is the map modeling the contents of array `bits`, which happens to have type `coloring`.

Upon termination, the program must have enumerated all colorings, each coloring being visited exactly once. Since the code is not storing the colorings, we extend it with *ghost* code to do that. A ghost reference, `visited`, is declared to hold the sequence of colorings enumerated so far:

```
val ghost visited: ref (seq coloring)
```

(Sequences are predefined in Why3 standard library.) The idea is that this reference is updated each time a new coloring is found, on line 10 of the program in Fig. 1.

To express that `main` enumerates all colorings exactly once, we specify that all colorings in `visited` are valid and pairwise distinct colorings, and that there are the expected number of colorings. The latter is easily defined recursively:

```
function count_forest (f: forest) : int = match f with
  | E          → 1
  | N _ f1 f2 → (1 + count_forest f1) * count_forest f2
  end
```

Indeed, an empty forest has exactly one coloring (the empty coloring), and colorings of a non-empty forest are obtained by combining any coloring for the first tree with any coloring for the remaining forest. Last, the coloring of a tree is either all white (hence 1) or a black root with any coloring of the children forest. The postcondition of `main` states that we have enumerated this number of colorings:

```
let main (bits: array color) (f0: forest)
  ensures { length !visited = count_forest f0 } ...
```

To be valid, a coloring must respect the constraint that if a node is colored white then its children forest must be all white. The predicate `valid_coloring` checks this constraint:

```
predicate valid_coloring (f: forest) (c: coloring) =
  match f with
  | E → true
  | N i f1 f2 →
      valid_coloring f2 c &&
      match c[i] with
      | White → white_forest f1 c
      | Black → valid_coloring f1 c
      end
  end
```

Each time a white node is reached, we use predicate `white_forest` to ensure that its children forest is white.

Comparing two colorings requires to ignore values outside of the array range. Thus we introduce predicate `eq_coloring` to state that two colorings coincide on a given range $0..n - 1$:

```
predicate eq_coloring (n: int) (c1 c2: coloring) =
  forall i. 0 ≤ i < n → c1[i] = c2[i]
```

We are now in position to give the full code and specification of function `main`:

```
let main (bits: array color) (f0: forest)
  requires { size_forest f0 = length bits }
  requires { valid_nums_forest f0 (size_forest f0) }
  requires { white_forest f0 bits.elts }
  ensures  { length !visited = count_forest f0 }
  ensures  { let n = length !visited in
              forall j. 0 ≤ j < n →
              valid_coloring f0 !visited[j] &&
              forall k. 0 ≤ k < n → j ≠ k →
                not (eq_coloring (length bits) !visited[j] !visited[k]) }
= visited := empty;
  enum bits f0 (Cons f0 Nil)
```

Note that `main` assigns `visited` to the `empty` sequence before calling `enum`. The forest `f0` is also passed to `enum` as an extra, ghost argument.

4 Proof

As shown in Fig. 1, program `main` simply amounts to a call to `enum`. So, in order to prove that `main` respects its specification we need to specify and prove correct function `enum`. In this section we go over the most subtle points in the specification and proof of `enum`. The complete specification for this function is shown in Fig. 2.

```
1  let rec enum (bits: array color) (ghost f0: forest) (st: list forest)
2    requires { st ≠ Nil }
3    requires { size_forest f0 = length bits }
4    requires { valid_nums_forest f0 (length bits) }
5    requires { sub st f0 bits.elts }
6    requires { any_stack st bits.elts }
7    requires { valid_coloring f0 bits.elts }
8    ensures  { forall i. not (mem_stack i st) → bits[i] = (old bits)[i] }
9    ensures  { inverse st (old bits).elts bits.elts }
10   ensures  { valid_coloring f0 bits.elts }
11   ensures  { stored_solutions f0 bits.elts st (old !visited) !visited }
12   variant  { size_stack st, st }
```

Fig. 2. Specification of function `enum`.

Function `enum` operates on a stack of forests, and we need to relate that stack to the original forest `f0` (which is passed to `enum` as a ghost argument). To do so, we introduce a predicate `sub` st f c that relates a stack st, a forest f, and a coloring c. It is defined with the following inference rules:

$$\frac{}{\text{sub } [f] \; f \; c} \qquad \frac{\text{sub } st \; f_2 \; c}{\text{sub } st \; (\text{N } i \; f_1 \; f_2) \; c} \qquad \frac{\text{sub } st \; f_1 \; c \quad c[i] = \text{Black}}{\text{sub } (st \mathbin{+\!\!+} [f_2]) \; (\text{N } i \; f_1 \; f_2) \; c}$$

The first rule states that a stack containing a single forest f is a sub-forest of f itself. ($[f]$ is a notation for a one-element list.) The second rule states that we can skip the left tree (i, f_1) of a forest $(\text{N } i \; f_1 \; f_2)$. The third rule states that we can plunge into f_1 provided $c[i]$ is black and f_2 appears at the end of the stack. (Operator `++` is list concatenation). In Why3, such a set of inference rules is defined as an inductive predicate:

```
inductive sub stack forest coloring =
| Sub_reflex:
    forall f, c. sub (Cons f Nil) f c
| Sub_brother:
    forall st i f1 f2 c.
    sub st f2 c → sub st (N i f1 f2) c
| Sub_append:
    forall st i f1 f2 c.
    sub st f1 c → c[i] = Black →
    sub (st ++ Cons f2 Nil) (N i f1 f2) c
```

We use this predicate in `enum`'s precondition, with the current stack, the initial forest `f0`, and the current coloring (line 5). Together with preconditions in lines 2–4, we are already in position to prove safety of function `enum`. Indeed, nodes found in the stack do belong to `f0`, according to `sub`, and thus are legal array indices.

To specify what `enum` does, we need to characterize the final coloring in the enumeration (*e.g.*, the bottom right coloring in the 15 colorings on page 1). Indeed, for the algorithm to work, it has to enumerate all colorings in a reverse order when called on such a final coloring, ending on a white forest. Since the algorithm is interleaving the colorings for the various trees of the forest, the final configuration depends on the parity of these numbers of colorings. So we first introduce a predicate `even_forest` `f` which means that forest `f` has an even number of colorings:

```
predicate even_forest (f: forest) = match f with
  | E         → false
  | N _ f1 f2 → not (even_forest f1) || even_forest f2
  end
```

Though we could define it instead as `count_forest` being even, we prefer this direct definition, which saves us some arithmetical reasoning. We can now define what is the final coloring of a forest:

```
predicate final_forest (f: forest) (c: coloring) = match f with
```

```
  | E → true
  | N i f1 f2 →
      c[i] = Black && final_forest f1 c &&
      if not (even_forest f1) then white_forest f2 c
      else final_forest f2 c
  end
```

Though we can see `final_forest` as the dual of `white_forest`, from the algorithm point of view, it is clear that a final forest is not a black forest (as one can see on page 1). Function `enum` requires all forests in the stack to be either white or final. To say so, we introduce the following recursive predicate:

```
  predicate any_stack (st: stack) (c: coloring) = match st with
  | Nil → true
  | Cons f st →
      (white_forest f c || final_forest f c) && any_stack st c
  end
```

It appears as a precondition on line 6.

From a big-step perspective, Koda-Ruskey's algorithm is switching from a white coloring to a final coloring and conversely. But `enum` is operating over a stack of forests and thus requires us to be more precise. For the tree on top of the stack, we are indeed switching states. However, for the next tree (its right sibling in the same forest, if any, or the next tree in the stack, otherwise), the state changes only if the first tree has an odd number of colorings. Otherwise, it is kept unchanged. To account for this inversion, we introduce the following predicate that relates a stack `st` and two colorings, namely the first coloring c_1 and the last coloring c_2:

```
  predicate inverse (st: stack) (c1 c2: coloring) =
    match st with
    | Nil → true
    | Cons f st' →
        (white_forest f c1 && final_forest f c2 ||
         final_forest f c1 && white_forest f c2) &&
        if even_forest f then
          unchanged st' c1 c2
        else
          inverse st' c1 c2
    end
```

Note that the coloring of the first forest in the stack is always inverted, while the inversion of the remaining of the stack depends on the parity of the first forest. The predicate `unchanged st' c1 c2` states that c_1 and c_2 coincide on any node in the stack `st'`. The postcondition on line 9 in Fig. 2 relates the initial contents of array `bits` (written `old bits`) to its final contents using predicate `inverse`.

We briefly go over the remaining clauses in the specification of `enum`. The stack is never empty (line 2). The initial forest `f0` has as many elements as the `bits` array (line 3) and is correctly numbered from 0 (line 4). In both pre- and post-state, the coloring must be valid w.r.t. `f0` (lines 7 and 10). A frame postcondition ensures that any element outside of the stack is left unchanged (line 8). We characterize the sequence of enumerated colorings with a predicate stored_solutions (line 11), not shown here. It means that visited has been augmented with new, valid, and pairwise distinct colorings, which coincide with array bits outside of the stack nodes. Finally, we ensure termination with a lexicographic variant (line 12). In all cases but one, the size of the stack is decreasing, when defined as its total number of nodes, as follows:

```
function size_stack (st: stack) : int = match st with
  | Nil → 0
  | Cons f st → size_forest f + size_stack st
  end
```

The last case is when the stack is of the form Cons E st', for which we perform a recursive call on st'. The number of nodes remains the same, but the stack is structurally smaller, hence the lexicographic variant.

Proof Statistics. To make the proof of enum and main fully automatic, we introduce 19 proof hints in the body of enum and 37 auxiliary lemmas. Many of these lemmas require a proof by induction, which is done in Why3 by first applying a dedicated transformation (interactively, from the Why3 IDE) and then calling automated theorem provers. The table below summarizes the number of VCs and the verification time.

	Number of VCs	Automatically proved	Verification time
lemmas	102	100 (98 %)	14.72 s
enum	94	94 (100 %)	47.51 s
main	7	7 (100 %)	0.07 s
Total	203	201 (99 %)	62.30 s

Two VCs are proved interactively using Coq. These proofs amount to 55 lines of Coq tactics, including the why3 tactic that allows to automatically discharge some Coq sub-goals using SMT solvers. All other VCs are proved automatically, using a combination of theorem provers as follows:

Prover	VCs proved
Alt-Ergo 1.01	139
CVC4 1.4	57
Z3 4.4.0	3
CVC3 2.4.1	1
Eprover 1.8-001	1

Our proof process consists in calling Alt-Ergo first. When it does not succeed, we switch to CVC4. And so on. So the numbers above should not be interpreted as "Alt-Ergo discharges 139 VCs and CVC4 only 57". Though we could call all provers on all VCs, we choose not to do this in practice to save time. A more detailed table is available on-line at http://toccata.lri.fr/gallery/koda_ruskey.en.html.

5   Conclusion

In this paper we presented a formal verification of an implementation of Koda-Ruskey's algorithm using Why3. To our knowledge, this is the first formal proof of this algorithm. The main contribution of this paper is the definition of the algorithm's invariants (mostly, the definition of predicates `any_stack` and `inverse`). We argue that such definitions could be readily reused in other proofs of this algorithm, whatever the choice of implementation and of verification tool (*e.g.*, Dafny [5], VeriFast [2], or Viper [6]).

We intend to improve our verification with a proof that `count_forest` is indeed the right number of colorings. One way to do that would be to implement a naive enumeration of all colorings, with an obvious soundness proof. We are also interested in verifying higher-order implementations of Koda-Ruskey's algorithm, such as the ones by Filliâtre and Pottier [1]. This means extending Why3 with support for effectful higher-order functions.

Acknowledgments. We thank Claude Marché for his comments on earlier versions of this paper.

References

1. Filliâtre, J.C., Pottier, F.: Producing all ideals of a forest, functionally. J. Funct. Program. **13**(5), 945–956 (2003)
2. Jacobs, B., Smans, J., Philippaerts, P., Vogels, F., Penninckx, W., Piessens, F.: VeriFast: a powerful, sound, predictable, fast verifier for C and java. In: Bobaru, M., Havelund, K., Holzmann, G.J., Joshi, R. (eds.) NFM 2011. LNCS, vol. 6617, pp. 41–55. Springer, Heidelberg (2011). doi:10.1007/978-3-642-20398-5_4
3. Knuth, D.E.: An implementation of Koda and Ruskey's algorithm (June 2001). http://www-cs-staff.stanford.edu/knuth/programs.html
4. Koda, Y., Ruskey, F.: A gray code for the ideals of a forest poset. J. Algorithms **15**, 324–340 (1993)
5. Leino, K.R.M.: Dafny: an automatic program verifier for functional correctness. In: Clarke, E.M., Voronkov, A. (eds.) LPAR 2010. LNCS (LNAI), vol. 6355, pp. 348–370. Springer, Heidelberg (2010). doi:10.1007/978-3-642-17511-4_20
6. Müller, P., Schwerhoff, M., Summers, A.J.: Viper: a verification infrastructure for permission-based reasoning. In: Jobstmann, B., Leino, K.R.M. (eds.) VMCAI 2016. LNCS, vol. 9583, pp. 41–62. Springer, Heidelberg (2016). doi:10.1007/978-3-662-49122-5_2

Constructing Semantic Models of Programs with the Software Analysis Workbench

Robert Dockins, Adam Foltzer, Joe Hendrix, Brian Huffman,
Dylan McNamee, and Aaron Tomb[(✉)]

Galois, Inc., Portland, OR, USA
{rdockins,acfoltzer,jhendrix,huffman,dylan,atomb}@galois.com

Abstract. The Software Analysis Workbench (SAW) is a system for translating programs into logical expressions, transforming these expressions, and using external reasoning tools (such as SAT and SMT solvers) to prove properties about them. In the implementation of this translation, SAW combines efficient symbolic execution techniques in a novel way. It has been used most extensively to prove that implementations of cryptographic algorithms are functionally equivalent to referencespecifications, but can also be used to identify inputs to programs that will lead to outputs with particular properties, and prove other properties about programs. In this paper, we describe the structure of the SAW system and present experimental results demonstrating the benefits of its implementation techniques.

Keywords: Equivalence checking · Cryptography · SAT · SMT · Symbolic execution · Verification

1 Introduction

The Software Analysis Workbench (SAW) is a suite of tools for transforming programs into *formal models* — logical representations of program semantics — and for subsequent analysis of those models. Such models are appropriate for mechanized reasoning about the functional behavior of programs. For example, SAW can be used to answer questions such as the following, with a high degree of automation:

- Is a tricky optimized program equivalent to a trusted reference specification?
- What is an input that will lead to a given location in a program?
- What inputs will yield outputs satisfying a given predicate?
- Did a refactoring cause any semantic change?
- What is an input for which program A, written in language L produces a different output than program B, written in language M?

SAW supports generating models from several source languages, including Java Virtual Machine (JVM) bytecode, Low-Level Virtual Machine (LLVM) bitcode, and Cryptol (a domain-specific language designed for the description of

© Springer International Publishing AG 2016
S. Blazy and M. Chechik (Eds.): VSTTE 2016, LNCS 9971, pp. 56–72, 2016.
DOI: 10.1007/978-3-319-48869-1_5

cryptographic algorithms [21]). As a result, SAW can generate models from C and Java programs, along with other languages that target the JVM or LLVM.

The formal models are represented in a dependently-typed functional language, SAWCore, that adopts the same general design as the internal representation used by proof assistants based on type theory.

The philosophy of SAW is to generate generic models of program semantics, independent of a specific analysis task, and then act as a bridge between programs and existing automated reasoning tools, allowing a wide range of transformations along the way. The goal is to be able to perform mostly-automated proofs about subtle code. SAW integrates existing tools with custom implementations of a number of known techniques, along with a variety of novel enhancements to those techniques.

1.1 The Structure of SAW

Translation from programs to formal models in SAWCore takes one of several forms. For programs that are originally written in functional style (such as Cryptol programs), the process is essentially a straightforward compilation into SAW-Core. For imperative programs, the current version of SAW depends primarily on symbolic execution with path merging to generate functional terms. When using symbolic execution, the resulting terms are "flat"; all iteration, whether originating from loops or recursive functions, is fully unrolled. If full unrolling is not possible, symbolic execution can simply fail to terminate.

Once programs have been translated to formal models, SAW supports transforming, composing, and evaluating these models in a variety of ways. A built-in rewriter can transform existing terms according to a chosen set of rewrite rules.

Transformation of formal models is generally used to prove properties about programs. The SAW tools have been tuned to proving functional equivalence between programs (and especially to the implementations of cryptographic algorithms), though the tools are well-suited to proving any relationship between the input and output of programs for which the model generation process succeeds.

The rewriting functionality built in to SAW can sometimes be used to complete a proof on its own. For instance, when performing equivalence proofs between similar programs written in different languages, the SAWCore terms generated from those programs are often very similar and require only minor transformations to become identical. Terms in SAWCore are represented as hash-consed Directed Acyclic Graphs (DAGs), so syntactically equivalent terms are immediately apparent, since they are guaranteed to be represented by the same node in the graph of the term. For proofs that cannot be completed with rewriting alone, SAW provides a connection to various automated and semi-automated external tools, including Boolean Satisfiability (SAT) and Satisfiability Modulo Theories (SMT) solvers, to offload proof tasks.

To improve the assurance of rewrite-based proofs, rewrite rules can be proven correct themselves. A rewrite rule can be built from an equality type in the logic, allowing a term of that type to serve as a witness to the validity of the rule.

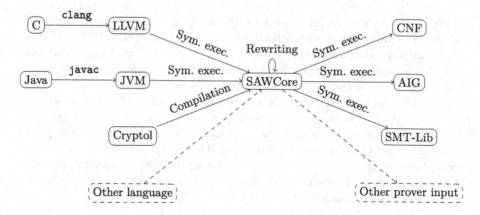

Fig. 1. Architecture of SAW. Source programs are translated to SAWCore, rewritten according to user-defined rules, and sent to external theorem provers. The process is controlled by programs in the SAWScript language.

In addition, SAT and SMT solvers can be used to prove the validity of rewrite rules. In cases where assurance requirements are lower, SAW also allows unproven rules.

The translations between source languages, SAWCore, and external theorem provers are illustrated in Fig. 1. The process of constructing models and orchestrating external theorem provers is controlled by a scripting language called SAWScript. It is a straightforward typed functional language with a large collection of built-in functions dedicated to extracting formal models from programs, manipulating those models, and interacting with external theorem provers.

In particular, SAW provides a novel combination of efficient symbolic execution techniques: a shared representation of symbolic program states; eager path merging; deeply-integrated rewriting; and deep integration with efficient bit-level provers based on an And-Inverter Graph (AIG) representation of boolean functions. These features allow it to construct complete semantic models of programs that include heavy use of bit-level operations. The key novelty of SAW is in this combination of techniques, and the primary contributions of our work include:

- Experimental results demonstrating the benefits of DAG term representations, compositional symbolic execution, and the use of a wide variety of back-end proof tools.
- Demonstration of symbolic execution for equivalence checking of cryptographic algorithms across multiple languages.
- A tool made publicly available to the community.

2   SAWCore

The formal models generated by SAW are represented in an internal modeling language called SAWCore. This language was designed to be an efficient, expressive representation for the semantics of programs originating in a variety of source languages, including languages with sophisticated type systems (such as Cryptol), general recursion (most languages), and complex memory models (such as those appropriate for JVM, LLVM, and most machine languages).

SAWCore is a dependently typed functional language, similar to the core calculi used by languages such as Coq [25], and Lean [22]. It supports user-defined inductive data types, but also has built-in support for a variety of special types such as Booleans, vectors (including extensive support for bit vectors), tuples, and records, for efficient modeling of constructs from software, and for compatibility with external tools that also have special support for these types.

Although SAWCore is intended primarily as an internal representation for program semantics, it also has a concrete syntax with some conveniences to simplify development of libraries of common operations and rewrite rules.

The ability to use high levels of abstraction in SAWCore makes models more compact and easier to transform according to the properties of those abstractions. Ultimately, however, many of the program analyses performed by SAW can largely be represented in first-order form (and the external provers we use generally operate on first-order formulas), so SAW includes back ends for translation of a subset of SAWCore into first-order representations such as the (AIGER) and SMT-Lib formats. Broadly speaking, the translatable subset consists of functions with domains and ranges that are made entirely of finite bit vectors (potentially aggregated into higher-level vectors, tuples, or records).

We are also considering adding the ability to export terms to Lean or Coq for interactive proof. These will stay at a high level of abstraction and make use of higher-order features, motivating a delay in lowering terms to first-order form.

3 Symbolic Execution

SAW makes heavy use of symbolic execution to translate imperative programs to SAWCore. Unlike most implementations of symbolic execution, we ultimately generate a single model of the symbolic state of a program, for all paths explored, rather than generating a separate symbolic state for each path. This has the advantage of capturing the entire semantics of a program, which is useful for functional correctness verification. However, it has the disadvantage of leading to more complex symbolic states, making it potentially less effective as a bug-finding tool for identifying potential assertion violations on specific paths. Therefore, SAW tends to be effective for programs that can be exhaustively explored by symbolic execution, but less scalable for programs that cannot. Our approach is similar to that used by bounded model checkers in this respect, though the bounds are all provided by the program rather than the model checker. Termination is determined by the satisfiability of loop conditions as each loop iteration executes, so symbolic execution will fail to terminate if the underlying program does not terminate, or if it has a sufficiently complex termination condition.

3.1   Shared Terms

The implementation of SAWCore uses a DAG structure to represent terms, and uses memoization to guarantee that identical subterms are represented with a single graph node. In addition, the SAW system uses a single term node database for all terms generated within a session. Therefore, when comparing two similar programs, semantically identical portions of those programs are immediately identified (even when the original programs are written in different languages). As detailed in Sect. 7.2, this representation is critical for symbolic execution of most cryptographic code, to avoid exponential blow-up. For non-cryptographic code without extensive iteration, the DAG representation is less critical, but still helpful for reducing model sizes.

3.2   Postdominator-Based Merging

To support generating a single model of program semantics, rather than a model of the symbolic state of each individual path, the symbolic execution infrastructure in SAW uses path merging at every node in the control-flow graph that immediately post-dominates more than one other node. To facilitate path merging, we translate the original program into a modified representation which includes special symbolic execution instructions in place of the original branch instructions. Each branch includes a merge point as well as an initial target, and each path that executes starting from that branch instruction will pause when it reaches the merge point. When all paths leading to a single merge target instruction have completed, the simulator merges their symbolic states. The result is a single logical formula describing the final state of the program in terms of its initial state (with free variables denoting arbitrary initial values).

3.3   Memory Models

One of the characteristics that tends to distinguish systems based on symbolic execution from those based on, for instance, weakest preconditions or strongest postconditions (the latter of which is roughly equivalent to symbolic execution), is the use an *implicit* instead of an *explicit* memory model. In an implicit memory model, the mapping between names and (potentially symbolic) values is tracked directly by the symbolic execution system, perhaps as a map data structure in the host language. Imperative updates, then, can be destructive updates to this map instead of existentially-quantified equalities in the generated verification conditions (as would be the case with strongest postconditions).

The ability to destructively update the internal simulator state can make symbolic execution more efficient than strongest postcondition calculation for typical imperative programs, and allows symbolic state expression to remain quantifier-free. However, if imperative updates occur to symbolic addresses, the size of verification conditions can explode with explicit case splitting expressions. Therefore, the ability to trade off between implicit and explicit memory models provides a flexibility advantage.

SAW currently has several implicit memory models, and does not implement an explicit memory model. As future work, we are considering implementing built-in data types in SAWCore that present similar functionality to the current implicit memory models but in a way that would allow them to be directly embedded into SAWCore terms, and therefore be used as part of an explicit memory model. Such terms might be difficult for SMT solvers, but could allow interactive provers to tackle more complex programs, rather than ruling out such cases entirely.

3.4 Path Feasibility Checking

Like many symbolic execution systems, SAW supports (optional) path feasibility checking. The process of executing a conditional branch instruction involves adding the relevant branch condition to the accumulated path condition of each path, and can include checking that condition for satisfiability.

For complex but satisfiable path conditions, full satisfiability checking can be expensive, so SAW also supports another option: translating the path condition term to AIG format and checking for syntactic equality with `False`. The translation to AIG form necessarily includes common simplifications such as constant folding and beta reduction as well as simple representations of bit-level operations such as shifting and masking. In code that uses bit-level manipulation heavily, this operation can frequently suffice to determine path feasibility. For example, consider a program that iteratively performs a logical right shift on a condition. For a bit vector of a fixed size, this operation will yield zero after a fixed number of iterations, making the condition `False` (for a C or LLVM program), and equivalence to `False` is often immediately apparent in AIG format.

3.5 Example

As a simple example of a task that SAW is ideally suited for, consider the POSIX Find First Set (FFS) function, for finding the index of the first bit set in a word. This function is implemented in many standard C library variants. Some implementations iterate over the bits of the word, such as shown in the left column of Fig. 2.

Other implementations avoid loops by masking off bits of the word in chunks, such as shown in the right column of Fig. 2. These two functions compute the same result using dramatically different techniques.

SAW can translate each of these programs to a formal model using symbolic execution and prove the models equivalent with a SAT solver in a fraction of a second (using the short script that appears in Sect. 5).

```
int ffs_ref(int w) {
  int cnt, i = 0;
  if(!w) { return 0; }
  for(cnt = 0; cnt < 32; cnt++) {
    if(((1 << i++) & w) != 0) {
      return i;
    }
  }
  return 0;
}
```

```
int ffs_imp(int w) {
  char n = 1;
  if (!(w & 0xffff)) {
    n += 16; w >>= 16;
  }
  if (!(w & 0x00ff)) {
    n += 8;  w >>= 8;
  }
  if (!(w & 0x000f)) {
    n += 4;  w >>= 4;
  }
  if (!(w & 0x0003)) {
    n += 2;  w >>= 2;
  }
  return (w) ? (n+((w+1) & 0x01)) : 0;
}
```

Fig. 2. Reference and efficient implementations of the FFS algorithm which compute the same result using different techniques.

4   Compositional Symbolic Execution

For functional languages, symbolic execution is naturally compositional. Symbolic execution essentially amounts to a non-standard reduction strategy, and any application expression with a name on the left-hand side can be either inlined or treated as uninterpreted.

For imperative languages, the problem is trickier. We would like to treat the target of a function call abstractly, referring to it with an uninterpreted function symbol in our logic. It would also be convenient to provide only some facts about that function, rather than a complete definition. However, doing this automatically is tricky in an imperative setting with an implicit memory model: although treating an imperative program as a pure function can often be straightforward when its inputs and outputs are known, it can in general be undecidable to determine those inputs and outputs automatically.

Therefore, our strategy to compositional verification is to allow users to provide descriptions of the inputs and outputs of a procedure in the imperative language, and then describe the logical function that transforms those inputs to outputs. This function can be an arbitrary expression, including, if desired, uninterpreted function symbols.

Given such a description, we can do two things. We can symbolically execute the procedure being described, given arbitrary contents of the inputs, to derive a term denoting the symbolic values of the outputs. We can then (attempt to) prove that this resulting term satisfies any property we desire.

Alternatively, we can use the same description of a procedure during the symbolic execution of one of its callers. When the symbolic execution engine encounters a function call, it can simply apply the provided expression to the appropriate (symbolic) values of the state elements that form its inputs, and store the resulting term in the portion of the simulator state corresponding to its outputs. Thus, the symbolic execution engine can process procedure calls without examining the callee, and may (as one option) simply use an uninterpreted function to describe the semantics of the callee.

A more general approach is also possible: the semantics of a procedure can be represented by a function that takes in all of that procedure's arguments plus the current heap and returns the procedure's return value plus a new heap. This allows automated composition, but trades off the efficiency possible with an implicit representation of the heap. For programs that use linked data structures or unbounded memory allocation, however, this approach would be effective in cases where the current one is not. We plan to explore this approach more in future work.

5 SAWScript

The process of model generation and transformation in SAW, and the interaction with third-party proof tools, is coordinated by a scripting language called SAWScript. The language is a simply-typed functional language, with an interpreter that can be used either in batch mode or through an interactive Read-Evaluate-Print Loop (REPL).

Many of the built-in functions in SAWScript have externally-visible effects, and these effectful commands are combined with a monad-like construct. Unlike other languages with this approach to combining effectful computations, SAWScript has no facility for user-defined monads, a decision we made to reduce cognitive load. To the SAWScript user, the types of effectful commands simply restrict their use to specific contexts.

One central built-in type in SAWScript is `Term`, representing a SAWCore term. Most built-in functions produce, modify, or consume `Term` values. From the SAWScript point of view, `Term` is a single type, but each `Term` also has a SAWCore type internally. Each `Term` is type-checked according to the SAWCore type system as it is constructed, but the internal type of a `Term` can change without the underlying SAWScript program changing if the structure of the program under analysis changes.

SAWScript also has a tight connection with Cryptol, a language originally developed for the high-level description of cryptographic algorithms, but which is also very convenient for description of any algorithm that operates on fixed-size bit vectors. Cryptol syntax provides a convenient way to construct SAWCore terms that provides type inference and has less syntactic overhead than SAWCore. Existing SAWCore terms can be used in subsequent Cryptol expressions, allowing Cryptol to be used as convenient "glue" around SAWCore terms extracted automatically from programs.

A variety of commands exist for extracting `Term` objects from imperative programs. The simplest work only on a limited set of programs but are completely automatic, translating an imperative function to a lambda abstraction with a type isomorphic to that of the original program. An alternative interface allows more control over symbolic execution, allowing the user to place either symbolic or concrete values into the program state, symbolically execute a function, and then read out components of the final state. The third interface allows for compositional reasoning following the approach described in Sect. 4.

Given a `Term`, SAWScript provides commands to perform rewriting with a given set of rules, unfold abstract named subterms, perform beta reduction, or export it in various external formats. Proving the validity of `Term` values is a central activity in SAW, and a `ProofScript` monad provides a mechanism for chaining simple tactics together to complete a proof. The final tactic in a `ProofScript` can be `trivial` to indicate that the preceding tactics should have reduced the term to `True`, or a tactic that invokes an external prover on the residual term. If a proof fails (or if a `Term` is satisfiable when using the `sat` command), counter-examples are presented in terms of variables from the original program.

Figure 3 shows a short script that compares the FFS implementations from Sect. 3.5 for equivalence. The `llvm_extract` command translates a simple LLVM function into SAWCore, and the `abc` primitive is a `ProofScript` value that instructs the system to perform the proof automatically using ABC. Expressions between double curly braces are in Cryptol syntax and automatically translated to SAWCore terms.

```
m <- llvm_load_module "ffs.bc";
ref <- llvm_extract m "ffs_ref" llvm_pure;
imp <- llvm_extract m "ffs_imp" llvm_pure;
let thm = {{ \x -> ref x == imp x }};
time (prove_print abc thm);
```

Fig. 3. SAWScript code to compare FFS implementations.

6   Implementation

The SAW implementation brings together a symbolic execution system for the JVM; a similar system for LLVM; an implementation of the SAWCore language, including a rewriting engine; an interpreter for the SAWScript language; and an interpreter for the Cryptol language. All of these components are written in Haskell, and total around 70 k Lines of Code (LOC). In addition to this Haskell code, SAW builds heavily on (and statically links with) the ABC system [5], which consists of around 480 k LOC in C. ABC is used in particular to represent AIG data structures.

The current implementation can export SAWCore models to ABC, other tools supporting the AIGER format, SAT solvers supporting the DIMACS Conjunctive Normal Form (CNF) format, model checkers that use sequential AIG models, and SMT solvers that use the SMT-Lib2 format (including invocation support for ABC, Boolector, CVC4, MathSAT, Yices, and Z3).

The entire SAW system is publicly available under the 3-clause BSD license:

- An overview and tutorial: http://saw.galois.com
- Complete source code: http://github.com/GaloisInc/saw-script

6.1 Current Limitations

Because the development of SAW has been driven by the goal of automatically proving properties about cryptographic algorithms, the scope of programs it can effectively model is currently restricted in several ways.

Symbolic Termination. Because symbolic execution is the key technique in SAW for translating imperative programs into formal models, we can successfully generate formal models only in cases where symbolic execution terminates. Symbolic execution is guaranteed to terminate when control flow does not depend on symbolic values (and when the program terminates for concrete values), but it may fail to terminate in other cases.

Memory Layout. The formal models generated by SAW must currently work over data composed of fixed-size bit vectors (potentially aggregated into larger data structures). Because of this, programs that operate over linked data structures such as lists or trees can only be analyzed for specific, fixed layouts.

Exceptions. Exceptions in both JVM and LLVM are largely unsupported. Code under analysis can throw exceptions, as a way of indicating invalid paths, but the symbolic execution engines do not track or invoke exception handlers.

Floating Point. The floating point instructions in JVM and LLVM are supported only for concrete values.

7 Experiments

SAW provides a novel combination of symbolic execution techniques. Although each has been at least proposed in prior work, the performance of each on concrete benchmarks is less well-understood. In this section, we describe how SAW performs on several benchmarks that show the benefits of its design choices. In all experiments, we set a time limit of 1500 s, and indicate times longer than this limit with "T/O".

7.1 Experimental Subjects

We have focused on using SAW for proofs about cryptographic algorithms and implementations, so the chosen benchmarks come from that domain.

FFS Two C implementations of the FFS algorithm (shown earlier), taken from standard C library implementations, compared for equivalence. The implementations are each a single function, so the proof of equivalence uses a monolithic strategy.

AES In-house implementations of the Advanced Encryption Standard (AES) block cipher in C and Cryptol, compared for equivalence using a monolithic proof strategy.

SHA-384 Three implementations of the SHA-384 hash function in C (from the `libgcrypt` library), Java (from Bouncy Castle), and Cryptol, compared for equivalence using both monolithic and compositional proof strategies. This proof covers just the inner loop of the compression function.

ZUC Implementations of two versions of the ZUC stream cipher, in C (from the official reference implementation) and Cryptol, compared for equivalence using both monolithic and compositional proof strategies. Version 1.4 of the algorithm had a bug related to non-injectivity of the key expansion function. We show a proof of the injectivity of the key expansion routine in version 1.5, and an example of non-injectivity in version 1.4 (by automatically producing two inputs for which the key expansion function returns the same output).

ECDSA In-house implementations of the Elliptic Curve Digital Signature Algorithm (ECDSA) over the NIST P-384 curve, written in Cryptol and Java, compared for equivalence using a compositional strategy. We also compare a subset of this implementation for equivalence using both a monolithic and a compositional strategy.

All of the in-house implementations are in the `examples` directory of the `saw-script` repository on GitHub cited in Sect. 6.

7.2 Shared Term Representation

Representing programs using shared (DAG) terms is one of the critical features of SAW. Because symbolic execution unrolls loops, many similar or identical subterms appear in the final program model. Table 1 shows how the shared and unshared sizes of the verification conditions for the following proofs compare. We also show the overall number of code lines, script lines, and total execution time required for each proof. In some cases, such as the SHA-384 equivalence proof, the improvement due to shared terms is simply a significant performance benefit; in other cases, such as the ECDSA equivalence proof, it makes proofs feasible that would otherwise be intractable.

Note that, although most of these benchmarks are equivalence proofs, two are not. The ZUC 1.4 example finds a specific input for which the key expansion function is not injective, and the ZUC 1.5 example shows that the improved key expansion function has been made injective. Both of these cases work directly on the C code without making use of a separate specification (other than a one-line statement of the injectivity property of the key expansion function).

7.3 Compositional Proofs

We show the effects of compositional reasoning on several examples on Table 2. Compositional reasoning can split one large proof into several smaller proofs. Because each proof must be processed separately, compositional reasoning can

Table 1. Shared and unshared term sizes, execution times, and script sizes for benchmarks. Proof times are for our original proof scripts, each of which may use several different provers.

Benchmark	Term Size		Lines		Proof time
	Shared	Unshared	Code	Script	
FFS equivalence	6.48×10^2	9.90×10^3	18	5	0.012 s
ZUC equivalence	3.96×10^4	3.550×10^6	620	152	6.443 s
ZUC 1.4 bug	1.83×10^4	1.27×10^7	263	79	1.692 s
ZUC 1.5 injectivity	1.83×10^4	1.30×10^7	263	78	7.047 s
AES equivalence	6.67×10^5	2.09×10^{38}	1301	55	901.923 s
SHA-384 equivalence	3.39×10^4	6.64×10^5	979	309	8.619 s
ECDSA equivalence	3.03×10^5	2.76×10^{273}	4305	1526	311.009 s

Table 2. Execution time for compositional and monolithic equivalence checking. These benchmarks use a single prover, rather than an optimized set, so the proof times differ from those in Table 1.

Benchmark	Prover	Proof time	
		Compositional	Monolithic
ZUC equivalence	ABC	13.873 s	13.064 s
ZUC equivalence	Z3	4.445 s	5.371 s
SHA-384 equivalence	ABC	T/O	T/O
SHA-384 equivalence	Z3	25.219 s	7.750 s
ECDSA equivalence (subset)	ABC	27.220s	105.284 s
ECDSA equivalence (subset)	Z3	75.385s	T/O

make small equivalence proofs slower to complete (as in the SHA-384 example). However, some proofs that are feasible monolithically are faster when done compositionally (such as ZUC using Z3 and the ECDSA subset using ABC). Most importantly, larger proofs tend to be intractable when done monolithically (such as the ECDSA proof using Z3) but become tractable using compositional reasoning. The full ECDSA proof mentioned in the previous section is compositional. A monolithic attempt at the same proof runs out of memory before even generating a theorem to prove, much less invoking a solver to discharge it.

7.4 Prover Comparison

We have included support for multiple provers within SAW because each tends to be efficient on a different class of applications. In particular, the purely propositional ABC tends to be the most efficient for small cryptographic primitives that primarily perform bit-level operations, whereas SMT solvers become more efficient for larger programs in which compositional verification is necessary.

Table 3. Relative prover efficiency. These are the same benchmarks as in Table 1, but with a single prover instead of potentially several. All proofs are monolithic, since ABC and Picosat do not support uninterpreted functions.

Benchmark	ABC	CVC4	Yices	Z3	Picosat
FFS equivalence	0.013 s	0.015 s	0.018 s	0.021 s	0.035 s
ZUC equivalence	14.451 s	T/O	4.196 s	6.952 s	11.311 s
ZUC 1.4 bug	1.692 s	3.073 s	0.599 s	1.991 s	2.961 s
ZUC 1.5 injectivity	7.047 s	T/O	2.051 s	1.679 s	4.629 s
AES equivalence	901.923 s	T/O	T/O	T/O	T/O
SHA-384 equivalence	T/O	T/O	56.368 s	8.813 s	T/O
ECDSA equivalence (subset)	26.743 s	T/O	42.925 s	74.591 s	35.470 s

Table 3 shows the time taken by each of five provers on several benchmarks. For the AES benchmark, we used the equivalence checking interface to ABC to compare two distinct circuits. For all other benchmarks, we generated a single formula for the property to be checked.

8 Related Work

Symbolic execution has been used since at least the 1970s as a technique for software analysis [17]. Many systems have used symbolic execution to prove properties about programs, detect bugs, and guide test generation. Of these, the KLEE tool [7] for LLVM is a representative example, and one of the most robust. Unlike SAW, KLEE focuses on checking specific properties of individual execution paths rather than generating complete models of programs that can be used for a variety of purposes. Others have investigated state merging in symbolic execution [15,19], but have used it more to improve the efficiency of path-based analysis based on symbolic execution, rather than for generation of complete semantic models.

The approach taken by bounded model checkers, such as CBMC [10] and LLBMC [13], is in some ways more similar to that of SAW. Bounded model checkers also tend to construct models of program semantics that are complete up to a certain bound. Model checkers frequently focus on temporal properties of concurrent systems, at the expense of efficiency when reasoning about complex, non-concurrent systems. SAW supports precise, efficient reasoning about sequential code but does not support concurrency or temporal properties.

Contract-based software verification tools such as Frama-C [18], VCC [11], the Java Modeling Language (JML) tools [6], and KeY [1] are very flexible with respect to the sorts of properties they can prove. They typically require significantly more manual effort than SAW for problems supported by both approaches (in the form of manual annotations or user-assisted proofs), but can handle a wider range of properties.

Unlike all of the verifiers mentioned so far, the goal of SAW is to construct a full model of the underlying program, separate from any specific verification task, and then perform any desired analysis on that model. However, some other tools have taken a similar approach to SAW. The most similar is Axe [24], which also aims at comparing cryptographic algorithms for equivalence. Axe uses ACL2 instead of type theory as its internal logic, and is not publicly available. Myreen et al. [23] and Hardin et al. [16] have both described decompilation of low-level imperative languages into logic, using techniques similar to those of SAW, though neither has a similar degree of integration. In the narrower domain of equivalence checking, LLVM-MD [26] used somewhat similar techniques for LLVM translation validation.

Both Why3 [14] and Boogie [20] have very similar goals to SAWCore. They are aimed at modeling the semantics of various source languages and providing easy connection to existing theorem provers. However, both languages use imperative constructs in the modeling language to encode the imperative constructs from the source language. Some standard program analysis techniques (e. g., dataflow analysis) are easier to implement on an imperative language, but verification must generally be annotation-based, and use, for instance, an approach like the weakest precondition calculus. Therefore, imperative modeling languages are not well-suited to the rewrite-based philosophy that we embrace. SAWCore tends to be well-suited to different classes of programs than Why3 or Boogie. Implementing a translator from either Why3 or Boogie to SAWCore could allow for the best of both worlds.

In the specific application domain of cryptography, several proof tools exist. One example is EasyCrypt [3], which allows high-level reasoning about cryptographic algorithms in the abstract, but does not allow proofs about existing concrete implementations.

In the realm of implementation verification, Appel recently proved the SHA-256 code in OpenSSL [2] equivalent to a high-level specification using the Verified Software Toolchain (VST), which provides a strong reasoning path between high-level cryptographic notions and concrete implementations written in C, depending on only the relatively small trusted code base (TCB) of the Coq theorem prover. The TCB of SAW is much larger. However, using VST to show equivalence between the abstract definition of SHA-256 and the C implementation required around 6,500 lines of manual proof, whereas equivalence proofs in SAW tend to be mostly automated. Our hope is that, in the long run, it will be possible to achieve a better balance between TCB size and automation, realizing the best of both worlds.

Relatedly, the miTLS project has created an implementation of Transport Layer Security TLS verified to be equivalent to a high-level specification [4]. The proof concerns a custom implementation written in F* and the tools could not be used to verify existing implementations in other languages.

The implementation of SAW described in this paper grew out of previous work on verifying Cryptol programs [12] and is the second iteration of a system briefly outlined in a previous extended abstract [8].

9 Conclusions and Future Work

We have shown that SAW can perform efficient equivalence checking and bug finding on a variety of real-world examples written in several programming languages. It achieves this by combining a collection of known but not previously integrated symbolic execution and program modeling techniques and connecting to a wide range of state-of-the art theorem provers.

Currently, however, SAW is most applicable to a restricted class of programs: those with finite, fixed input and output types that terminate under symbolic execution. Our primary intended direction of future work is to relax the restrictions. To ease the restriction on termination under symbolic execution, we plan to translate at least some iterative programs into explicit uses of fixpoint operations in the logic. This will allow us to generate models of more programs at the expense of more difficult reasoning about the resulting models. To allow general recursion in the context of our logic, while still allowing the logic to be used for proofs, we are considering adopting the approach of Zombie [9].

To ease the restriction on finite, fixed input and output types, we plan to extend SAW with the ability to generate formal models that include the heap as an explicit parameter and result. In conjunction with explicit fixpoint operations, this change should allow SAW to generate models of essentially arbitrary programs. It will, however, place a higher burden on the proof infrastructure required to do analysis of those models. Inductive proofs and complex reasoning about arrays will become much more important. Therefore, proofs about such models may only be feasible with interactive or semi-interactive proof tools, and we plan to explore emitting SAWCore models in the language of a proof assistant such as Coq or Lean.

Acknowledgments. Much of the work on SAW and Cryptol has been funded by, and design input was provided by the team at the NSA's Trusted Systems Research Group, including Brad Martin, Frank Taylor, Sean Weaver, and Jared Ziegler.

References

1. Ahrendt, W., Beckert, B., Bruns, D., Bubel, R., Gladisch, C., Grebing, S., Hähnle, R., Hentschel, M., Herda, M., Klebanov, V., Mostowski, W., Scheben, C., Schmitt, P.H., Ulbrich, M.: The KeY platform for verification and analysis of Java programs. In: Giannakopoulou, D., Kroening, D. (eds.) VSTTE 2014. LNCS, vol. 8471, pp. 55–71. Springer, Heidelberg (2014). doi:10.1007/978-3-319-12154-3_4

2. Appel, A.W.: Verification of a cryptographic primitive: SHA-256. ACM Trans. Program. Lang. Syst. **37**(2), 7:1–7:31 (2015)

3. Barthe, G., Grégoire, B., Heraud, S., Béguelin, S.Z.: Computer-aided security proofs for the working cryptographer. In: Rogaway, P. (ed.) CRYPTO 2011. LNCS, vol. 6841, pp. 71–90. Springer, Heidelberg (2011). doi:10.1007/978-3-642-22792-9_5

4. Bhargavan, K., Fournet, C., Kohlweiss, M., Pironti, A., Strub, P.Y.: Implementing TLS with verified cryptographic security. In: Proceedings of the 2013 IEEE Symposium on Security and Privacy (SP), pp. 445–459, May 2013

5. Brayton, R., Mishchenko, A.: ABC: an academic industrial-strength verification tool. In: Touili, T., Cook, B., Jackson, P. (eds.) CAV 2010. LNCS, vol. 6174, pp. 24–40. Springer, Heidelberg (2010). doi:10.1007/978-3-642-14295-6_5
6. Burdy, L., Cheon, Y., Cok, D.R., Ernst, M.D., Kiniry, J.R., Leavens, G.T., Leino, K.R.M., Poll, E.: An overview of JML tools and applications. Intl. J. Softw. Tools Technol. Transf. **7**(3), 212–232 (2005)
7. Cadar, C., Dunbar, D., Engler, D.: KLEE: Unassisted and automatic generation of high-coverage tests for complex systems programs. In: Proceedings of the 8th USENIX Conference on Operating Systems Design and Implementation (OSDI 2008), pp. 209–224. USENIX Association, Berkeley (2008)
8. Carter, K., Foltzer, A., Hendrix, J., Huffman, B., Tomb, A.: SAW: the software analysis workbench. In: Proceedings of the 2013 ACM SIGAda Annual Conference on High Integrity Language Technology (HILT 2013), pp. 15–18 (2013)
9. Casinghino, C., Sjöberg, V., Weirich, S.: Combining proofs and programs in a dependently typed language. In: Proceedings of the 41st ACM SIGPLAN-SIGACT Symposium on Principles of Programming Languages (POpPL 2014), pp. 33–45 (2014)
10. Clarke, E., Kroening, D., Lerda, F.: A tool for checking ANSI-C programs. In: Jensen, K., Podelski, A. (eds.) TACAS 2004. LNCS, vol. 2988, pp. 168–176. Springer, Heidelberg (2004). doi:10.1007/978-3-540-24730-2_15
11. Cohen, E., Dahlweid, M., Hillebrand, M., Leinenbach, D., Moskal, M., Santen, T., Schulte, W., Tobies, S.: VCC: a practical system for verifying concurrent C. In: Berghofer, S., Nipkow, T., Urban, C., Wenzel, M. (eds.) TPHOLs 2009. LNCS, vol. 5674, pp. 23–42. Springer, Heidelberg (2009). doi:10.1007/978-3-642-03359-9_2
12. Erkök, L., Matthews, J.: Pragmatic equivalence and safety checking in Cryptol. In: Proceedings of the 3rd Workshop on Programming Languages Meets Program Verification (PLpPV 2009), pp. 73–82 (2009)
13. Falke, S., Merz, F., Sinz, C.: The bounded model checker LLBMC. In: Proceedings of the 28th IEEE/ACM International Conference on Automated Software Engineering, (ASE 2013), pp. 706–709. IEEE (2013)
14. Filliâtre, J.-C., Paskevich, A.: Why3 — where programs meet provers. In: Felleisen, M., Gardner, P. (eds.) ESOP 2013. LNCS, vol. 7792, pp. 125–128. Springer, Heidelberg (2013). doi:10.1007/978-3-642-37036-6_8
15. Hansen, T., Schachte, P., Søndergaard, H.: State joining and splitting for the symbolic execution of binaries. In: Bensalem, S., Peled, D.A. (eds.) RV 2009. LNCS, vol. 5779, pp. 76–92. Springer, Heidelberg (2009). doi:10.1007/978-3-642-04694-0_6
16. Hardin, D.S.: Reasoning about LLVM code using Codewalker. In: Proceedings of the 13th International Workshop on the ACL2 Theorem Prover and Its Applications. Electronic Proceedings in Theoretical Computer Science, vol. 192, pp. 79–92, October 2015
17. King, J.C.: Symbolic execution and program testing. Commun. ACM **19**(7), 385–394 (1976)
18. Kirchner, F., Kosmatov, N., Prevosto, V., Signoles, J., Yakobowski, B.: Frama-C: a software analysis perspective. Formal Aspects Comput. **27**(3), 573–609 (2015)
19. Kuznetsov, V., Kinder, J., Bucur, S., Candea, G.: Efficient state merging in symbolic execution. In: Proceedings of the 33rd ACM SIGPLAN Conference on Programming Language Design and Implementation (PLDI 2012), pp. 193–204 (2012)
20. Leino, K.R.M.: This is Boogie 2. Technical report, Microsoft Research (2008)
21. Lewis, J., Martin, B.: Cryptol: high assurance, retargetable crypto development and validation. In: Proceedings of the IEEE Military Communications Conference (MILCOM 2003), vol. 2, pp. 820–825, October 2003

22. de Moura, L., Kong, S., Avigad, J., van Doorn, F., von Raumer, J.: The Lean theorem prover. In: Proceedings of the 25th International Conference on Automated Deduction (CADE-25), Berlin, Germany (2015)
23. Myreen, M.O., Gordon, M.J.C., Slind, K.: Decompilation into logic - improved. In: Proceedings of the 12th International Conference on Formal Methods in Computer-Aided Design (FMCAD 2012), pp. 78–81. IEEE (2012)
24. Smith, E.W.: Axe: an automated formal equivalence checking tool for programs. Ph.D. thesis, Stanford University (2011)
25. The Coq development team: The Coq Proof assistant reference manual. LogiCal Project, version 8.0 (2004). http://coq.inria.fr
26. Tristan, J.B., Govereau, P., Morrisett, G.: Evaluating value-graph translation validation for LLVM. In: Proceedings of the 32nd ACM SIGPLAN Conference on Programming Language Design and Implementation (PLDI 2011), pp. 295–305 (2011)

Bidirectional Grammars for Machine-Code Decoding and Encoding

Gang Tan[1]([⊠]) and Greg Morrisett[2]

[1] Pennsylvania State University, State College, USA
gtan@cse.psu.edu
[2] Cornell University, Ithaca, USA
jgm19@cornell.edu

Abstract. Binary analysis, which analyzes machine code, requires a decoder for converting bits into abstract syntax of machine instructions. Binary rewriting requires an encoder for converting instructions to bits. We propose a domain-specific language that enables the specification of both decoding and encoding in a single bidirectional grammar. With dependent types, a bigrammar enables the extraction of an executable decoder and encoder as well as a correctness proof showing their consistency. The bigrammar DSL is embedded in Coq with machine-checked proofs. We have used the bigrammar DSL to specify the decoding and encoding of a subset of x86-32 that includes around 300 instructions.

1 Introduction

Much recent research has been devoted to binary analysis, which performs static or dynamic analysis on machine code for purposes such as malware detection [5], vulnerability identification [14], and safety verification [16]. As a prominent example, Google's Native Client (NaCl [16]) statically checks whether a piece of machine code respects a browser sandbox security policy, which prevents buggy or malicious machine code from corrupting the Chrome browser's state, leaking information, or directly accessing system resources.

When analyzing machine code, a binary analysis has to start with a disassembly step, which requires the decoding of bits into abstract syntax of machine instructions. For some architectures, decoding is relatively trivial. But for an architecture as rich as the x86, building a decoder is incredibly difficult, as it has thousands of unique instructions, with variable lengths, variable numbers of operands, a large selection of addressing modes, all of which can be prefixed with a number of different byte sequences that change the semantics. Flipping just one bit leads to a totally different instruction, and can invalidate the rest of binary analysis.

In our previous work [10], we developed a Domain-Specific Language (DSL) for constructing high-fidelity machine-code decoders. It allows the specification of a machine-code decoder in a declarative grammar. The specification process in the DSL is user friendly in that a user can take the decoding tables from an architecture manual and use them to directly construct patterns in the decoder

© Springer International Publishing AG 2016
S. Blazy and M. Chechik (Eds.): VSTTE 2016, LNCS 9971, pp. 73–89, 2016.
DOI: 10.1007/978-3-319-48869-1_6

DSL. Furthermore, the decoder DSL comes with a denotational and operational semantics, and a proof of adequacy for the two semantics. Finally, we can automatically extract efficient recognizers and parsers from grammars in the DSL, with a proof of correctness about the extraction process based on the semantics.

The inverse of machine-code decoding is encoding: going from the abstract syntax of instructions to bits. Machine-code encoding is also important for some applications. For instance, binary rewriting has often been used to enforce security properties on untrusted code by inserting security checks before dangerous instructions [15]. After binary rewriting, the new code needs to be encoded into bits. Following the spirit of the previous decoder DSL, the machine-code encoding process should also be specified in some grammar with formal semantics. More importantly, we should be able to show the consistency between the decoder and the encoder: ideally, if we encode an instruction into bits and then decode those bits, we should get the instruction back (and also the other way around).

In this paper, we propose a DSL that allows the specification of both machine-code encoding and decoding in the same bidirectional grammar. The DSL is equipped with formal semantics. From a bidirectional grammar, we can extract a decoder and an encoder, as well as a machine-checked consistency proof that relates the decoder and encoder. Major contributions of the paper is as follows:

– We propose a bidirectional grammar (abbreviated as bigrammar) DSL that allows simultaneous specification of decoding and encoding. Using dependent types, it enables correctness by construction: if a bidirectional grammar in the DSL can be type checked, then the extracted decoder and encoder must be consistent. Our consistency definition takes into consideration that practical parsers may lose information during parsing and may produce values in loose semantic domains.
– We have used the bigrammar DSL to specify the decoding and encoding of an x86-32 model, which demonstrates the practicality of our proposed DSL. In this process we identified a dozen bugs in our previous x86 encoder and decoder, which were written separately and without a correctness proof.
– The bigrammar DSL and its semantics are formally encoded in Coq [6] and all proofs are machine-checked.

Machine decoding is an instance of parsing and encoding is an instance of pretty-printing. There has been previous work in the Haskell community on unifying parsing and pretty printing using invertible syntax [1,7,12]. In comparison, since our DSL is embedded in Coq, consistency proofs between decoding and encoding are explicitly represented as part of bigrammars and machine checked. Previous work in Haskell relies on paper and pencil consistency proofs. Another difference is on the consistency definition. Early work [1,7] required that parsers and pretty-printers are complete inverses (i.e., they form bijections). Rendel and Ostermann [12] argued that the bijection requirement is too strong in practice and proposed a consistency definition based on partial isomorphisms. We further simplify the requirement by eliminating equivalence relations in partial isomorphisms; details will be in Sect. 3.

2   Background: The Decoder DSL

We next briefly describe the decoder DSL, upon which the bidirectional DSL is based. The decoder DSL was developed as part of RockSalt [10], a machine-code security verifier with a formal correctness proof mechanized in Coq. The decoder language is embedded into Coq and lets users specify bit-level patterns and associated semantic actions for transforming input strings of bits to outputs such as abstract syntax. The pattern language is limited to regular expressions, but the semantic actions are arbitrary Coq functions. The decoder language is defined in terms of a small set of constructors given by the following type-indexed datatype:

$$
\begin{aligned}
&\text{Inductive grammar}\ :\text{Type} \to \text{Type} := \\
&\mid\ \text{Char}:\ \text{ch} \to \text{grammar ch} \\
&\mid\ \text{Eps}:\ \text{grammar unit} \\
&\mid\ \text{Zero}:\ \forall t, \text{grammar}\ t \\
&\mid\ \text{Cat}:\ \forall t_1\ t_2, \text{grammar}\ t_1 \to \text{grammar}\ t_2 \to \text{grammar}\ (t_1 * t_2) \\
&\mid\ \text{Alt}:\ \forall t_1\ t_2, \text{grammar}\ t_1 \to \text{grammar}\ t_2 \to \text{grammar}\ (t_1 + t_2) \\
&\mid\ \text{Map}:\ \forall t_1\ t_2, (t_1 \to t_2) \to \text{grammar}\ t_1 \to \text{grammar}\ t_2 \\
&\mid\ \text{Star}:\ \forall t, \text{grammar}\ t \to \text{grammar}\ (\text{list}\ t)
\end{aligned}
$$

A grammar is parameterized by ch, the type for input characters. For machine decoders, the ch type contains bits 0 and 1. A value of type "grammar t" represents a relation between input strings and semantic values of type t. Alternatively, we can think of the grammar as matching an input string and returning a set of associated semantic values. Formally, the denotation of a grammar is the least relation over strings and values satisfying the following equations:

$$
\begin{aligned}
[\![\text{Char}\ c]\!] &= \{(c::\text{nil}, c)\} \\
[\![\text{Eps}]\!] &= \{(\text{nil}, \text{tt})\} \\
[\![\text{Zero}]\!] &= \emptyset \\
[\![\text{Cat}\ g_1\ g_2]\!] &= \{((s_1 s_2), (v_1, v_2)) \mid (s_i, v_i) \in [\![g_i]\!]\} \\
[\![\text{Alt}\ g_1\ g_2]\!] &= \{(s, \text{inl}\ v_1) \mid (s, v_1) \in [\![g_1]\!]\} \cup \{(s, \text{inr}\ v_2) \mid (s, v_2) \in [\![g_2]\!]\} \\
[\![\text{Map}\ f\ g]\!] &= \{(s, f(v)) \mid (s, v) \in [\![g]\!]\} \\
[\![\text{Star}\ g]\!] &= [\![\text{Map}\ (\lambda\_.\,\text{nil})\ \text{Eps}]\!]\ \cup [\![\text{Map}\ (::)\ (\text{Cat}\ g\ (\text{Star}\ g))]\!]
\end{aligned}
$$

Grammar "Char c" matches strings containing only the character c, and returns that character as the semantic value. Eps matches only the empty string and returns tt (Coq's unit value). Grammar Zero matches no strings and thus returns no values. When g_1 is a grammar that returns values of type t_1 and g_2 is a grammar that returns values of type t_2, then "Alt $g_1\ g_2$" matches a string s if either g_1 or g_2 matches s; it returns values of the sum type $t_1 + t_2$. "Cat $g_1\ g_2$" matches a string if it can be broken into two pieces that match the grammars. It returns a pair of the values computed by the grammars. Star matches zero or more occurrences of a pattern, returning the result as a list.

Map is the constructor for semantic actions. When g is a grammar that returns t_1 values, and f is a function of type $t_1 \to t_2$, then "Map $f\ g$" is the grammar

```
Definition INC_p : grammar instr :=
   ("1111" $$ "111" $$ anybit $ "11000" $$ reg) @
      (fun p => let (w,r) := p in INC w (Reg_op r))
|| ("0100" $$ "0" $$ reg) @
      (fun r => INC true (Reg_op r))
|| ("1111" $$ "111" $$ anybit $ ext_op_modrm_noreg "000") @
      (fun p => let (w,addr) := p in INC w (Address_op addr)
```

Fig. 1. Parsing specification for the INC instruction.

that matches the same set of strings as g, but transforms the outputs from t_1 values to t_2 values using f.

Figure 1 gives an example grammar for the x86 INC instruction. We use Coq's notation mechanism to make the grammar more readable. Next we list the definitions for the notation used.

$g \mathbin{@} f := \mathsf{Map}\, f\, g$
$g_1 \mathbin{\$} g_2 := \mathsf{Cat}\, g_1\, g_2$
$\mathtt{literal}\, [c_1, \ldots, c_n] := (\mathsf{Char}\, c_1)\, \$ \ldots \$\, (\mathsf{Char}\, c_n)$
$g_1 \mathbin{\$\$} g_2 := ((\mathtt{literal}\, g_1)\, \$\, g_2) \mathbin{@} \mathsf{snd}$
$g_1 \mathbin{\|} g_2 := (\mathsf{Alt}\, g_1\, g_2) @ (\lambda v.\ \mathtt{match}\ v\ \mathtt{with}\ \mathtt{inl}\ v_1 \Rightarrow v_1 \mid \mathtt{inr}\ v_2 \Rightarrow v_2\ \mathtt{end})$

Note that "$g_1 \| g_2$" uses the union operation and assumes both g_1 and g_2 are of type "grammar t" for some t. It throws away information about which branch is taken.

At a high-level, the grammar in Fig. 1 specifies three alternatives that can build an INC instruction. Each case includes a pattern specifying literal sequences of bits (e.g., "1111"), followed by other components like anybit or reg that are themselves grammars that compute values of an appropriate type. For example, in the first case, we take the bit returned by anybit and the register returned by reg and use them to build the abstract syntax for a version of the INC instruction with a register operand.

The denotational semantics allows formal reasoning about grammars, but it cannot be directly executed. The operational semantics of grammars is defined using the notion of *derivatives* [4]. Informally, the derivative of a grammar g for an input character c is a residual grammar that returns the same semantic values as g and takes the same input strings except c. Using the notion of derivatives, we can build a parsing function that takes input strings and builds appropriate semantic values according to the grammar. We have also built a tool that constructs an efficient, table-driven recognizer from a grammar. Details about derivatives and table-driven recognizers can be found in our previous paper [10].

3   Relating Parsing and Pretty-Printing

A machine decoder is a special parser and a machine encoder is a special pretty printer. In general, a parser accepts an input string s and constructs a semantic value v according to a grammar. A pretty printer goes in the reverse direction, taking a semantic value v and printing a string s according to some grammar. In this section, we discuss how parsers and pretty printers should be formally related. We will first assume an unambiguous grammar g: that is, for a string s, there is at most one v so that $(s, v) \in [\![g]\!]$. In Sect. 5, we will present how to generalize to ambiguous grammars.

Ideally, a parser and its corresponding pretty printer should form a bijection [1, 7]: (i) if we parse some string s to get some semantic value v and then run the pretty printer on v, we should get the same string s back, and (ii) if we run the pretty printer on some v to get string s and then run the parser on s, we should get value v back. While some simple parsers and pretty printers do form bijections, most of them do not, because of the following two reasons.

Information loss during parsing. Parsing is often forgetful, losing information in the input. A simplest example is that a source-code parser often forgets the amount of white spaces in the AST produced by the parser. Another typical example happens when the union operator (i.e., $\|$) is used during parsing. For example, the INC grammar in Fig. 1 forgets which branch is taken because of the uses of the union operator. Our x86 decoder grammar has many such uses.

Because information is lost in a typical parser, multiple input strings may be parsed to the same semantic value. Therefore, for such a semantic value, the pretty printer has to either list all possible input strings, or choose a particular one, which may not be the same as the original input string. In this work, we take the second option since listing all possible input strings can be challenging for certain parsers (e.g., x86 has many bit-string encodings for the same instructions and operands; enumerating all of them during encoding is troublesome at least).

Loose semantic domains. A parser produces semantic values in some domain. For uniformity the semantic domain may include values that cannot be possible parsing results. Here is a contrived example: a parser takes strings that represent even numbers and converts them to values in the natural-number domain; the result domain is loose as the parser cannot produce odd numbers. Our x86 decoder has many examples, especially with respect to instruction operands. In the x86 syntax, operands can be immediates, registers, memory addresses, etc.; an instruction can take zero or several operands. A two-operand instruction cannot use memory addresses for both operands, but for uniformity our decoder just uses the operand domain for both operands. Similarly, some instructions cannot take all registers but only specific registers, but our decoder also uses the operand domain for these instructions.

Some of these issues can be fixed by tightening semantic domains so that they match exactly the set of possible parse results. While this is beneficial in some cases, it would in general require the introduction of many refined semantic domains, which would make the abstract syntax and the processing following parsing messy. For the example of x86 operands, we would need to define extra syntax for different groups of operands and, when we defined the semantics of instructions, we would need to introduce many more interpretation functions for those extra groups of operands.

The implication of loose semantic domains is that the pretty printer has to be partial: it cannot convert all possible semantic values back to input strings.

Formalizing consistency between parsing and pretty printing. The following diagram depicts the relationship between the domain of input strings and the output semantic domain for a parser: because of information loss during parsing, multiple input strings can be parsed to the same semantic value; because of loose semantic domains, some values may not be possible parsing results; finally, a typical parser is partial and may reject some input strings during parsing.

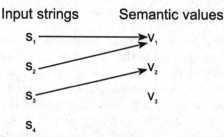

With the above diagram in mind, we next formalize the properties we desire from a parser and its corresponding pretty printer. Both the parser and the pretty printer are parameterized by a grammar of type "bigrammar t", which stands for bidirectional grammars that produce semantic values of type t. We will present the details of our bidirectional grammars in the next section; for now we just discuss the desired properties about the parser and the pretty printer that are derived from a bigrammar. These properties will be used to motivate the design of bigrammars.

Formally, a parser turns an input string (as a list of chars) to a possible value[1] of type t, according to a grammar indexed by t. A pretty printer encodes a semantic value in a possible string, according to a grammar.

$$\text{parse} : \forall t, (\text{bigrammar } t) \rightarrow \text{list ch} \rightarrow \text{option } t$$
$$\text{pretty-print} : \forall t, (\text{bigrammar } t) \rightarrow t \rightarrow \text{option (list ch)}$$

Two consistency properties that relate a parser and a pretty printer for the same grammar g of type "bigrammar t" are as follows:

Definition 1. *(Consistency between parsers and pretty printers)*

Prop1: If parse g s = Some v, *then exists* s' *so that* pretty-print g v = Some s'.
Prop2: If pretty-print g v = Some s, *then* parse g s = Some v.

Property 1 says that if a parser turns an input string s to a semantic value v, then the pretty printer should encode that value into some input string s';

---

[1] Our parser implementation actually returns a list of values during parsing, for simplicity of presentation we ignore that aspect in this paper.

however, s and s' may be different—this is to accommodate the situation when multiple input strings may correspond to the same semantic value. The property allows the pretty printer to choose one of them (the pretty printer cannot just pick an arbitrary string that is unrelated to v because of property 2).

Property 2 says that if the pretty printer encodes value v in string s, then the parser should parse s into the same value. Note that it places no restriction when the pretty printer cannot invert v—this is to accommodate a loose semantic domain in which some semantic values are not possible parsing results.

Rendel and Ostermann [12] proposed to use partial isomorphisms to relate parsers and pretty-printers. A partial isomorphism requires the same Property 2, but also requires s' and s are in some equivalence relation in Property 1. While it is mathematically appealing, requiring an extra equivalence relation would require adding unintuitive equivalence relations for many of our examples. For instance, x86 often has multiple bit-string encodings for the same instruction; for each case, we would have to define a special equivalence relation that just relates those bit strings. In our approach, the information about equivalence is actually contained in the bigrammar; the equivalence relation relates all bit strings that are parsed to the same semantic value. We could build an additional layer on top of our design and provide additional checking, but at the price of a programmer specifying the equivalence relations explicitly.

4   A Bidirectional Grammar

It would certainly be possible to write a parser and a pretty printer separately and then develop a correctness proof based on the consistency definition we presented. We actually developed an encoder separately from the x86-32 decoder (extracted from the decoder grammar). However, we realized that developing a correctness proof this way was rather difficult. Since the decoder and the encoder were developed separately, their internal structures were not designed to match closely and thus not amenable to a proof that relates them.

More importantly, the reverse pretty-printing functions for most constructors in our decoder DSL can be automatically calculated, but the separate encoder does not take advantage of that. For instance, the parser for "Cat g_1 g_2" parses the input string to construct a pair of values (v_1, v_2), the reverse pretty-printing function is then to encode v_1 to get s_1 according to g_1, encode v_2 to get s_2 according to g_2, and return s_1 followed by s_2. In fact, if a grammar forgoes the use of Map, then the semantic value returned by the grammar represents the input as a parse tree, which loses no information; the pretty printer can easily takes the parse tree and the grammar to reconstruct the input string.

Our bigrammar DSL takes advantage of the above observation and requires an inverse function only for the map case. Both a parser and a pretty printer are extracted from a bigrammar. Furthermore, the extracted parser and the pretty printer meet the consistency requirement. Therefore, it enables correctness by construction of parsers and pretty printers.

Figure 2 presents the bigrammar DSL syntax. We use lower-case constructors for bigrammars to distinguish them from grammar constructors. They are almost

```
Inductive bigrammar : Type → Type :=
| char : ch → bigrammar ch
| eps : bigrammar unit
| zero : ∀t, bigrammar t
| cat : ∀t₁ t₂, bigrammar t₁ → bigrammar t₂ → bigrammar (t₁ * t₂)
| alt : ∀t₁ t₂, bigrammar t₁ → bigrammar t₂ → bigrammar (t₁ + t₂)
| map : ∀t₁ t₂ (f₁ : t₁ → t₂)(f₂ : t₂ → option t₁)(g : bigrammar t₁)
           (pf : invertible(f₁, f₂, g)), bigrammar t₂
| star : ∀t, bigrammar t → bigrammar (list t)
```

where $\texttt{invertible}(f_1, f_2, g) \triangleq$
$$\big(\forall v : t_1, v \in \text{rng}(g) \Rightarrow \exists v', f_2 \; (f_1 \; v) = \texttt{Some} \; v' \wedge v' \in \text{rng}(g)\big) \wedge$$
$$\big(\forall v : t_1 \; \forall w : t_2, v \in \text{rng}(g) \Rightarrow f_2 \; w = \texttt{Some} \; v \Rightarrow f_1 \; v = w\big)$$

Fig. 2. Bigrammar DSL syntax.

the same as those in the decoder DSL, except that the map case requires an additional partial inverse function that goes from values of t_2 to values of type "option t_1" as well as a proof showing that the map function f_1 and the inverse function f_2 are invertible (we will discuss the invertible definition later). The inverse function is partial to accommodate loose semantic domains; i.e., some values cannot be possible results of the map function.

The denotational semantics of bigrammars is the same as the denotational semantics of the decoder DSL in Sect. 2, except that the map case ignores the inverse function and the proof; therefore, we do not repeat it. We still use g for a bigrammar. As before, notation $[\![g]\!]$ is the denotation of g and contains all pairs of (s, v) according to the denotational semantics. We write rng(g) to be the set $\{v \mid \exists s, (s, v) \in [\![g]\!]\}$.

Figure 3 presents the pretty printer for bigrammars. It takes a bigrammar and a semantic value, and returns an optional string s for the semantic value according to the bigrammar. We comment only on a few cases next. For "char c", since it is impossible for "char c" to produce a char that is different from c, the pretty printer tests if the semantic value c' is the same as c; if so, the input string must be a single-char string that contains c; otherwise, it returns None. Since pretty-print returns an optional value, we use an option monad and use the Haskell-style monadic notation ($\leftarrow$ and ret) to simplify the syntax of propagating None values.[2] Take the case of "cat g_1 g_2" as an example: if running pretty-print on g_1 produces None, then it returns None for the cat grammar; otherwise, the returned string is bound to s_1 and pretty-print is run on g_2; it either returns None or some s_2; in the first case, None is returned; in the second case, return $s_1 + + s_2$, which is s_1 concatenated with s_2. For "map f_1 f_2 g pf", the inverse function f_2 is first used to convert v to a possible v'; if it succeeds, pretty-print is run on v' according to g. Only the map case uses an explicit

---

[2] That is, "ret s" is defined as Some s; and "$s_1 \leftarrow v; f$" is defined as
match v with | None $\Rightarrow$ None | Some $s_1 \Rightarrow f \; s_1$ end.

$$
\begin{aligned}
\texttt{pretty-print (char } c) &= \lambda c'. \text{ if } c = c' \text{ then } \textbf{Some } (c :: \texttt{nil}) \text{ else } \textbf{None} \\
\texttt{pretty-print eps} &= \lambda\_. \ \textbf{Some nil} \\
\texttt{pretty-print (zero } t) &= \lambda\_. \ \textbf{None} \\
\texttt{pretty-print (cat } g_1 \ g_2) &= \lambda v. \ s_1 \leftarrow \texttt{pretty-print } g_1 \ (\texttt{fst } v); \\
&\qquad\quad s_2 \leftarrow \texttt{pretty-print } g_2 \ (\texttt{snd } v); \\
&\qquad\quad \texttt{ret } (s_1\texttt{++}s_2) \\
\texttt{pretty-print (alt } g_1 \ g_2) &= \lambda v. \ \texttt{match } v \text{ with} \\
&\qquad\quad |\ \texttt{inl } v_1 \Rightarrow \texttt{pretty-print } g_1 \ v_1 \\
&\qquad\quad |\ \texttt{inl } v_2 \Rightarrow \texttt{pretty-print } g_2 \ v_2 \text{ end} \\
\texttt{pretty-print (map } f_1 \ f_2 \ g \ pf) &= \lambda v. \ v' \leftarrow f_2 \ v; \ \texttt{pretty-print } g \ v' \\
\texttt{pretty-print (star } g) &= \texttt{fix } \lambda pp \ v. \ \texttt{match } v \text{ with} \\
&\qquad\quad |\ \texttt{nil} \Rightarrow \textbf{Some nil} \\
&\qquad\quad |\ hd :: tl \Rightarrow \\
&\qquad\qquad\quad s_1 \leftarrow \texttt{pretty-print } g \ hd; s_2 \leftarrow pp \ tl; \\
&\qquad\qquad\quad \texttt{ret } (s_1\texttt{++}s_2) \text{ end}
\end{aligned}
$$

Fig. 3. The pretty-print function for bigrammars.

inverse function; other cases' inverse functions are completely determined by the shapes of the bigrammar and the semantic value.

In "map $f_1 \ f_2 \ g \ pf$", a proof that the map function and the inverse function are invertible is required. The definition of invertibility is formulated so that the parser and the pretty printer for a bigrammar should meet the correctness properties in Definition 1. Therefore, the two conditions closely follow the two properties in Definition 1. The definition also takes g as a parameter and quantifies over all values in the range of g; this is to accommodate the situation when the range of g is a strict subset of the values in t_1. Requiring that the property holds for all values in t_1 would be too strong and unnecessary (and make the invertibility conditions unprovable for certain useful bigrammars).

Now we show how to prove that the parser and the pretty printer for a bigrammar meet the consistency requirement. With the help of denotational semantics, we can decouple the correctness proof of the parser from the correctness proof of the pretty printer. The correctness of the parser extracted from a grammar has been shown in the RockSalt paper [10] for a derivative-based parser; in the same way, a derivative-based parser can be extracted from a bigrammar with a similar correctness proof:

Theorem 1. *(Parser correctness.)*

$$(s, v) \in [\![g]\!] \ if \ and \ only \ if \ \texttt{parse } g \ s = \textbf{Some } v.$$

The second theorem is about pretty-printer correctness.

Theorem 2. *(Pretty-printer correctness.)*

(1) If $(s, v) \in [\![g]\!]$, then exists s' so that $\texttt{pretty-print } g \ v = \textbf{Some } s'$.
(2) If $\texttt{pretty-print } g \ v = \textbf{Some } s$, then $(s, v) \in [\![g]\!]$.

The proof of the above theorem is straightforward, based on induction over the syntax of g. With the theorems about parser and pretty-printer correctness, it can be checked easily that the consistency requirement in Definition 1 is a corollary.

The following notation is also introduced to simplify bigrammar construction:

$$g @ f_1 \& f_2 \& pf := \texttt{map } f_1 \ f_2 \ g \ pf \qquad\qquad g_1 + g_2 := \texttt{alt } g_1 \ g_2$$

5   Generalization to Ambiguous Grammars

An ambiguous bigrammar g can relate the same input string s to multiple semantic values. A simple example is "$\texttt{alt } (\texttt{char } c) \ (\texttt{char } c)$", where c is some character; it relates the single-character string c to "$\texttt{inl } c$" and "$\texttt{inr } c$". Because of ambiguity, the type of the parser is changed to the following:

$$\texttt{parse} : \forall t, (\texttt{bigrammar } t) \rightarrow \texttt{list ch} \rightarrow \texttt{list } t$$

It takes a possibly ambiguous bigrammar and an input string, and returns a list of values of type t. Correspondingly, the correctness theorem for the parser has to change:

Theorem 3. *(Parser correctness for ambiguous bigrammars.)*

$$(s, v) \in [\![g]\!] \ if \ and \ only \ if \ v \in \texttt{parse } g \ s.$$

We write "$v \in \texttt{parse } g \ s$" to mean that v is in the list produced by $\texttt{parse } g \ s$.

The type signature of the pretty printer and its correctness formulation are as before. With parser and pretty-printer correctness, we can show the following consistency theorem:

Theorem 4. *(Consistency between parsers and pretty printers for ambiguous grammars.)*

Prop1: If $v \in \texttt{parse } g \ s$, then exists s' so that $\texttt{pretty-print } g \ v = \texttt{Some } s'$.
Prop2: If $\texttt{pretty-print } g \ v = \texttt{Some } s$, then $v \in \texttt{parse } g \ s$.

6   Engineering Bigrammars for x86 Decoding and Encoding

We previously defined a 32-bit x86 grammar in the decoder DSL and used the grammar to extract a decoder. We retrofitted the grammar into a bigrammar by adding inverse functions and invertibility proofs to where Map is used. In the process we often needed to tweak grammar rules (sometimes with substantial changes) and introduce new constructors to make it easier to develop invertibility proofs and make the encoder more efficient. Using representative examples, we next discuss this experience about how we engineered the x86-32 decoder/encoder bigrammar.

Tighten semantic domains. Most of the changes were because the map functions used in the original decoder grammar are not surjective, causing loose semantic domains. Some of those instances can be fixed by having a tightened semantic domain. Here is a typical example. The grammar for parsing immediate values takes either 32 bits or 16 bits, depending on an operand-override flag, and returns an immediate operand:

```
Definition imm_p (opsize_override:bool): grammar operand_t :=
    match opsize_override with
      | false => word @ (fun w => Imm_op w)
      | true => halfword @ (fun w => Imm_op (sign_extend16_32 w))
    end.
```

To convert it to a bigrammar, we need to add one inverse function for each of the two cases. However, the operand domain contains not just immediate operands, but also other kinds of operands such as register operands. So the inverse function, which takes an operand value, has to first check if the value is an immediate operand. For instance, the inverse function for the first case is:

```
fun op => match op with | Imm_op w => Some w | _ => None end
```

Furthermore, we need a lemma that says operands produced by imm_p must be immediate operands and use the lemma in other bigrammars that use imm_p.

The problem is that the map functions in imm_p are not surjective and the resulting **operand** domain is loose. The fix is to change imm_p to return 32-bit immediates and any client of it applies Imm_op in its map functions when necessary. This makes the inverse function more efficient by avoiding some runtime tests. In particular, the imm_b bigrammar is as follows (in this and following examples, invertibility proofs are omitted and are represented as _).

```
Program Definition imm_b (opsize_override:bool):
    bigrammar word_t :=
    match opsize_override with
      | false => word
      | true => halfword @ (fun w => sign_extend16_32 w)
                       & (fun w =>
                            if repr_in_signed_halfword_dec w then
                              Some (sign_shrink32_16 w)
                            else None)
                       & _
    end.
```

Eliminating the uses of the union operator. Not all instances of loose semantic domains can be fixed easily, because of the extensive use of the union operator in the x86 decoder grammar. Many instructions' grammars have multiple cases. We have seen a typical example about the INC instruction in Fig. 1, which has three cases. Each case uses a map function and the three cases are combined through union, which throws away information about which case is taken during parsing.

To turn the INC grammar to a bigrammar, one possible way is to add an inverse function for each of the three cases. For instance, the inverse function for the first case (copied below) would pattern match the two arguments; if they are of the form "w, (Reg_op r)", return Some (w,r); otherwise, return None.

```
"1111" $$ "111" $$ anybit $ "11000" $$ reg @
    (fun p => let (w,r) := p in INC w (Reg_op r))
```

The three cases can then be combined using a special union operator that constructs bigrammars:

```
Program Definition union t (g1 g2:bigrammar t): bigrammar t :=
    (g1 + g2)
    @ (fun w => match w with inl v1 => v1 | inr v2 => v2 end)
    & (fun v: t =>
         match pretty_print g1 v with
         | Some _ => Some (inl v)
         | None =>
            match pretty_print g2 v with
                | Some _ => Some (inr v) | None => None end
       end)
    & _.
```

The inverse function for the union operator implements a backtracking semantics: it uses the pretty printer to first try the left branch; if it succeeds, inject v to the left branch; if it fails, it tries the right branch. The union constructor is biased toward the left branch if v can be produced by both branches.

Although the use of union is convenient for converting grammars to bigrammars, it is terribly inefficient. If the union is used to convert the INC grammar to a bigrammar, each case needs an inverse function that performs strict pattern matches and the inverse function in the union sequentially tries each case and checks which one succeeds. It comes with many runtime tests. Things get worse for instructions that have more cases; for instance, the grammar for MOV has a dozen cases. In general, if g is the result of combining n bigrammars via union and each bigrammar is of size m, then running the pretty printer on g takes $O(n * m)$ time in the worst case since it may try all n possibilities and pretty printing each bigrammar may take time $O(m)$. Therefore, the use of the union operator should be avoided as much as possible and it would be much more efficient to have some test at the top of the inverse function and use the test result to dispatch to *one of* the m cases, which leads to a complexity of $O(n+m)$. Our first version of the x86 bigrammar used the union operator for convenience, but in a subsequent version all uses of union were eliminated. We next discuss how this was achieved via the INC example.

In the following INC bigrammar, we combine cases using the disjoint-sum operator alt (abbreviated as +). Essentially, the three cases are combined to produce a parse tree and a single map function is used to convert the parse tree into arguments for INC. A single inverse function then converts arguments for INC to a parse tree. We will discuss later why the map function constructs arguments for INC instead of INC instructions.

```
Program Definition INC_b: bigrammar (pair_t bool_t operand_t) :=
(    "1111" $$ "111" $$ anybit $ "11000" $$ reg
  + "0100" $$ "0" $$ reg
  + "1111" $$ "111" $$ anybit $ ext_op_modrm_noreg "000")
  @ (fun v => match v with
                | inl (w,r) => (w, Reg_op r)
                | inr (inl r) => (true, Reg_op r)
                | inr (inr (w,addr)) => (w, Address_op addr)
              end)
  & (fun u => let (w,op):=u in
         match op with
           | Reg_op r =>
             if w then Some (inr (inl r)) else Some (inl (w,r))
           | Address_op addr => Some (inr (inr (w,addr)))
           | _ => None
         end)
  & _.
```

Since the above pattern is used over and over again in many instructions, we have constructed specialized Coq tactics for facilitating the process. Suppose we have a list of n bigrammars and bigrammar g_i is of type "bigrammar t_i" and function f_i is of type $t_i \to t$. For instance, the INC example has three cases:

```
Grammar 1:"1111" $$ "111" $$ anybit $ "11000" $$ reg
Map 1: fun v => let (w,r):=v in (w, Reg_op r)
Grammar 2: "0100" $$ "0" $$ reg
Map 2: fun r => (true, Reg_op r)
Grammar 3: "1111" $$ "111" $$ anybit $ ext_op_modrm_noreg "000"
Map 3: fun v => let (w,addr):=v in (w, Address_op addr)
```

Bigrammars g_1 to g_n can then be combined through repeated uses of alt and a single map function can be produced based on f_1 to f_n. We have automated the process by introducing tactics that combine bigrammars and for producing the map function based on f_1 to f_n. The inverse function needs to perform case analysis over values of type t and construct appropriate parse trees. A special tactic is introduced to facilitate the writing of the inverse function; it takes a case number and a value and produces a parse tree by inserting appropriate inl and inr constructors.

Our tactics construct balanced parse trees when combining bigrammars via the disjoint-sum operator; this makes a substantial difference for the speed of checking proofs of the combined bigrammar. To see why, one naive way would be to combine bigrammars in a right-associative fashion (or similarly in a left-associative fashion): $g = g_1 + (g_2 + (\ldots + (g_{n-1} + g_n)))$. However, to inject a value v_i produced by g_i into a parse tree, an average of $O(n)$ number of inl and inr constructors would be used. In contrast, our tactics balance the sizes of branches when combining bigrammars. For instance, g_1 to g_4 are combined to be $(g_1 + g_2) + (g_3 + g_4)$. This way, an average of $O(\log n)$ number of inls and inrs are used to inject a value to a parse tree. When developing proofs about g, this makes a substantial difference in the speed of proof checking. For instance, bigrammar reg_no_esp accepts the encoding of all registers except for esp and has therefore seven cases; it would take five seconds in Coq 8.4 to finish checking the bigrammar definition for the right-associative combination and take only two seconds for the balanced combination.

Combining instruction bigrammars. After individual instruction bigrammars have been developed, we need to combine them into a global bigrammar for all instructions. This was relatively easy to achieve when we developed grammars (without inverse functions): each instruction grammar produced values of the instr type and instruction grammars were combined through union. We have seen an example instruction grammar in Fig. 1, which returns INC instructions.

When constructing bigrammars, the situation is more complicated because of the desire of eliminating the use of union. To achieve that, we make our instruction bigrammars return arguments for instructions instead of instructions; then instruction bigrammars are combined via the disjoint-sum operator. That is, the global instruction bigrammar produces a parse tree; this is similar to the technique for dealing with cases in individual instruction bigrammars. We next illustrate this using an instruction set of only two instructions:

```
Inductive instr :=
  | AAA | INC (w:bool)(op1:operand).
Definition AAA_b : bigrammar unit_t := ...
Definition INC_b : bigrammar (pair_t bool_t operand_t) := ...
Program Definition instr_b : bigrammar instr_t :=
  (AAA_b + INC_b)
  @ (fun v =>
      match v with | inl _ => AAA | inr (w,op) => INC w op end)
  & (fun i =>
      match i with | AAA => inl tt | INC w op => inr (w,op) end)
  & _ .
```

As before, part of instr_b can be automatically generated using special Coq tactics.

However, during development we encountered the difficulty of running out of memory in Coq when checking instr_b. This was because our x86 model had around 300 instructions and it used a flat instruction syntax in which the instr definition has around 300 cases, one for each instruction. The resulting instr_b had an enormous number of uses of inls and inrs; each use had an implicit type parameter (the type parameter of inl/inr tells the type of the right/left branch of the sum type). As a result, Coq ran out of memory when checking the invertibility proof in instr_b and this was the case even after using balanced parse trees and employing special tricks in Coq to save memory (e.g., using the abstract tactic). To deal with the situation, we introduced hierarchical abstract syntax for instructions. For instance, floating-point instructions are grouped into a separate instruction type and a bigrammar is developed for floating-point instructions; as there are much fewer floating-point instructions, Coq was able to type check the bigrammar. Then, we have a bigrammar that converts the hierarchical instruction syntax into the flat instruction syntax (and also an inverse function for going the other direction).

Statistics of the x86 bigrammar. Our x86 bigrammar specifies the decoding and encoding of 297 instructions, including all x86 integer, floating-point, SSE, and MMX instructions. It also allows prefixes that can be added in the front of instructions. So for each decoding operation the decoder returns (p, i), where p is the set of prefixes and i is the instruction.

The following table lists the lines of Coq code for our previous decoder grammar, a separately developed encoder, and our new bigrammar for x86 encoding and decoding. Since our bigrammars enforce correctness by construction, the x86 bigrammar implies its extracted decoder and encoder are consistent. In contrast, the separately developed decoder and encoder lacked the correctness proof that relates them. We have also extracted executable OCaml decoder and encoder code from our x86 bigrammar and are using them in a separate OCaml project.

	Lines of Coq code
Decoder grammar	2,194
Encoder	2,891
Decoder/Encoder bigrammar	7,254

During the construction of the x86 bigrammar, we found around a dozen bugs in the previous decoder grammar and encoder. The decoder grammar was extensively tested in RockSalt [10], so most of the identified bugs were in the encoder. For example, the old encoder for MOVBE disallows the combination of using registers for both of its two operands (i.e., the encoder maps the case to None), but the decoder can actually produce operands of that combination. When developing the proof for the corresponding bigrammar, we could not prove the first condition in the invertibility definition and this was fixed by modifying the inverse function. As another example, the old encoders for instructions BT/BTC/BTR/BTS allow the combination of using a register for the first operand and a memory address for the second operand; however, this combination is not a possible decoding result for those instructions. As a result, we could not prove the second condition in the invertibility definition and this was fixed by mapping the combination to None in the inverse function. Even though the old decoder grammar was extensively tested, we did find a couple of bugs. For instance, the old decoder for the `Test` instruction had a case as follows:

```
"1010" $$ "1000" $$ byte @
  (fun b => TEST true (Reg_op EAX) (Imm_op (zero_extend8_32 b)))
```

The first parameter of `Test` tells whether the test operation should be for 32-bit words (when the parameter's value is true) or for 8-bit bytes (when the parameter's value is false). The above case actually compares bytes, so the first argument should be `false`.

Before we started migrating the x86 grammar, we wanted to determine whether or not moving from an established grammar and abstract syntax to a bigrammar required extensive changes. Our x86 experience tells us that the answer is yes, especially when one wants to eliminate the use of union. On the other hand, some of those changes could be alleviated through clever tactics.

7   Related Work

Specialized DSLs have been designed for declarative machine-code decoding (e.g., [13]); most of them do not allow a bidirectional syntax. Similar to bigrammars, SLED [11] allows specifying both encoding and decoding in a bidirectional syntax; however, consistency requirements are not formally spelled out and proofs are not represented and machine checked, leaving room for errors.

There are many general parsing and pretty-printing libraries. However, in general they do not allow a single syntax for both parsing and pretty-printing (other than [1,7,12], which we previously discussed). There has also been many bidirectional languages that have been designed for mapping between different data formats including XML processing [3,8] and pickling/unpickling [9]. They all require the forward and the backward directions form bijections, which are too strong for practical parsing and pretty-printing. Boomerang [2] provides bidirectional lenses that can run backwards. However, a bidirectional lens is motivated by the view-update problem in the database community and the backward direction takes both an abstract value and the original concrete value as input, while a pretty printer takes only the abstract value as input.

8   Conclusions

Our bigrammar DSL allows declarative specification of decoding and encoding of machine instructions, with machine-checked proofs that show the consistency between decoding and encoding. We have shown how to migrate a grammar for x86 decoding to a bigrammar for decoding and encoding. As future work, we plan to use the bigrammar DSL to specify the decoding/encoding of other machine architectures such as ARM. We also plan to extend the bigrammar DSL to support more expressive grammars such as parsing-expression grammars and context-free grammars.

The bigrammar development and the x86-32 bigrammar are open sourced and available at the following URL: https://github.com/gangtan/CPUmodels/tree/master/x86model/Model.

Acknowledgement. We thank the anonymous reviewers for their comments. This research is supported by NSF grants CCF-1217710, CCF-1149211, and CNS-1408826.

References

1. Alimarine, A., Smetsers, S., van Weelden, A., van Eekelen, M., Plasmeijer, R.: There and back again: arrows for invertible programming. In: Proceedings of the ACM SIGPLAN Workshop on Haskell, pp. 86–97 (2005)
2. Bohannon, A., Foster, J.N., Pierce, B.C., Pilkiewicz, A., Schmitt, A.: Boomerang: resourceful lenses for string data. In: 35th ACM Symposium on Principles of Programming Languages (POPL), pp. 407–419 (2008)
3. Brabrand, C., Møller, A., Schwartzbach, M.I.: Dual syntax for XML languages. In: Bierman, G., Koch, C. (eds.) DBPL 2005. LNCS, vol. 3774, pp. 27–41. Springer, Heidelberg (2005). doi:10.1007/11601524_2
4. Brzozowski, J.A.: Derivatives of regular expressions. J. ACM **11**, 481–494 (1964)
5. Christodorescu, M., Jha, S.: Static analysis of executables to detect malicious patterns. In: 12th Usenix Security Symposium. pp. 169–186 (2003)
6. The Coq proof assistant. https://coq.inria.fr/
7. Jansson, P., Jeuring, J.: Polytypic compact printing and parsing. In: Swierstra, S.D. (ed.) ESOP 1999. LNCS, vol. 1576, pp. 273–287. Springer, Heidelberg (1999). doi:10.1007/3-540-49099-X_18
8. Kawanaka, S., Hosoya, H.: biXid: a bidirectional transformation language for XML. In: ACM International Conference on Functional Programming (ICFP), pp. 201–214 (2006)
9. Kennedy, A.: Pickler combinators. J. Funct. Program. **14**(6), 727–739 (2004)
10. Morrisett, G., Tan, G., Tassarotti, J., Tristan, J.B., Gan, E.: Rocksalt: better, faster, stronger SFI for the x86. In: ACM Conference on Programming Language Design and Implementation (PLDI), pp. 395–404 (2012)
11. Ramsey, N., Fernández, M.F.: Specifying representations of machine instructions. ACM Trans. Program. Lang. Syst. **19**(3), 492–524 (1997)
12. Rendel, T., Ostermann, K.: Invertible syntax descriptions: unifying parsing and pretty printing. In: Proceedings of the Third ACM Haskell Symposium on Haskell, pp. 1–12 (2010)
13. Sepp, A., Kranz, J., Simon, A.: GDSL: a generic decoder specification language for interpreting machine language. In: Tools for Automatic Program Analysis, pp. 53–64 (2012)
14. Song, D., Brumley, D., Yin, H., Caballero, J., Jager, I., Kang, M.G., Liang, Z., Newsome, J., Poosankam, P., Saxena, P.: BitBlaze: a new approach to computer security via binary analysis. In: Proceedings of the 4th International Conference on Information Systems Security (2008)
15. Wartell, R., Mohan, V., Hamlen, K.W., Lin, Z.: Securing untrusted code via compiler-agnostic binary rewriting. In: Proceedings of the 28th Annual Computer Security Applications Conference, pp. 299–308 (2012)
16. Yee, B., Sehr, D., Dardyk, G., Chen, B., Muth, R., Ormandy, T., Okasaka, S., Narula, N., Fullagar, N.: Native client: a sandbox for portable, untrusted x86 native code. In: IEEE Symposium on Security and Privacy (S&P), May 2009

Automated Verification of Functional Correctness of Race-Free GPU Programs

Kensuke Kojima[1,2]($\boxtimes$), Akifumi Imanishi[1], and Atsushi Igarashi[1,2]

[1] Kyoto University, Kyoto, Japan
kozima@fos.kuis.kyoto-u.ac.jp
[2] JST CREST, Tokyo, Japan

Abstract. We study an automated verification method for functional correctness of parallel programs running on GPUs. Our method is based on Kojima and Igarashi's Hoare logic for GPU programs. Our algorithm generates verification conditions (VCs) from a program annotated by specifications and loop invariants and pass them to off-the-shelf SMT solvers. It is often impossible, however, to solve naively generated VCs in reasonable time. A main difficulty stems from quantifiers over threads due to the parallel nature of GPU programs. To overcome this difficulty, we additionally apply several transformations to simplify VCs before calling SMT solvers.

Our implementation successfully verifies correctness of several GPU programs, including matrix multiplication optimized by using shared memory. In contrast to many existing tools, our verifier succeeds in verifying fully parameterized programs: parameters such as the number of threads and the sizes of matrices are all symbolic. We empirically confirm that our simplification heuristics is highly effective for improving efficiency of the verification procedure.

1 Introduction

General-purpose computation on graphics processing units (GPGPU) is a technique to utilize GPUs, which consist of many cores running in parallel, to accelerate applications not necessarily related to graphics processing. GPGPU is one of the important techniques in high-performance computing, and has a wide range of applications [21]. However, it is hard and error-prone to hand-tune GPU programs for efficiency because the programmer has to consider cache, memory latency, memory access pattern, and data synchronization.

In this paper we study an automated verification technique for functional correctness of GPU programs. The basic idea is standard: our algorithm first generates verification conditions (VCs) from a program annotated with specification and loop invariants and then passes the generated VCs to off-the-shelf SMT solvers to check their validity. We empirically show that our technique can be applied to actual GPU programs, such as a matrix multiplication program optimized by using shared memory. Because shared memory optimization is a technique that is widely used when writing GPU programs, we believe that it is an encouraging result that we could verify a typical example of such programs.

S. Blazy and M. Chechik (Eds.): VSTTE 2016, LNCS 9971, pp. 90–106, 2016.
DOI: 10.1007/978-3-319-48869-1_7

We focus on race-free programs, relying on race detection techniques that have been studied elsewhere [1,16]. Race-freedom allows us to assume an arbitrary scheduling of threads without changing the behavior of a program. In particular, we can safely assume that all threads are executed in *complete lockstep* (that is, all threads execute the same instruction at the same time). Kojima and Igarashi [10] observed that such an assumption makes it possible to analyze a program similarly to the sequential setting and developed Hoare logic for GPGPU programs executed in lockstep. We adapt their logic for VC generation.

Even under the race-freedom assumption, however, the generated VCs are often too complex for SMT solvers to solve in a reasonable amount of time. VCs tend to involve many quantifiers over threads and multiplication over integers. Quantifiers over threads arise from assignment statements. When an assignment is executed on a GPU, it modifies more than one element of an array at a time. This means that the VC corresponding to an assignment says "if there exists a thread writing into this index, ..., and otherwise, ..." Also, the termination condition of a loop involves a quantifier over threads, saying "there is no thread satisfying the guard." Multiplications over integers often appears in GPGPU programs as computation of offsets of arrays in a complicated way. This also increases the difficulty of the verification problem because nonlinear integer arithmetic is undecidable in general. To overcome this difficulty, we devise several transformations to simplify VCs. Some of the simplification methods are standard (e.g., quantifier elimination) but others are specific to the current problem.

We implement a verifier for (a subset of) CUDA C, conduct experiments, and show that our method successfully verifies a few realistic GPU programs. Specifically, the correctness of an optimized matrix multiplication program using shared memory is verified, without instantiating parameters such as sizes of matrices and thread blocks. We also empirically confirm that our simplification heuristics is indeed highly effective to improve the verification process.

Contributions. Our main contributions are: (1) a VC generation algorithm for (race-free) GPU programs; (2) several simplification procedures to help SMT solvers discharge VCs; (3) implementation of a verifier based on (1) and (2); and (4) experiments to show that our verification method can indeed be applied to realistic GPU programs. Our approach can successfully handle fully parameterized programs, that is, we do not need to fix parameters such as the number of threads and sizes of arrays, unlike much of the existing work (for example, GPUVerify [1] requires the user to specify the number of threads).

Organization. The rest of the paper is organized as follows. Section 2 explains the execution model of GPU programs on which our verification method is based. Section 3 describes our VC generation algorithm. Section 4 introduces several methods to simplify generated VCs. Section 5 reports our implementation and experimental results. Section 6 discusses related work, and finally we summarize the paper and discuss future directions in Sect. 7.

2   Execution Model of GPU Programs

Compute Unified Device Architecture (CUDA) is a development environment provided by NVIDIA [22] for GPGPU. It includes a programming language CUDA C, which is an extension of C for GPGPU. A CUDA C program consists of host code, which is executed on a CPU, and device code, which is executed on a GPU. Host code is mostly the same as usual C code, except that it can invoke a function defined in device code. Such a function is called a *kernel function* (or simply kernel). The device code is also similar to usual C code, but it includes several special constants and functions specific to GPU, such as thread identifiers and synchronization primitives. The kernel function is executed on GPUs by the specified number of threads in parallel. The number of threads is specified in host code and does not change during the execution of a kernel function. When all the threads finish the execution, the result becomes available to host code. In this paper we focus on the verification of kernel functions invoked by host code (so we do not consider kernel functions called from device code).

As is mentioned in Sect. 1, we assume each instruction is executed in complete lockstep by all threads during the execution of device code. When the control branches during the execution, both branches are executed sequentially with threads irrelevant to branches being disabled. After both branches are completed, all the threads are enabled again. We say a thread is *inactive* if it is disabled, and *active* otherwise. This execution model is simplified from the so-called SIMT execution model, an execution model of CUDA C [22], in which threads form hierarchically organized groups and only threads that belong to the smallest group (called warp) are executed in lockstep. However, for race-free programs, there are not significant differences (except barrier divergence, which is an error caused by threads executing barrier synchronization at different program points).

Let us consider the kernel given in Fig. 1, which we call ArrayCopy, and use it as a running example. This program copies the contents of a shared array (pointed to by) a to another shared array (pointed to by) b, both of length len. N is the number of threads, and tid is a thread identifier, which ranges from 0 to $N - 1$. The first two lines specify a precondition and a postcondition, and

```
/*@ requires len == m * N;
    ensures  \forall int j; 0 <= j < len ==> b[j] == a[j]; */
void ArrayCopy (int *a, int *b, int len) {
  int i = tid;
  /*@ loop invariant i == N * loop_count + tid;
      loop invariant
         \forall int j; 0 <= j < N * loop_count ==> b[j] == a[j]; */
  while (i < len) {
    b[i] = a[i];
    i = i + N;
}}
```

Fig. 1. Running example: ArrayCopy

the three lines above the loop declare loop invariants used for verification of the specification. These specifications will be used later but we ignore them for the moment because they are not used during the execution.

If len is 6 and N is 4, the execution takes place as follows.[1] The local variable i is initialized to tid, so its initial value equals t at thread t $(0 \leq t < 4)$. In the first iteration of the loop body, the first four elements are copied from a to b, and the value of i at thread t becomes $t + 4$. Then, the guard i < len is satisfied by only threads 0 and 1; therefore, threads 2 and 3 become inactive and the loop body is iterated again. Because active threads are only 0 and 1, the fourth and fifth elements of a are copied, and the values of i at threads $0, 1, 2, 3$ becomes $8, 9, 6, 7$, respectively. Now, no threads satisfy the guard, so the loop is exited and the program terminates with the expected result.

3   Verification Condition Generation

In this section we describe how VCs are generated from a program annotated with specifications, using the example ArrayCopy in Fig. 1. Before discussing VC generation, let us take a look at the specification. The first line declares a precondition that the length of arrays is a multiple of the number of threads. A variable m, whose declaration is omitted, is a specification variable, which is a variable used only in the specification. We also assume implicitly that a and b do not overlap, and have length (at least) len. The second line declares the postcondition asserting that the contents of a are indeed copied into b. The loop contains two declarations of loop invariants. In the invariant we allow a specification variable loop_count, which stands for how many times the loop body has been executed. This variable is not present in CUDA C, but we have introduced it for convenience. It allows us to express the value of variables explicitly in an invariant. The first invariant specifies the value of the variable i on each iteration, and the second asserts that at the beginning of l-th iteration (counting from 0) the first $N \cdot l$ elements of a have been already copied to b.

We present verification condition generation as symbolic execution of the axiomatic semantics of SIMT programs by Kojima and Igarashi [10]. We do not review the previous work here but believe that the description below is detailed enough (and self-contained), with the concrete execution model described in the last section in mind. Constructs that do not appear in this example are explained at the end of the section.

First, generate specification variables i_0 and len_0, which represent the initial values of i and len, respectively, and a_0 and b_0, which represent the contents of arrays pointed to by a and b, respectively. Here, i_0, a_0, and b_0 has the type of maps from int to int, and len_0 has type int. Since a_0 and b_0 represent arrays, they are naturally represented as maps. The reason that i_0 also has a map type is that it corresponds to a local variable whose value varies among

---

[1] We choose these initial values to explain what happens when the control branches. These initial values do not satisfy the precondition on the first line, so the asserted invariant is not preserved during execution.

threads. So, expression $i_0(t)$ stands for the value of i at thread t. We also need m which is a specification variable of type int. The precondition in the first line is translated into the formula $len_0 = m \cdot N$, so we assume this equation holds. In the next line the value of i is updated to tid in all threads. In general every time we encounter an assignment we introduce a new variable that represents the value of the variable being assigned after this assignment. In the case of i = tid we introduce a new variable i_1 of the same type as i_0, and assume $\forall t.0 \leq t < N \rightarrow i_1(t) = t$, that is, its value on thread t equals t. For later use, let us denote by Γ_{entry} the list consisting of the two constraints we have introduced so far:

$$\Gamma_{\text{entry}} \overset{\text{def}}{=} len_0 = m \cdot N, \forall t.0 \leq t < N \rightarrow i_1(t) = t.$$

So, Γ_{entry} represents possible states of the program at the beginning of the loop. Since two invariants are declared in this loop, we have to check that they are true at the entry, so we generate two conditions to be verified:

$$\Gamma_{\text{entry}} \vdash \forall t.0 \leq t < N \rightarrow i_1(t) = N \cdot 0 + t, \tag{T1}$$

$$\Gamma_{\text{entry}} \vdash \forall j.0 \leq j < N \cdot 0 \rightarrow b_0(j) = a_0(j). \tag{T2}$$

Below we call a condition of the form $\Gamma \vdash \varphi$ a *task*, and φ the *goal*. Tasks (T1) and (T2) assert that the first and second invariants are true at the loop entry, respectively. The right-hand sides of these tasks are obtained from loop invariants by simply replacing loop_count with 0, the initial value of the loop counter.

Next, we have to encode the execution of the loop, but in general it is impossible to know how many times the loop body is executed. Rather than iterating the loop, we directly generate a constraint that abstracts the final state of the loop, relying on the invariants supplied by the programmer [8]. Also we have to verify that the supplied invariants are indeed preserved by iterating the loop. To do this we first introduce a new variable for each program variable being modified in the loop body. In the case of our example, variables being modified are b and i, so we generate fresh b_1 and i_2. We also introduce l corresponding to the loop counter. Let Γ_{loop} be the following list of formulas:

$$\Gamma_{\text{loop}} \overset{\text{def}}{=} \Gamma_{\text{entry}}, 0 \leq l, \forall t.0 \leq t < N \rightarrow i_2(t) = N \cdot l + t,$$
$$\forall j.0 \leq j < N \cdot l \rightarrow b_1(j) = a_0(j).$$

Γ_{loop} consists of three additional constraints. The first one, $0 \leq l$, says that the loop counter is not negative. The second and third ones correspond to invariants, and they assert that invariants are true for variables b_1, i_2, and l we just have introduced. Note that in Γ_{loop} it is not yet specified whether the loop is already exited or not.

Consider the case the loop is continued. Then, there is at least one thread that satisfies the loop guard i < len, which is expressed: $\exists t.0 \leq t < N \wedge i_2(t) < len_0$. Since the loop body contains assignments to b and i, we generate new variables b_2 and i_3 and add constraints expressing that these variables are the result of executing these assignments. Writing down such constraints is a little more involved than before, because these assignments are inside the loop body, and therefore there may be several threads that are inactive (actually in this example such a situation never happens, but to describe how VCs are generated in a general case, let us proceed as if we do not know this fact). We use the notation $assign(b_2, i_2 < len_0, b_1, i_2, a_0(i_2))$ for such a constraint.[2] This intuitively means that b_2 is the result of executing b[i] = a[i] with the values of b and i being b_1 and i_2 respectively, and active threads t being precisely those that satisfy $i_2(t) < len_0$. The first argument is the new value of the variable being assigned, the second specifies which threads are active, the third is the original value of the variable being assigned, the fourth is the index being written (in general, this is an n-tuple if the array being assigned is n-dimensional, and the 0-tuple · if the variable is scalar), and the last is the value of the right-hand side of the assignment. It can be written out as

$$\forall n. (\exists t.0 \le t < N \wedge i_2(t) < len_0 \wedge i_2(t) = n \wedge b_2(n) = a_0(i_2(t))) \vee \\ ((\forall t.\neg(0 \le t < N \wedge i_2(t) < len_0 \wedge i_2(t) = n)) \wedge b_2(n) = b_1(n)), \quad (1)$$

but the concrete definition does not matter here. For general cases, readers are referred to Kojima and Igarashi [10]. Putting these constraints together we obtain Γ_{iter} defined as follows:

$$\Gamma_{\text{iter}} \stackrel{\text{def}}{=} \Gamma_{\text{loop}}, \exists t.0 \le t < N \wedge i_2(t) < len_0,$$
$$assign(b_2, i_2 < len_0, b_1, i_2, a_0(i_2)), assign(i_3, i_2 < len_0, i_2, \cdot, i_2 + N).$$

Using Γ_{iter} we can write the tasks corresponding to the invariant preservation as follows:

$$\Gamma_{\text{iter}} \vdash \forall t.0 \le t < N \to i_3(t) = N \cdot (l+1) + t, \quad (\text{T3})$$

$$\Gamma_{\text{iter}} \vdash \forall j.0 \le j < N \cdot (l+1) \to b_2(j) = a_0(j). \quad (\text{T4})$$

The right-hand sides of these tasks are obtained by replacing loop_count, b, and i in the invariants with their values after the iteration, namely $l+1$, b_2, and i_3, respectively.

Finally we consider the case loop is exited, in which case the loop guard is false in all threads. Therefore we put

$$\Gamma_{\text{exit}} \stackrel{\text{def}}{=} \Gamma_{\text{loop}}, \forall t.0 \le t < N \to \neg(i_2(t) < len_0).$$

Since there are no more statements to be executed, it only remains to verify that the postcondition holds under this constraint. So the final task is as follows:

$$\Gamma_{\text{exit}} \vdash \forall j.0 \le j < len_0 \to b_1(j) = a_0(j). \quad (\text{T5})$$

---

[2] Some of the terms appearing in this expression are not well-typed. We could write $assign(b_2, (\lambda t.i_2(t) < len_0), b_1, (\lambda t.i_2(t)), (\lambda t.a_0(i_2(t))))$, but for brevity we abbreviate it as above.

To summarize, we generate tasks (T1–T5) as VCs for our example program. (T1) and (T2) ensure that the invariants hold when the loop is entered, (T3) and (T4) ensure that the invariants are preserved by executing the loop body, and (T5) ensures that the postcondition is satisfied when the program terminates.

Finally let us mention two more constructs: if-statements and barrier synchronization. As mentioned before, an if-statement is executed sequentially with switching active threads. When a statement if b then P else Q is encountered, we first process P, and then Q (because we assume race-freedom, the order does not matter). When processing P we have to bear in mind that active threads are restricted to those at which b evaluates to true, and similarly for Q. Barrier synchronization is, since we assume the execution is complete lockstep, considered as an assertion that all threads are active at that program point. We can generate an extra task $\Gamma \vdash \forall t.0 \leq t < N \rightarrow \mu(t)$, where $\mu(t)$ is a formula expressing that thread t is currently active, to verify that the synchronization does not fail. For example, if there were synchronization at the end of the loop body in ArrayCopy, $\mu(t)$ would be $i_2(t) < len_0$.

4   Simplifying Verification Conditions

Unfortunately, SMT solvers often fail to discharge VCs generated by the algorithm described in the previous section. In this section, we describe a few schemes to simplify VCs used in our verifier implementation.

The main difficulty stems from universal quantifiers, which are typically introduced by assignment statements and loop invariants. When these universally quantified formulas are put on the left-hand side of the tasks, the solvers have to instantiate them with appropriate terms, but it is often difficult to find them. To overcome this difficulty, in Sects. 4.1 and 4.2 we introduce two strategies that find appropriate instances of these quantified variables and rewrite VCs using these instances.

Another difficulty stems from multiplication over integers that often arises from indices of arrays. This makes VCs harder to discharge automatically, since nonlinear integer arithmetic is undecidable (even without quantifiers). The transformation described in Sect. 4.3 simplifies formulas involving both quantifiers and multiplication in a certain form.

A standard approach to the first problem would be to provide SMT solvers with patterns (triggers) to help them find appropriate instances. However, we could not verify programs by using triggers instead of the first two methods introduced in this section. This is because the third transformation (described in Sect. 4.3) often works only after the first two have been applied, that is, instantiation and rewriting have to be performed before this transformation. Because all of our transformations are performed before calling SMT solvers, they cannot be replaced by triggers.

4.1 Eliminating *assign*

One of the important transformations is what we call *assign*-elimination. During VC generation, we introduce a new assumption involving *assign* for each assignment statement. As we have seen in (1), *assign* is universally quantified and therefore has to be instantiated by appropriate terms. The main objective of *assign*-elimination is to find all necessary instances automatically, and rewrite the VC using such instances (as a result, *assign* may be removed from the task). Since (1) is introduced to specify the value of b_2, we instantiate (1) by every term u such that $b_2(u)$ appears in VCs. By enumerating such u's (including those inside quantifiers) we would find all instances for n that are necessary to prove VCs.

There are two cases to consider: assignments to local variables and shared variables. As an example of the local case, let us consider i_3 appearing in (T3). Its value is specified by $assign(i_3, i_2 < len_0, i_2, \cdot, i_2 + N)$ in Γ_{iter}, which implies: (a) if t is a thread ID that is active (that is, $i_2(t) < len_0$), then the value of i_3 at t is $i_2(t) + N$, and (b) otherwise the value of i_3 at t is $i_2(t)$. In case (a), $i_3(t) = N \cdot (l+1) + t$ is equivalent to $i_2(t) + N = N \cdot (l+1) + t$, and in case (b) it is equivalent to $i_2(t) = N \cdot (l+1) + t$. Therefore by doing case splitting, we can rewrite the right-hand side of (T3) into:

$$\forall t.(0 \leq t < N \rightarrow i_2(t) < len_0 \rightarrow i_2(t) + N = N \cdot (l+1) + t) \wedge$$
$$(0 \leq t < N \rightarrow \neg(i_2(t) < len_0) \rightarrow i_2(t) = N \cdot (l+1) + t).$$

The first and the second conjuncts correspond to cases (a) and (b), respectively.

For the case of shared variables, consider b_2 in task (T4). Similarly to the previous case, for each j either (a) there exists a thread t such that $i_2(t) < len_0$, $i_2(t) = j$, and $b_2(j) = a_0(i_2(t))$, or (b) there is no such thread t, and $b_2(j) = b_1(j)$. We obtain the following formula by rewriting the right-hand side of (T4):

$$\forall j.(0 \leq j < N \cdot (l+1) \rightarrow$$
$$\quad \forall t.0 \leq t < N \wedge i_2(t) < len_0 \wedge i_2(t) = j \rightarrow a_0(i_2(t)) = a_0(j)) \wedge$$
$$(0 \leq j < N \cdot (l+1) \rightarrow \tag{2}$$
$$\quad (\forall t.\neg(0 \leq t < N \wedge i_2(t) < len_0 \wedge i_2(t) = j)) \rightarrow b_1(j) = a_0(j)).$$

Following this strategy we can rewrite the VC so that the first argument of *assign* does not appear in the resulting VC, thus SMT solvers do not have to search for instances of *assign* any more.

4.2 Rewriting Using Equalities with Premises

Invariants often involve a quantified and guarded equality that specifies the values of program variables, as we can see in ArrayCopy. Let us illustrate how such an equality can be used to rewrite and then simplify the formula. The method described below applies to both goals and assumptions.

Consider b_1 in the task (T5). Using the invariant $\forall j.0 \leq j < N \cdot l \rightarrow b_1(j) = a_0(j)$, we can rewrite $b_1(j)$ into $a_0(j)$, but only under the assumption that $0 \leq j < N \cdot l$. Taking this condition into account, we can see that the goal $\forall j.0 \leq j < len_0 \rightarrow b_1(j) = a_0(j)$ can be changed to:

$$\forall j.0 \leq j < len_0 \rightarrow (0 \leq j < N \cdot l \wedge a_0(j) = a_0(j)) \vee \tag{3}$$
$$(\neg(0 \leq j < N \cdot l) \wedge b_1(j) = a_0(j)).$$

After this transformation, we can use several simplifications to transform the task into an easier one that can be solved automatically. Let us demonstrate how this can be done. We have both $\forall t.0 \leq t < N \rightarrow \neg(i_2(t) < len_0)$ and $\forall t.0 \leq t < N \rightarrow i_2(t) = N \cdot l + t$ in Γ_{exit}; therefore, rewriting $i_2(t)$ in the same way as above, we can see that it follows from Γ_{exit} that

$$\forall t.0 \leq t < N \rightarrow \neg((0 \leq t < N \rightarrow N \cdot l + t < len_0) \wedge$$
$$(\neg(0 \leq t < N) \rightarrow i_2(t) < len_0)).$$

By using laws of propositional logic we can simplify this as $\forall t.0 \leq t < N \rightarrow \neg(N \cdot l + t < len_0)$, and by eliminating the quantifier we obtain $len_0 \leq N \cdot l$. From this, (3) is easily derived by SMT solvers.

Similarly, (2) can be simplified as follows: the first conjunct is easily proved; in the second conjunct we can replace $i_2(t)$ with $N \cdot l + t$, and then eliminate $\forall t$ to obtain

$$\forall j.0 \leq j < N \cdot (l+1) \rightarrow \neg(0 \leq j - N \cdot l < N \wedge j < len_0) \rightarrow b_1(j) = a_0(j).$$

In general, we first search for an assumption of the form

$$\forall x_1.\gamma_1 \rightarrow \forall x_2.\gamma_2 \rightarrow \cdots \rightarrow \forall x_m.\gamma_m \rightarrow f(s_1, \ldots, s_n) = s' \tag{4}$$

where f is a function symbol. For each such assumption, find another formula (either one of the assumptions or the goal) in which f occurs. Such a formula can be written as $\psi[\varphi(f(t_1, \ldots, t_n))]$, where every variable occurrence of $t_1, \ldots, t_n$ is free in $\varphi(f(t_1, \ldots, t_n))$. Then by rewriting f we obtain:

$$\psi[(\exists x_1 \ldots x_m.\gamma_1 \wedge \cdots \wedge \gamma_m \wedge s_1 = t_1 \wedge \cdots \wedge s_n = t_n \wedge \varphi(s')) \vee$$
$$(\forall x_1 \ldots x_m.\neg(\gamma_1 \wedge \cdots \wedge \gamma_m \wedge s_1 = t_1 \wedge \cdots \wedge s_n = t_n)) \wedge \varphi(f(t_1, \ldots, t_n))].$$

Intuitively, this can be read as follows. If there are $x_1, \ldots, x_n$ that satisfy $\gamma_1, \ldots, \gamma_n$ and $s_i = t_i$ for every i, then by (4) we can replace $\varphi(f(t_1, \ldots, t_n))$ with $\varphi(s')$ (the first disjunct). If there are no such $x_1, \ldots, x_n$, then we leave $\varphi(f(t_1, \ldots, t_n))$ unchanged (the second disjunct).

4.3 Merging Quantifiers

Aside from standard transformations on formulas such as quantifier elimination, we exploit a procedure which merges two quantifiers into a single one.

Typical example is the following: if x and y range over integers, $\forall x.0 \le x <$ $a \to \forall y.0 \le y < b \to \varphi(x + ay)$ (or equivalently, $\forall x.0 \le x \le a - 1 \to \forall y.0 \le$ $y \le b - 1 \to \varphi(x + ay)$) is equivalent to $0 < a \to \forall z.0 \le z < ab \to \varphi(z)$ (the antecedent $0 < a$ is necessary because otherwise if both a and b are negative the former is trivially true while the latter would not). This pattern often arises when computing an index of an array.

Let us illustrate how this helps simplify a VC. This transformation typically applies when a thread hierarchy and/or two-dimensional arrays are involved. Consider the following program, which is a variant of ArrayCopy.

```
/*@ requires len == m * N;
    ensures  \forall int j; 0 <= j < len ==> b[j] == a[j]; */
i = bid * bsize + tid;
/*@ loop invariant i == N * loop_count + bid * bsize + tid;
    loop invariant
        \forall int j; 0 <= j < N * loop_count ==> b[j] == a[j]; */
while (i < len) {
  b[i] = a[i];
  i = i + N;
}
```

Here we assume that threads are grouped into *blocks*, as in actual CUDA C or OpenCL programs. Each block consists of an equal number of threads. In the program above, bsize is the number of threads contained in one block, and bid is the identifier for a block, called block ID. When bid is evaluated on a certain thread, the result is the block ID of the block to which the thread belongs. N is, as before, the number of threads, and now equals the product of bsize and the number of blocks.

Let us consider the termination condition of the loop:

$$\forall t.0 \le t < T \to \forall b.0 \le b < B \to \neg(N \cdot l + b \cdot T + t < len)$$

where T denotes the number of threads per block, and B the number of blocks (we replaced i with $N \cdot l + b \cdot T + t$ using the first invariant). By merging two quantifiers, we obtain

$$0 < T \to \forall z.0 \le z < T \cdot B \to \neg(N \cdot l + z < len).$$

The quantification over z is now easily eliminated, and we obtain $0 < T \to$ $T \cdot B \le 0 \lor len \le N \cdot l$.

Up to now we have assumed that the quantifiers that can be merged have the form $\forall x.0 \le x < a \to \ldots$, but in general this is not the case. Other simplification procedures (quantifier elimination, in our implementation) may convert formulas to their normal forms. After that, the guard $0 \le x < a$ may be modified, split, or moved to other places. This significantly makes the quantifier merging algorithm complicated. Because guards do not necessarily follow quantifiers, it is not straightforward to find a pair of quantifiers that can be merged as described above.

Our strategy in the general case is the following. (I) For every quantified subformula $\forall x.\varphi(x)$, find a such that $\forall x.\varphi(x)$ is equivalent to $\forall x.0 \le x < a \to \varphi(x)$. We call such a a *bound* of x. (II) For each subformula $\forall x.\forall y.\varphi(x, y)$, where x and y have bounds a and b, respectively, find $\psi(z)$ such that $\varphi(x, y)$ is equivalent to $\psi(x+ay)$ (or $\psi(y+bx)$). Then we can replace $\forall x.\forall y.\varphi(x, y)$ with an equivalent formula $0 < a \to \forall z.0 \le z < ab \to \psi(z)$, as desired. For the existential case, use $\land$ instead of $\to$. There may be multiple (actually infinitely many) bounds, and only some of them can be used as a in step (II). We collect as many bounds as possible in step (I), and try step (II) for every bound a of x we found. Below we simply write φ rather than $\varphi(x)$ if no confusion arises.

For step (I), note that if $\neg(0 \le x)$ implies φ and $\neg(x < a)$ implies φ, then $\forall x.\varphi$ if and only if $\forall x.0 \le x < a \to \varphi$. Similarly, if φ implies both $0 \le x$ and $x < a$, then $\exists x.\varphi$ if and only if $\exists x.0 \le x < a \land \varphi$. Therefore we can split the problem as follows: for the universal case, (i) check that $\neg(0 \le x)$ implies φ, and (ii) find a such that $\neg(x < a)$ implies φ; for the existential case, (i) check that φ implies $0 \le x$, and (ii) find a such that φ implies $x < a$. Because both of them can be solved similarly, we shall focus on (ii).

Let us say that a is a $\forall$-bound ($\exists$-bound) of x in φ if $\neg(x < a)$ implies φ (φ implies $x < a$, respectively). Then we are to find $\forall$- and $\exists$-bounds of x in a given φ. The procedure is given recursively. If φ is atomic, then the problem is easy, although there are tedious case distinctions. For example, $\forall$-bound of $x \ge t$ is t,[3] $\forall$-bound of $x < t$ does not exist, and $\exists$-bound of $x \le t$ is $t+1$. If φ is atomic but not an inequality, then we consider there are no bounds. If φ is $\varphi_1 \land \varphi_2$, then $\forall$-bounds of φ is the intersection of those of φ_1 and φ_2 (this may miss some bounds, but we confine ourselves to this approximation), and $\exists$-bounds are the union of those of φ_1 and φ_2. The $\forall$- and $\exists$-bounds of $\neg\varphi$ are $\exists$- and $\forall$-bounds of φ, respectively. Bounds of $\forall y.\varphi$ are those of φ. We omit $\lor$, $\to$, and $\exists$ since they are derived from other connectives by the laws of classical logic.

Step (II) is done by verifying that all atomic formulas depends only on $x+ay$. First, consider $s(x, y) < t(x, y)$ where s and t are polynomials in x, y. There is a simple sufficient condition: if there exists a polynomial $u(z)$ such that $t(x, y) - s(x, y) = u(x+ay)$, then $s(x, y) < t(x, y)$ is equivalent to $0 < u(x+ay)$. Therefore it is sufficient to check that $s(x, y) - t(x, y)$ can be written as a polynomial of $x + ay$, which is not difficult. If s and t are not polynomials, or a predicate other than inequalities is used, then we check whether all arguments of the predicate or function symbols can be written as $u(x + ay)$.

4.4 Extra Heuristics

It is sometimes the case that the simplified goal is not still provable by SMT solvers, but the following transformations help proving the task (they are sound but not complete, i.e. they may replace a provable goal with an unprovable one).

---

[3] In this case $t+1, t+2, \ldots$ are also $\forall$-bounds, but we do not take them into account. Practically, considering only t seems sufficient in many cases.

– If an equality $f(s_1, \ldots, s_n) = f(t_1, \ldots, t_n)$ occurs in a positive position, then we may replace it with $s_1 = t_1 \land \cdots \land s_n = t_n$.
– A subformula occurring in a positive (negative) position of a task may be replaced by False (True, respectively). We try this for a subformula of the form $f(t_1, \ldots, t_n) = t$ where f corresponds to a program variable.

By applying them to a subformula inside a quantifier, we can rewrite a nonlinear formula into a linear one. After that we can use quantifier elimination to simplify the resulting formula.

5   Implementation and Experiment

We have implemented the method described above and conducted an experiment on three kernels. Our implementation takes source code annotated with specifications (pre- and post-conditions and loop invariants) as an input and checks whether the specification is satisfied. The input language is a subset of CUDA C, but we slightly modified the syntax so that we can use an existing C parser without modification. This is just to simplify the implementation.

The verifier first generates VCs as described in Sect. 3, and performs the simplification in Sect. 4 roughly in the following order: (1) *assign*-elimination (Sect. 4.1); (2) rewriting (Sect. 4.2); (3) merge quantifiers (Sect. 4.3). In addition to these operations, we also use standard simplification methods such as quantifier elimination. After that, for each task, it calls several SMT solvers at once, and run them in parallel. The task is considered completed when one of the solvers successfully proves it. For tasks that none of the solvers can prove, it applies heuristics in Sect. 4.4 followed by calls to SMT solvers and repeats these steps at most 10 times. If there is still a task that remains unsolved, the verification fails.

The front-end is written in OCaml. We use Cil [20] to parse the input, and the syntax tree is converted into tasks using Why3 [3] API. Simplification of formulas is implemented as a transformation on data structures of Why3, and SMT solvers are called through Why3 API functions.[4] We use Alt-Ergo, CVC3, CVC4, E Theorem Prover, and Z3 as back-ends.[5]

Using our implementation we have verified the functional correctness of three programs: vector addition, matrix multiplication, and stencil computation (diffusion equation in one dimension) programs. The matrix multiplication program is taken from NVIDIA CUDA Samples [22] and slightly modified without changing the essential part of the algorithm. The vector addition program computes the sum of two vectors in a similar way to ArrayCopy. The matrix multiplication and diffusion programs are optimized by using shared memory.

We did not concretize any of the parameters in programs, such as the number of threads and blocks, length of vectors, and size of matrices. Throughout the

---

[4] Currently we use Why3 only for manipulating formulas and calling SMT solvers, although it provides a programming language WhyML.
[5] alt-ergo.lri.fr,   www.cs.nyu.edu/acsys/cvc3,   cvc4.cs.nyu.edu,   www.eprover.org, z3.codeplex.com.

Table 1. The number of proved/generated tasks, time spent for VC generation and SMT solving (sec), and size of VC, with and without VC simplification. LOC excludes blank lines and annotations.

Program	Simplify	Result	VC generation	SMT solving	Size of VC
vectorAdd	Y	7/7	0.1488	0.8154	9836
(9 LOC)	N	3/7	0.0064	8.9177	9879
matrixMul	Y	19/19	1.4101	10.4927	34754
(29 LOC)	N	15/17	0.0271	5.3835	38416
Diffusion	Y	112/112	9264.9941	17.7110	163819
(20 LOC)	N	1/4	0.0063	3.7122	6511

experiments, we set time limit to 1 s through Why3 API for each solver call (but CVC4 seems to run for two seconds; we do not know the reason). We also set memory limit to 4000 MB, but it seems that it is almost impossible to exhaust this amount of memory in 1 s. Experiments are conducted on a machine with two Intel Xeon processors E5-2670 (with eight cores, 2.6 GHz) and 128 GB of main memory. The OCaml modules are compiled with `ocamlopt` version 4.02.3.

The result is summarized in Table 1. We compared the performance of our method with and without the simplification introduced in Sect. 4 (shown in the second column). For the case where no simplification is applied, we have provided triggers that would help solvers finding an instance used in *assign*-elimination and rewriting (such as $b_2(n)$ in (1) and $i_2(t)$ in $\forall t.0 \leq t < N \rightarrow i_2(t) = N \cdot l + t$). The size of a VC is the sum of the size of all formulas in it and the size of a formula is the number of nodes in its abstract syntax tree. The number of tasks increases when simplification is enabled, because simplification may split a task into smaller tasks.

Our implementation with the simplification successfully verified realistic GPU kernels, whereas it could not verify any of the three programs without simplification. We also ran SMT solvers for one hour on each task without simplification, and confirmed that the numbers of proved tasks did not change in any of the three cases. These results show that our simplification strategy is indeed effective. We also tried applying only some of the simplifications introduced in Sect. 4; solvers could discharge one more task for vectorAdd under some combinations of simplification, but verification failed unless all of the simplifications are applied.

The result also suggests a limitation of our current implementation. As we can see from the VC-generation time and size for diffusion with the simplification, our method occasionally generates very large VCs, which are time- and memory-consuming to generate. This is mainly caused by iterated applications of the *assign*-elimination which, in the worst case, doubles the size of the formula every time. We expect that the generation time can be reduced by further optimization, because during *assign*-elimination many redundant formulas are generated, and removed afterwards (indeed, in the case of diffusion, the intermediate VC has size approximately 1.1×10^7, which is nearly 70 times larger than the final VC).

6   Related Work

Functional correctness of GPU programs. Some of the existing tools support functional correctness verification by assertion checking or equivalence checking. PUG [14] and GKLEE [16] support assertion checking (as well as detecting other defects such as data races), but they cannot verify fully parameterized programs. Both of them require the user to specify the number of threads, and they duplicate each instruction by the specified number of threads to simulate lockstep behavior as a sequential program. PUG_{para} [15] supports equivalence checking of two parameterized programs. They report results on equivalence checking of unoptimized and optimized kernels; equivalence checking of a parameterized matrix-transpose program resulted in timeout, so they had to concretize some of the variables.

Deductive approaches to functional correctness. Regarding deductive verification of GPU programs, two approaches have been proposed. Kojima and Igarashi adapted the standard Hoare Logic to GPU programs [10]. Our work is based on theirs, although we do not use their inference rules as they are. Blom, Huisman and Mihelčić applied permission-based separation logic to GPU programs [2]. Their logic is implemented in the VerCors tool set.[6] Their approach, in addition to functional correctness, can reason about race-freedom by making use of the notion of permission (but it requires more annotations than ours).

Automated race checking. Race checking is one of the subject intensively-studied in verification of GPU programs, and many tools have been developed so far [1, 6, 14, 15, 17, 18]. Although they use SMT solvers, their encoding methods for race-checking are different from ours in several ways. In particular, it is not necessary to consider all threads at a time, but only two threads suffice. This is because if there is a race, then there has to be a pair of threads that are to perform conflicting read/write (this is an important observation for optimization which, to our knowledge, first mentioned in [14] and detailed discussion on this technique is given in [1]). Therefore they model the behavior of a pair of threads (whose thread identifiers are parameterized), rather than all threads.

Reasoning about arrays. There is a technique to eliminate existential quantification over arrays, which is applied to the verification of C program involving arrays [11]. Although we did not consider quantifier elimination over arrays explicitly, the effect of *assign*-elimination is similar to the quantifier elimination: if a variable a representing an intermediate value of some array and a does not appear in the postcondition, then we can regard a as an existentially quantified variable. Because *assign*-elimination removes a from the VC, it could be seen as a quantifier-elimination procedure. Further investigation on relationship to their idea and possibility of adapting it to our setting is left for future work.

---

[6] Several examples are found at https://fmt.ewi.utwente.nl/redmine/projects/vercors-verifier/wiki/Examples.

7   Conclusion

We have presented an automated verification method of race-free GPGPU programs. Our method is based on symbolic execution and (manual) loop abstraction. In addition to the VC generation method, we have proposed several simplification methods that can help SMT solvers prove generated VCs. We have empirically confirmed that our method successfully verifies several realistic kernels without concretizing parameters and that the simplification method is effective for improving efficiency of the verification procedure. We expect that it is a feasible approach to the verification of functional correctness to check race-freedom by using the existing tools first, and then verifying functional correctness by using our method.

Automatically inferring loop invariants is one of the interesting and important problems left for future work. Various methods to generate invariants have been proposed in the literature [5,9,12,19]. Although they mainly target sequential programs, we expect that they can be adapted to GPU programs. To our knowledge, there is no previous work on applying these invariant generation methods to GPU programs (GPUVerify [1] uses Houdini algorithm [7] to find invariants, and PUG [14] uses predefined set of syntactic rules that can automatically derive an invariant if the program fragment matches a common pattern).

Other important future work is to improve our manipulation of formulas of nonlinear arithmetic, from which a difficulty often arises. Sometimes SMT solvers cannot solve a problem that seems quite easy for humans. For example, if a, x, x', y, y' are integers, $0 \leq x < a \wedge 0 \leq x' < a \wedge x + ay = x' + ay'$ implies $x = x'$. Similar inferences are often needed to reason about GPU programs because it arises from the computation of an index of arrays. As far as we have tried, this type of inference is hard to automate. We conjecture that nonlinear expressions (such as $x + ay$ above) that appear during verification have some patterns in common, and we can find a suitable strategy to handle them, enabling us to automatically prove the correctness of more complicated programs. One of the possible direction would be to investigate the relationship to decidable nonlinear extensions of linear arithmetic [4,13]. Although we do not expect that all the VCs are expressed in such theories, it would be interesting if these theories and their decision procedures bring us a new insight into the manipulation of non-linear VCs.

Improving the strategy of simplification on VCs is also vital for scalability of our verification method. As we have discussed in Sect. 5, our simplification method sometimes produces extremely large VCs, or even fails to generate VCs in a reasonable amount of time. Also, there seems to be room for optimization in the *assign*-elimination procedure. We expect that optimizing this part greatly reduces the amount of time spent for verification, because *assign*-elimination is one of the most time-consuming part of our verification method.

References

1. Betts, A., Chong, N., Donaldson, A.F., Ketema, J., Qadeer, S., Thomson, P., Wickerson, J.: The design and implementation of a verification technique for GPU kernels. ACM Trans. Program. Lang. Syst. **37**(3), 10:1–10:49 (2015)
2. Blom, S., Huisman, M., Mihelčić, M.: Specification and verification of GPGPU programs. Sci. Comput. Prog. **95**(3), 376–388 (2014)
3. Bobot, F., Filliâtre, J.C., Marché, C., Paskevich, A.: Why3: shepherd your herd of provers. In: 1st International Workshop on Intermediate Verification Languages, Boogie 2011, pp. 53–64, Wroclaw, Poland (2011)
4. Bozga, M., Iosif, R.: On decidability within the arithmetic of addition and divisibility. In: Sassone, V. (ed.) FoSSaCS 2005. LNCS, vol. 3441, pp. 425–439. Springer, Heidelberg (2005). doi:10.1007/978-3-540-31982-5_27. http://dx.doi.org/10.1007/b106850
5. Cachera, D., Jensen, T.P., Jobin, A., Kirchner, F.: Inference of polynomial invariants for imperative programs: a farewell to Gröbner bases. Sci. Comput. Prog. **93**, 89–109 (2014)
6. Collingbourne, P., Cadar, C., Kelly, P.H.J.: Symbolic testing of OpenCL code. In: Eder, K., Lourenço, J., Shehory, O. (eds.) HVC 2011. LNCS, vol. 7261, pp. 203–218. Springer, Heidelberg (2012). doi:10.1007/978-3-642-34188-5_18
7. Flanagan, C., Leino, K.R.M.: Houdini, an annotation assistant for ESC/Java. In: Oliveira, J.N., Zave, P. (eds.) FME 2001. LNCS, vol. 2021, pp. 500–517. Springer, Heidelberg (2001). doi:10.1007/3-540-45251-6_29
8. Flanagan, C., Saxe, J.B.: Avoiding exponential explosion: generating compact verification conditions. In: Proceedings of ACM POPL, pp. 193–205 (2001)
9. Garg, P., Löding, C., Madhusudan, P., Neider, D.: ICE: a robust framework for learning invariants. In: Biere, A., Bloem, R. (eds.) CAV 2014. LNCS, vol. 8559, pp. 69–87. Springer, Heidelberg (2014). doi:10.1007/978-3-319-08867-9_5
10. Kojima, K., Igarashi, A.: A hoare logic for SIMT programs. In: Shan, C. (ed.) APLAS 2013. LNCS, vol. 8301, pp. 58–73. Springer, Heidelberg (2013). doi:10.1007/978-3-319-03542-0_5
11. Komuravelli, A., Bjørner, N., Gurfinkel, A., McMillan, K.L.: Compositional verification of procedural programs using Horn clauses over integers and arrays. In: Formal Methods in Computer-Aided Design, FMCAD 2015, pp. 89–96, Austin, Texas, USA, 27–30 September 2015
12. Kovács, L., Voronkov, A.: Finding loop invariants for programs over arrays using a theorem prover. In: Chechik, M., Wirsing, M. (eds.) FASE 2009. LNCS, vol. 5503, pp. 470–485. Springer, Heidelberg (2009). doi:10.1007/978-3-642-00593-0_33
13. Lechner, A., Ouaknine, J., Worrell, J.: On the complexity of linear arithmetic with divisibility. In: Proceedings of 30th Annual ACM/IEEE Symposium on Logic in Computer Science, (LICS 2015), pp. 667–676 (2015)
14. Li, G., Gopalakrishnan, G.: Scalable SMT-based verification of GPU kernel functions. In: Proceedings of the 18th ACM SIGSOFT International Symposium on Foundations of Software Engineering (FSE 2010), pp. 187–196. ACM (2010)
15. Li, G., Gopalakrishnan, G.: Parameterized verification of GPU kernel programs. In: IPDPS Workshop on Multicore and GPU Programming Models, Languages and Compilers Wokshop, pp. 2450–2459. IEEE (2012)
16. Li, G., Li, P., Sawaya, G., Gopalakrishnan, G., Ghosh, I., Rajan, S.P.: GKLEE: concolic verification and test generation for GPUs. In: Proceedings of ACM PPoPP, pp. 215–224 (2012)

17. Li, P., Li, G., Gopalakrishnan, G.: Parametric flows: automated behavior equivalencing for symbolic analysis of races in CUDA programs. In: Proceedings of the International Conference on High Performance Computing, Networking, Storage and Analysis (SC 2012). IEEE Computer Society Press (2012)
18. Li, P., Li, G., Gopalakrishnan, G.: Practical symbolic race checking of GPU programs. In: Proceedings of International Conference for High Performance Computing, Networking, Storage and Analysis (SC 2014), pp. 179–190 (2014)
19. McMillan, K.L.: Quantified invariant generation using an interpolating saturation prover. In: Ramakrishnan, C.R., Rehof, J. (eds.) TACAS 2008. LNCS, vol. 4963, pp. 413–427. Springer, Heidelberg (2008). doi:10.1007/978-3-540-78800-3_31
20. Necula, G.C., McPeak, S., Rahul, S.P., Weimer, W.: CIL: intermediate language and tools for analysis and transformation of C programs. In: Horspool, R.N. (ed.) CC 2002. LNCS, vol. 2304, pp. 213–228. Springer, Heidelberg (2002). doi:10.1007/3-540-45937-5_16
21. Nguyen, H.: GPU Gems 3, 1st edn. Addison-Wesley Professional, Reading (2007). http://developer.nvidia.com/object/gpu-gems-3.html
22. NVIDIA: NVIDIA CUDA C Programming Guide (2014). http://docs.nvidia.com/cuda/cuda-c-programming-guide/index.html

The Matrix Reproved (Verification Pearl)

Martin Clochard[1,2], Léon Gondelman[1,2(✉)], and Mário Pereira[1,2]

[1] Lab. de Recherche en Informatique, Univ. Paris-Sud, CNRS, 91405 Orsay, France
{martin.clochard,leon.gondelman,mario.pereira}@lri.fr
[2] INRIA, Université Paris-Saclay, 91893 Palaiseau, France

Abstract. In this paper we describe a complete solution for the first challenge of the VerifyThis 2016 competition held at the 18th ETAPS Forum. We present the proof of two variants for the multiplication of matrices: a naive version using three nested loops and the Strassen's algorithm. The proofs are conducted using the Why3 platform for deductive program verification, and automated theorem provers to discharge proof obligations. In order to specify and prove the two multiplication algorithms, we develop a new Why3 theory of matrices and apply the proof by reflection methodology.

1   Introduction

In this paper we describe a complete solution for the first challenge of the VerifyThis 2016 competition using the Why3 platform for deductive verification.

As it was asked in the original challenge, we prove the correctness of two different implementations of matrix multiplication. First, we specify and prove a naive algorithm which runs in cubic time; then the more efficient Strassen's algorithm. To our knowledge, this is the first proof of Strassen's algorithm for square matrices of arbitrary size in a program verification environment based on automated theorem provers.

Wishing to make our solutions both concise and generic, we devised in Why3 an axiomatic theory for matrices and showed various algebraic properties for their arithmetic operations, in particular multiplication distributivity over addition and associativity (which was asked in the challenge second task). Our full development is available online[1].

It turns out that proving Strassen's algorithm was virtually impossible for automated theorem provers due to their incapacity to perform reasoning on algebraic matrix equations. To overcome this obstacle, we devise an algebraic expression simplifier in order to conduct proof by reflection.

This work is partly supported by the Bware (ANR-12-INSE-0010, http://bware.lri.fr/) and VOCAL (ANR-15-CE25-008, https://vocal.lri.fr/) projects of the French national research organization (ANR) and by the Portuguese Foundation for the Sciences and Technology (grant FCT-SFRH/BD/99432/2014).
[1] http://toccata.lri.fr/gallery/verifythis_2016_matrix_multiplication.en.html.

© Springer International Publishing AG 2016
S. Blazy and M. Chechik (Eds.): VSTTE 2016, LNCS 9971, pp. 107–118, 2016.
DOI: 10.1007/978-3-319-48869-1_8

This paper is organized as follows. The Sect. 2 presents briefly Why3. The Sect. 3 describes our solution for naive matrix multiplication. Then, the Sect. 4 presents our solution for the second task and for that purpose introduces our axiomatic matrix theory. We specify and prove Strassen's algorithm in Sects. 5 and 6. We discuss related work in Sect. 7.

2   Why3 in a Nutshell

The Why3 platform proposes a set of tools allowing the user to implement, formally specify, and prove programs. It comes with a programming language, WhyML [6], an ML dialect with some restrictions in order to get simpler proof obligations. This language offers some features commonly found in functional languages, like pattern-matching, algebraic types and polymorphism, but also imperative constructions, like records with mutable fields and exceptions. Programs written in WhyML can be annotated with contracts, that is, pre- and postconditions. The code itself can be annotated, for instance, to express loop invariants or to justify termination of loops and recursive functions. It is also possible to add intermediate assertions in the code to ease automatic proofs. The WhyML language features ghost code [5], which is used only for specification and proof purposes and can be removed with no observable modification in the program's execution. The system uses the annotations to generate proof obligations thanks to a weakest precondition calculus.

Why3 uses external provers to discharge proof obligations, either automatic theorem provers (ATP) or interactive proof assistants such as Coq, Isabelle, and PVS. The system also allows the user to manually apply *transformations* to proof obligations before they are sent to provers, in order to make proofs easier.

The logic used to write formal specifications is an extension of first-order logic with rank-1 polymorphic types, algebraic types, (co-)inductive predicates and recursive definitions [4], as well as a limited form of higher-order logic [2]. This logic is used to write theories for the purpose of modeling the behavior of programs. The Why3 standard library is formed of many such logic theories, in particular for integer and floating point arithmetic, sets, and sequences.

The entire standard library, numerous verified examples, as well as a more detailed presentation of Why3 and WhyML are available on the project web site, http://why3.lri.fr.

3   Naive Matrix Multiplication

The VerifyThis 2016 first challenge starts with a proposal to verify a naive implementation of the multiplication of two matrices using three nested loops, though in non-standard order. In this section we present our solution to this part of the challenge.

We first write the WhyML equivalent of the challenge code for multiplication of two matrices a and b:

```
let mult_naive (a b: matrix int) : matrix int
= let rs = make (rows a) (columns b) 0 in
  for i = 0 to rows a - 1 do
    for k = 0 to rows b - 1 do
      for j = 0 to columns b - 1 do
        set rs i j (get rs i j + get a i k * get b k j)
      done;
    done;
  done;
  rs
```

To encode matrices, we use two-dimensional arrays as provided in the Why3 standard library. Operations `get` and `set` have the usual semantics, and `make` carries out creation and initialization. Such arrays are represented by the following abstract type, whose fields can only be accessed in specifications.

```
type matrix 'a
  model { rows: int; columns: int; mutable elts: map int (map int 'a) }
```

Let us now specify the multiplication procedure

```
let mult_naive (a b: matrix int) : matrix int
  requires { a.columns = b.rows }
  ensures  { result.rows = a.rows ∧ result.columns = b.columns }
  ensures  { matrix_product result a b }
```

The `matrix_product` predicate mimics the mathematical definition of matrix product $(AB)_{ij} = \sum_{k=0}^{m-1} A_{ik} B_{kj}$:

```
function mul_atom (a b: matrix int) (i j: int) : int → int =
  \k. a.elts[i][k] * b.elts[k][j]
predicate matrix_product (m a b: matrix int) =
  forall i j. 0 ≤ i < m.rows → 0 ≤ j < m.columns →
    m.elts[i][j] = sum 0 a.columns (mul_atom a b i j)
```

In order to define this predicate concisely we use higher-order features and the `sum` function from Why3 standard library. This function returns the sum of `f n` for n ranging between `a` and `b`, as defined by the following axioms:

```
function sum (a b: int) (f: int → int) : int
axiom sum_def1: forall f a b. b ≤ a → sum a b f = 0
axiom sum_def2: forall f a b. a < b →
  sum a b f = sum a (b - 1) f + f (b - 1)
```

The last argument we give to `sum` is a first-class function $\lambda k.M$. Why3 supports such definitions by translating them to first-order values [2].

To prove that `mult_naive` meets its specification, we give suitable loop invariants. There are two kinds of invariant per loop. The first one is the frame invariant, which describes the part of the matrix that is left unchanged. The second one describes the contents of cells affected by the loop. Let us illustrate this with the inner loop. In that case, the loop has the effect of writing a partial sum into cells 0 to `j-1` of the `i`-th row, leaving other cells unchanged.

```
'I: for j = 0 to columns b - 1 do
   invariant { forall i0 j0. 0 ≤ i0 < rows a ∧ 0 ≤ j0 < columns b  →
      (i0 ≠ i  ∨  j0 ≥ j) → rs.elts[i0][j0] = (at rs 'I).elts[i0][j0] }
   invariant { forall j0. 0 ≤ j0 < j →
      rs.elts[i][j0] = sum 0 (k+1) (mul_atom a b i j0) }
```

With the given specification all the generated verification conditions are discharged in a fraction of second using the Alt-Ergo SMT solver.

4   From Multiplication Associativity to a Matrix Theory

The next task was to show that matrix multiplication is associative. More precisely, participants were asked to write a program that performs the two different computations $(AB)C$ and $A(BC)$, and then prove the corresponding results are always the same. In our case, this corresponds to prove the following:

```
let assoc_proof (a b c: matrix int) : unit
   requires { a.columns = b.rows ∧ b.columns = c.rows }
= let ab_c = mult_naive (mult_naive a b) c in
  let a_bc = mult_naive a (mult_naive b c) in
  assert { ab_c.rows = a_bc.rows ∧ ab_c.columns = a_bc.columns ∧
     forall i j. 0 ≤ i < ab_c.rows ∧ 0 ≤ j < ab_c.columns →
        ab_c.elts[i][j] = a_bc.elts[i][j] }
```

As one can guess, the proof of associativity relies essentially on the linearity properties of the sum operator and Fubini's principle. Let us illustrate how we establish the additivity of the sum (the homogeneity of the sum and Fubini's principle are done in a similar way). First we define a higher-order function addf which, given two integer functions f and g, returns a function \x. f x + g x. Then, we state the additivity as a lemma function:

```
let rec lemma additivity (a b: int) (f g: int → int) : unit
   ensures { sum a b (addf f g) = sum a b f + sum a b g }
   variant { b - a }
= if b > a then additivity a (b-1) f g
```

The fact that we write the lemma not as a logical statement but as a recursive function allows us to do two important things. First, we simulate the induction hypothesis via a recursive call, which is useful since the ATPs usually do not support reasoning by induction. Second, writing a lemma as a program function allows us to call it with convenient arguments later, which amounts to giving instances. Notice that the lemma is given an explicit variant clause. Indeed, when one writes a lemma function, Why3 verifies that it is effect-free and terminating.

Now, a possible way to complete the second task would be to show the associativity directly for the multiplication implemented by the naive algorithm from task one. However, such a solution would be *ad hoc*: each time we implement the matrix multiplication differently, the associativity must be reproved.

To make our solution more general, we opt for a different solution which consists roughly of two steps. First, we provide an axiomatized theory of matrices where we prove that matrix product, as a mathematical operation, is associative. Second, we create a model function from program matrices to their logical representation in our theory. Finally, we show that from the model perspective naive multiplication implements the mathematical product. When all this is done, we have the associativity of naive multiplication for free.

We split our matrix axiomatization in two modules. The first module introduces a new abstract type and declares the following functions

```
type mat 'a
function rows (mat 'a) : int
function cols (mat 'a) : int
function get (mat 'a) int int : 'a
function set (mat 'a) int int 'a : mat 'a
function create (r c: int) (f: int → int → 'a) : mat 'a
```

and adds a set of axioms that describes their behavior. We add the `create` function to build new matrices by comprehension. Additionally, we have an extensionality axiom, *i.e.* that for any pair of matrices m1, m2, we have m1 == m2 → m1 = m2 where m1 == m2 means that both matrices have the same dimensions and the content of their cells are the same.

The second module defines arithmetic operations over integer matrices as straightforward instances of `create`, and exports various proved lemmas about their algebraic properties, including associativity and distributivity. Although we are looking for associativity, the other properties are expected in such a theory, and we will use some of them in later sections. A typical proof amounts to writing the following:

```
function mul_atom (a b: mat int) (i j:int) : int → int =
  \k. get a i k * get b k j
function mul (a b: mat int) : mat int =
  create (rows a) (cols b) (\i j. sum 0 (cols a) (mul_atom a b i j))
let lemma mul_assoc_get (a b c: mat int) (i j: int)
  requires { cols a = rows b ∧ cols b = rows c }
  requires { 0 ≤ i < rows a ∧ 0 ≤ j < cols c }
  ensures  { get (mul (mul a b) c) i j = get (mul a (mul b c)) i j }
= ...
lemma mul_assoc: forall a b c. cols a = rows b → cols b = rows c →
    mul a (mul b c) =  mul (mul a b) c
  by mul a (mul b c) == mul (mul a b) c
```

The `by` connective in the last line instruments the lemma with a logical cut for its proof, to show the desired instance of extensionality. It follows by the auxiliary lemma function `mul_assoc_get`, whose proof is omitted here.

Once we formalized the matrix theory and proved associativity, it remains to connect it to the implementation by a model function:

```
function mdl (m: matrix 'a) : mat 'a = create m.rows m.columns (get m)
```

Then, we change the specification of `mult_naive` to use the model. This turns the postcondition to `mdl result = mul (mdl a) (mdl b)`. The proof of this new specification is immediate and makes the second task trivial.

5   Strassen's Algorithm in **Why3**

The last (and optional) part in the VerifyThis challenge was to verify Strassen's algorithm for power-of-two square matrices. We prove a more general implementation that uses a padding scheme to handle square matrices of any size.

5.1   Implementation

The principle behind Strassen's Algorithm is to use 2×2 block multiplication recursively, using a scheme that uses 7 sub-multiplications instead of 8. More precisely, it works in 3 phases. It first partitions both input matrices in 4 equal-sized square matrices. Then, it computes 7 products of matrices obtained by additions and subtractions. Finally, it obtains a similar partition of the result using addition and subtractions from those products. The details can be found in Appendix B.

For even sizes, our implementation closely follows Strassen's recursive scheme. To this end, we first implement and prove a few simple matrix routines:

- Matrix addition (`add`) and subtraction (`sub`);
- Matrix block-to-block copy (`blit`);
- Sub-matrix extraction (`block`).

For odd sizes, the recursive scheme cannot be applied. This is typically solved by peeling or zero-padding, either statically or dynamically to recover an even size. We use a dynamic padding solution. In case the matrices have odd size, we add a zero row and column to recover an even size, make a recursive call and extract the relevant sub-matrices.

When the size gets below an arbitrary cutoff we use naive matrix multiplication. Although we used a concrete value, the code is correct for any positive cutoff. We ensure this by wrapping the cutoff value under an abstract block, which hides its precise value in verification conditions.

5.2   Specification and Proof

Except for the additional requirements that the matrices are square, we give the same specification for Strassen's algorithm as for naive multiplication.

As for the proof, let us first focus on the correctness of Strassen's recursive scheme. We break down that proof in two parts. First, we prove that the usual 2×2 block decomposition of matrix product is correct. Then, we prove that the efficient computation scheme that uses seven multiplication indeed computes that block decomposition. That second part boils down to checking four ring equations, which we will cover in details in Sect. 6.

In order to prove block decomposition, we introduce a dedicated module where sub-matrix extraction is defined by comprehension. It extracts a rectangle from a matrix, given the low corner at coordinates `r, c` and with dimensions `dr, dc`:

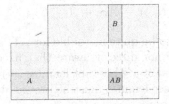 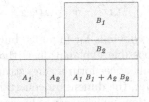

Fig. 1. Relations between sub-matrices and product

```
function block (a: mat int) (r dr c dc: int) : mat int =
  create dr dc (\i j. get a (r+i) (c+j))
```

The module essentially proves two lemmas about relations between sub-matrix extraction and product, which are best seen graphically as in Fig. 1. One expresses sub-matrices of the product as products of sub-matrices, while the other decomposes products into sums of sub-matrices products. We then expect to obtain the desired block decomposition by two successive partitioning steps, but there is a catch. Our implementation extracts directly the 4 input sub-matrices, while using those lemmas implies extracting from intermediate sub-matrices. We bridge the gap by reducing successive sub-matrix extraction to single ones. In practice, we do this by proving and then calling a lemma function with the following postcondition:

```
ensures { block (block a.mdl r1 dr1 c1 dc1) r2 dr2 c2 dc2 =
            block a.mdl (r1+r2) dr2 (c1+c2) dc2 }
```

This is sufficient to prove the algebraic relations between the partition of the product and the partitions of the input matrices. Also, note that we can readily reuse the same proof scheme for padding correctness. Indeed, it amounts to checking that the block we extract from the product of padded matrices is the right one. This follows immediately from the relevant block decomposition of the matrix product.

Finally, there is only one non-trivial remaining part: termination. It is non-trivial because our padding scheme increases the matrix size. This does not cause any problem, because the next step will halve it. We prove termination by introducing an extra ghost argument identifying matrices that will not require padding:

```
requires { 0 ≤ flag }
requires { flag = 0 → a.mdl.cols = 1  ∨  exists k. a.mdl.cols = 2 * k }
variant  { a.mdl.cols + flag, flag } (* lexicographic order *)
```

All generated VCs for the described specification are automatically discharged using a combination of Alt-Ergo, CVC4, and Z3 SMT solvers.

6   Proving Validity of Ring Equations by Reflection

Once we got rid of block matrix multiplication, proving validity of algebraic equations was the major difficulty. Indeed, Strassen's algorithm relies on equations like

$$A_{1,1}B_{1,2} + A_{1,2}B_{2,2} = A_{1,1}(B_{1,2} - B_{2,2}) + (A_{1,1} + A_{1,2})B_{2,2}$$

which is obvious for humans, but turns out to be quite a trouble for ATPs.

A possible explanation is that ATPs are not directly aware that fixed-size square matrices form a ring, struggling to instantiate relevant lemmas correctly. Moreover, the dimension constraints from those lemmas must be proved at each application, which makes the situation even worse.

One possible solution would be to add assertions about intermediate equations inside the code until they are easy enough to be exploitable by ATPs to bridge the gap. However, after trying to go this way, we found that even for the equality above (the easiest one), the gap was too large for ATPs which were still spending too much time to discharge the proof obligations.

Without support of automated provers, making use of an interactive one (typically Coq) would be a standard choice. If the interactive prover has support for proving ring equations, then it would suffice to embed our matrix theory inside the prover's ring structure. However, we were curious to see if we could embed some kind of similar ring support inside Why3 itself. That leads us to the technique known as proof by reflection. The methodology we follow is actually very similar to the one presented in [1, Chap. 16].

To carry out proof by reflection of algebraic equations, we have to do two things. First, we have to *reflect* (translate) the original expressions on each side by equivalent syntactical forms. Second, we need a procedure that normalizes a syntactical form so that the comparison of algebraic expressions becomes trivial. This can be implemented in Why3 logic, and run using the `compute_specified` transformation. This transformation normalizes a given goal, making boolean and integer arithmetic simplifications, and applying user-defined rewrite rules (in the source code one can add declarations to configure the transformation). To complete the proof, we need a lemma saying that the normalization procedure preserves the interpretation of the syntactic form. Let us now describe how we carry out these two phases in more detail.

6.1 Reflecting Algebraic Expressions by Ghost Tagging

Essentially, the reflection phase amounts to building an equivalent syntactic form for each algebraic expression. In our case, we achieve that by tagging each matrix with a ghost symbolic expression:

```
type with_symb = { phy : matrix int;
                   ghost sym : expr; (* reflection *) }

predicate with_symb_vld (env:env) (ws:with_symb) =
  e_vld env ws.sym ∧ (* internal dimension conditions *)
  e_mdl env ws.sym = ws.phy.mdl ∧ (* Model correlation *)
  ws.sym.e_rows = ws.phy.mdl.rows ∧ (* Dimensions correlation *)
  ws.sym.e_cols = ws.phy.mdl.cols
```

Notice that the representation predicate above is parametrized by an environment, which binds expression variables to matrices. Also, as field sym is ghost, it will not incur any extra runtime cost.

It remains then to provide, for each arithmetic operation, a tagging combinator that wraps in parallel the corresponding matrix computations and symbolic executions on their reflection. For instance, the combinator for addition is defined by:

```
let add_ws (ghost env:env) (a b:with_symb) : with_symb
  requires { a.phy.mdl.rows = b.phy.mdl.rows }
  requires { a.phy.mdl.cols = b.phy.mdl.cols }
  requires { with_symb_vld env a ∧ with_symb_vld env b }
  ensures { result.phy.mdl = add a.phy.mdl b.phy.mdl }
  ensures { result.sym = symb_add a.sym b.sym }
  ensures { with_symb_vld env result }
= { phy = add a.phy b.phy;
    sym = ghost symb_add env a.sym b.sym }
```

Introduction of variables is carried out by a similar combinator on top of submatrix extraction.

6.2 Normalizing Algebraic Expressions

In practice, we choose not to reflect completely algebraic expressions as syntactic objects. Instead, we implement in Why3 logic smart constructors that maintain normal forms, and reflect algebraic expressions as a computation tree made of those constructors. This has the advantage that we can use the ghost tagging mechanism to instantiate correctness lemmas as well. Also, this reduces the proof work to first write an assertion like

```
assert { e_mdl e m11.sym = e_mdl e egm11 }
```

then to apply the transformation on the associated goal. This completely reduces both computation trees and interprets back the results as standard expressions. Since they are in normal form, the equation becomes trivial and is reduced to true by the transformation directly.

The normal form we choose for algebraic expressions is a sorted sequence of signed variable products (monomials), interpreted as the sum of those monomials. We represent them using Why3 algebraic datatype of lists, and integers for variables. To correlate variables with effective matrices, we use a simple environment composed of a mapping and a symbol generator.

```
type mono = { m_prod : list int; m_pos : bool }
type expr = { e_body : list mono; e_rows : int; e_cols : int }
type env = { mutable ev_f : int → mat int; mutable ev_c : int }
```

The smart constructor implementations are fairly straightforward. For instance, addition is done by merging sorted lists followed by collapsing opposite terms. Multiplication is reduced to addition by distributing. We carried out smart constructors correctness proof by writing ghost procedures that mimic the control structure of the logical functions. Those procedures are then called in the ghost tagging combinators.

Note that we only prove that the simplifications are correct, not that we indeed compute normal forms. Although it may be desirable, it is not necessary if our goal is to prove algebraic equations. We only need both sides to be reduced to the same term. This also makes the aforementioned correctness proofs very easy, as the simplifications we carry out mirror the lemmas of our matrix theory.

All generated proof obligations for the correctness of smart constructors are automatically discharged using a combination of Alt-Ergo and CVC4 SMT solvers. The algebraic equations involved in Strassen's algorithm are directly eliminated by `compute_specified`.

7   Related Work

There are other works in the literature that tackle the proof of matrix multiplication algorithm similar to Strassen's. The closest to our work is that of Dénès *et al.* [3]. They propose a refinement-based mechanism to specify and prove efficient algebraic algorithms in the Coq proof assistant. The authors report on the use of Coq's `ring` tactic to ease the proof of Winograd's algorithm (a variant of Strassen's with fewer additions and subtractions), a similar approach to our proof by reflection. To cope with the case of odd-sized matrices they implemented dynamic peeling to remove extra rows or columns.

Another work is the proof of Strassen's algorithm in the ACL2 system [7]. The use of ACL2 with suitable rewriting rules and proper ring structure allows a high degree of automation in the proof process. However, they use an *ad hoc* definition of matrices whose sizes can only be powers of 2.

Srivastava *et al.* propose a technique for the synthesis of imperative programs [8] where synthesis is regarded as a verification problem. Verification tools are then used with a two-folded purpose: to synthesize programs and their correctness proof. One case-study presented for this technique is Strassen's algorithm for 2×2 integer matrices, for which the authors have been able to synthesize the additions and subtractions operations over block matrices.

8   Conclusion

We presented our solution for the first challenge of the VerifyThis 2016 competition. While presenting our solutions in detail, we took the opportunity to illustrate some interesting features of Why3, among which are higher-order functions in logic, lemma functions, ghost code, and proof obligation transformations. It would be interesting to see whether the proof by reflection methodology we use in this work can be helpful for verification of some other case studies, especially in a context which favours ATPs. .

Acknowledgements. We thank Arthur Charguéraud, Jean-Christophe Filliâtre, and Claude Marché for their comments and remarks.

A   Challenge 1 Original Text

Consider the following pseudocode algorithm, which is naive implementation of matrix multiplication. For simplicity we assume that the matrices are square.

```
int[][] matrixMultiply(int[][] A, int[][] B) {
    int n = A.length;

    // initialise C
    int[][] C = new int[n][n];

    for (int i = 0; i < n; i++) {
        for (int k = 0; k < n; k++) {
            for (int j = 0; j < n; j++) {
                C[i][j] += A[i][k] * B[k][j];
            }
        }
    }
    return C;
}
```

Tasks.

1. Provide a specification to describe the behaviour of this algorithm, and prove that it correctly implements its specification.
2. Show that matrix multiplication is associative, i.e., the order in which matrices are multiplied can be disregarded: $A(BC) = (AB)C$. To show this, you should write a program that performs the two different computations, and then prove that the result of the two computations is always the same.
3. [Optional, if time permits] In the literature, there exist many proposals for more efficient matrix multiplication algorithms. Strassen's algorithm was one of the first. The key idea of the algorithm is to use a recursive algorithm that reduces the number of multiplications on submatrices (from 8 to 7), see Strassen_algorithm on wikipedia for an explanation. A relatively clean Java implementation (and Python and C++) can be found here. Prove that the naive algorithm above has the same behaviour as Strassen's algorithm. Proving it for a restricted case, like a 2×2 matrix should be straightforward, the challenge is to prove it for arbitrary matrices with size 2^n.

B   Strassen Recursion Scheme

Given three matrices A, B and $M = AB$ partitioned as:

$$A = \left[\begin{array}{c|c} A_{1,1} & A_{1,2} \\ \hline A_{2,1} & A_{2,2} \end{array}\right] \quad B = \left[\begin{array}{c|c} B_{1,1} & B_{1,2} \\ \hline B_{2,1} & B_{2,2} \end{array}\right] \quad M = \left[\begin{array}{c|c} M_{1,1} & M_{1,2} \\ \hline M_{2,1} & M_{2,2} \end{array}\right]$$

Then we can compute the partition of M from the two others as follow:

$$M_{1,1} = X_1 + X_4 - X_5 + X_7 \qquad\qquad M_{2,1} = X_2 + X_4$$
$$M_{1,2} = X_3 + X_5 \qquad\qquad\qquad\quad M_{2,2} = X_1 - X_2 + X_3 + X_6$$

With

$$X_1 = (A_{1,1} + A_{2,2})\,(B_{1,1} + B_{2,2}) \qquad X_2 = (A_{2,1} + A_{2,2})\,B_{1,1}$$
$$X_3 = \qquad\quad A_{1,1}\,(B_{1,2} - B_{2,2}) \qquad X_4 = \qquad\quad A_{2,2}\,(B_{2,1} - B_{1,1})$$
$$X_5 = (A_{1,1} + A_{1,2})\,B_{2,2} \qquad\qquad X_6 = (A_{2,1} - A_{1,1})\,(B_{1,1} + B_{1,2})$$
$$X_7 = (A_{1,2} - A_{2,2})\,(B_{2,1} + B_{2,2})$$

References

1. Bertot, Y., Castéran, P.: Interactive Theorem Proving and Program Development. Springer, Heidelberg (2004)
2. Clochard, M., Filliâtre, J.-C., Marché, C., Paskevich, A.: Formalizing semantics with an automatic program verifier. In: Giannakopoulou, D., Kroening, D. (eds.) VSTTE 2014. LNCS, vol. 8471, pp. 37–51. Springer, Heidelberg (2014). doi:10.1007/978-3-319-12154-3_3
3. Dénès, M., Mörtberg, A., Siles, V.: A refinement-based approach to computational algebra in Coq. In: Beringer, L., Felty, A. (eds.) ITP 2012. LNCS, vol. 7406, pp. 83–98. Springer, Heidelberg (2012). doi:10.1007/978-3-642-32347-8_7
4. Filliâtre, J.-C.: One logic to use them all. In: Bonacina, M.P. (ed.) CADE 2013. LNCS (LNAI), vol. 7898, pp. 1–20. Springer, Heidelberg (2013). doi:10.1007/978-3-642-38574-2_1
5. Filliâtre, J.-C., Gondelman, L., Paskevich, A.: The spirit of ghost code. In: Biere, A., Bloem, R. (eds.) CAV 2014. LNCS, vol. 8559, pp. 1–16. Springer, Heidelberg (2014). doi:10.1007/978-3-319-08867-9_1
6. Filliâtre, J.-C., Paskevich, A.: Why3 — where programs meet provers. In: Felleisen, M., Gardner, P. (eds.) ESOP 2013. LNCS, vol. 7792, pp. 125–128. Springer, Heidelberg (2013). doi:10.1007/978-3-642-37036-6_8
7. Palomo-Lozano, F., Medina-Bulo, I., Alonso-Jiménez, J.: Certification of matrix multiplication algorithms. Strassen's algorithm in ACL2. In: Supplemental Proceedings of the 14th International Conference on Theorem Proving in Higher Order Logics, pp. 283–298. Edinburgh, Scotland (2001)
8. Srivastava, S., Gulwani, S., Foster, J.S.: From program verification to program synthesis. In: Proceedings of the 37th Annual ACM SIGPLAN-SIGACT Symposium on Principles of Programming Languages, POPL 2010, pp. 313–326. ACM, New York (2010). doi:10.1145/1706299.1706337

Enabling Modular Verification
with Abstract Interference Specifications
for a Concurrent Queue

Alan Weide[1]([✉]), Paolo A.G. Sivilotti[1], and Murali Sitaraman[2]

[1] The Ohio State University, Columbus, OH 43221, USA
weide.3@osu.edu, paolo@cse.ohio-state.edu
[2] Clemson University, Clemson, SC 29634, USA
murali@clemson.edu

Abstract. When concurrent threads of execution do not modify shared data, their parallel execution is trivially equivalent to their sequential execution. For many imperative programming languages, however, the modular verification of this independence is often frustrated by (i) the possibility of aliasing between variables mentioned in different threads, and (ii) the lack of abstraction in the description of read/write effects of operations on shared data structures. We describe a specification and verification framework in which abstract specifications of functional behavior are augmented with abstract interference effects that permit verification of client code with concurrent calls to operations of a data abstraction. To illustrate the approach, we present a classic concurrent data abstraction: the bounded queue. Three different implementations are described, each with different degrees of entanglement and hence different degrees of possible synchronization-free concurrency.

1 Introduction

Parallel programming is important for both large-scale high performance systems and, increasingly, small-scale multi-core commodity software. Programming with multiple threads, however, is error-prone. Furthermore, when errors are made, they can be difficult to debug and correct because parallel programs are often nondeterministic. Non-trivial parallel programs designed with software engineering consideration will be invariably composed from reusable components, often ones that encapsulate data abstractions.

Given this context, we propose a specification and verification framework to guarantee entanglement-free execution of concurrent code that invokes operations on data abstractions. Guaranteeing, simultaneously, modularity of the verification process and the independence of concurrent threads is complicated by two key problems. The first of these is the possibility of aliasing between objects involved in different threads. The second problem concerns guaranteeing safe parallel execution of data abstraction operations on an object without violating abstraction.

© Springer International Publishing AG 2016
S. Blazy and M. Chechik (Eds.): VSTTE 2016, LNCS 9971, pp. 119–128, 2016.
DOI: 10.1007/978-3-319-48869-1_9

At the core of a solution to the aliasing problem is a notion of *clean* operation calls whereby effects of calls are restricted to objects that are explicit parameters or to global objects that are explicitly specified as affected. Under this notion, regardless of the level of granularity, syntactically independent operation calls are always safe to parallelize. While both the problem and the solution are of interest, this paper focuses only on a solution to the second problem.

To illustrate the ideas, the paper presents a bounded queue data abstraction and outlines three different implementations that vary in their potential for parallelism among different queue operations. The data abstraction specification is typical, except that it is designed to avoid unintended aliasing. To capture the parallel potential in a class of implementations we augment the data abstraction specification with an interference specification that introduces additional modeling details to facilitate guarantees of safe execution of concurrent client code. The second-level specification is typically still quite abstract and is devoid of concrete implementation details. The novelty of the proposed solution is that it modularizes the verification problem along abstraction boundaries. Specifically, verification of implementation code with respect to both its data abstract and interference specification is done once in the lifetime of the implementation. Verification of client code relies strictly on the specifications.

This paper is strictly work in progress. We outline, for example, the specification and verification framework, but do not include formal proof rules. The rest of the paper is organized as follows. Section 2 summarizes the most related work. Section 3 describes the central example and alternative implementations. Section 4 describes the solution. It begins with a presentation of the interference specification that forms the basis for the subsequent discussion on verification. The last section summarizes and gives directions for further research.

2   Related Work

The summary here is meant to be illustrative of the type of related work, not exhaustive.

Classical solutions to the interference problem (e.g., [3]) would involve defining and using locks, but neither the solutions nor the proofs of absence of interference here involve abstraction or specification. Lock-free solutions built using atomic read-write-modify primitives (e.g., compare-and-swap) allow finer granularity of parallelism, but the proofs of serializability in that context are often not modular and do not involve complex properties.

The objective of modular verification is widely shared. The work in [1], for example, involves specifying interference points. For data abstractions, the interference points would be set at the operation level, meaning two operations may not execute concurrently on an object, even if they are disentangled at a "fine-grain" level. The work by Rodriguez, et al. [7] to extend JML for concurrent code makes it possible to specify methods to be atomic through locking and other properties. Using JML* and a notion of dynamic frames, the work in [6] address safe concurrent execution in the context of more general solutions to address aliasing and sharing for automated verification. The work in [9] makes it possible to specify memory locations that fall within the realm of an object's lock. Chalice allows specification of various types of permissions and includes a notion of permission transfer [5]. Using them, it is possible to estimate an upper bound on the location sets that may be affected by a thread in Chalice.

3   A Bounded Queue Data Abstraction

3.1   RESOLVE Background

RESOLVE [8] is an imperative, object-based programming and specification framework designed to support modular verification of sequential code. *Contracts* contain functional specifications and invariants in terms of abstract state. Abstract state is given in terms of mathematical types, such as sets or strings.[1] *Realizations* provide executable implementations as well as correspondence information connecting concrete and abstract state. The fundamental data movement operation is swap $(:=:)$, a constant-time operator that avoids introducing aliasing while also avoiding deep or shallow copying [2].

In addition to pre- and post-condition based specifications, operation signatures in contracts include *parameter modes*, whereby the modification frame is defined. For example, the value of a restores-mode parameter is the same at the end of the operation as it was the beginning. In the realm of concurrency, restore-mode alone is not sufficient to ensure noninterference since it does not preclude the temporary modification of a parameter during the execution of an operation. Other parameter modes include clears (changed to be an initial value), replaces (can change, incoming value is irrelevant), and updates (can change, incoming value may be relevant).

3.2   Abstract Specification

The BoundedQueueTemplate concept models a queue as a mathematical string of items. This concept defines queue operations including Enqueue, Dequeue, SwapFirstEntry, Length, and RemCapacity. The operations have been designed and specified to avoid aliasing that arises when queues contain non-trivial objects [2] and to facilitate clean semantics [4].

The operations in the contract are given in the listing below. For Enqueue, the requires clause says that there must be space in the queue for the new element $(|q| < \text{MAX\_LENGTH})$. The ensures clause says that the outgoing value of q is the string concatenation of the incoming value of q (i.e., #q) and the string consisting of a single item, the old value of e. Less formally, Enqueue puts e at the end of the queue. The parameter mode for e defines its outgoing value: an initial value for its type.

---

[1] A string is a sequence of values such as $<1, 2, 1, 3>$. The string concatenation operator is o.

> **operation** Enqueue (**clears** e: Item, **updates** q: Queue)
>   **requires** |q| < MAX_LENGTH
>   **ensures** q = #q o <#e>
>
> **operation** Dequeue (**replaces** r: Item, **updates** q: Queue)
>   **requires** q /= empty_string
>   **ensures** #q = <r> o q
>
> **operation** SwapFirstEntry (**updates** e: Item, **updates** q: Queue)
>   **requires** q /= empty_string
>   **ensures**   •
>   <e> = substring(#q, 0, 1) **and**
>   q = <#e> o substring(#q, 1, |#q|)
>
> **operation** Length (**restores** q: Queue) : Integer
>   **ensures** Length = |q|
>
> **operation** RemCapacity (**restores** q: Queue) : Integer
>   **ensures** RemCapacity = MAX_LENGTH − |q|

Listing 1.1. Contracts for queue operations

The requires clause for Dequeue says that q must not be empty. The ensures clause says that the concatenation of the resulting element r and outgoing value of q is the original value of q.

The SwapFirstEntry operation makes it possible to retrieve or update the first entry, without introducing aliasing.

The functions Length and RemCapacity behave as expected: Length returns an integer equal to the number of elements in the queue, and RemCapacity returns an integer equal to the number of free slots left in the queue before it becomes full. Neither modifies the queue.

3.3   Alternative Implementations

We have developed three alternative implementations of the bounded queue specified above, each with different parallelization opportunities. All three are based on a circular array. In the first two implementations, the length of the underlying array is equal to the maximum length of the queue, MAX_LENGTH, while in the third the length of the array is one greater (Fig. 1).

The first implementation has two Integer fields, front and length, where front is the index of the first element of the queue and length is the number of elements in the queue. This implementation cannot handle concurrent calls to Enqueue and Dequeue without synchronization because both of those calls must necessarily write to length. A client can, however, make concurrent calls to SwapFirstEntry and Enqueue when the precondition for both methods is met before the parallel block (that is, if 0 < |q| and |q| < MAX_LENGTH. These two methods may be

a. Realization #1   b. Realization #2   c. Realization #3

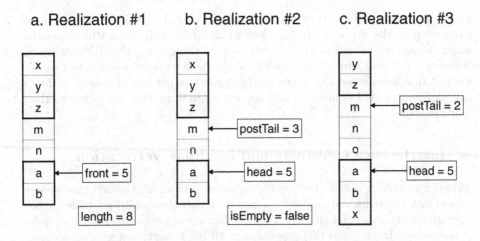

Fig. 1. Three alternatives for implementing a bounded queue on a circular array.

executed in parallel because SwapFirstEntry touches only the head of the queue and does not modify length, while Enqueue will write length and touch the end of the queue (which we know is different from the head of the queue because there was already an element in the queue before Enqueue was called). An empty queue in this implementation has length $= 0$ **and** $0 <=$ front $<$ MAX_LENGTH, and a full queue has length $=$ MAX_LENGTH **and** $0 <=$ front $<$ MAX_LENGTH.

The second implementation also has two Integer fields: head and postTail, and an additional Boolean field isEmpty. While head is the index of the array at which the first element of the queue is located, postTail is the index of the first element of the array after the last element of the queue. The boolean isEmpty is necessary to distinguish between a full queue and an empty queue since in both cases, head $=$ postTail. As in implementation 1, a client can concurrently call Enqueue and SwapFirstEntry as long as both preconditions are satisfied. However, because the length of the queue is computed from the head and postTail fields (and not another variable written by both Enqueue and Dequeue), we can also concurrently call Enqueue and Dequeue, but only in a more limited set of circumstances than is described by their respective preconditions: the queue must have at least 2 entries in it and there must be at least 2 "free" slots in the array. This restriction is important because both Enqueue and Dequeue must at least read isEmpty to determine if the queue is empty when head $=$ postTail. By restricting concurrent calls to these two methods to those situations when isEmpty will not be changed by either method (that is, when the queue will be made neither full nor empty by either Enqueue or Dequeue), we can guarantee deterministic behavior when they are executed in parallel.

The third and final implementation is similar to the second in that its two Integer fields are head and postTail (and they represent the same things), but in lieu of a Boolean isEmpty field, there is a sentinel node added to the array so that when head $=$ postTail it can only be the case that the queue is empty (a full queue has head = (postTail + 1) **mod** (MAX_LENGTH + 1)). Because the length of the array is greater than MAX_LENGTH, there will always be some element of the array that is not part of the queue. This differentiation between a full and empty queue without the need to have a separate variable ensures that even when the queue might become either full or empty during a call to Enqueue or Dequeue, it will not write anything that the other method reads or writes.

4   Interference Contracts and Modular Verification

Modular reasoning about the safe execution of concurrent threads can be separated into three distinct parts: (i) a description of the conditions under which operations are independent, (ii) a proof that client code ensures these independence conditions, and (iii) a proof that an implementation guarantees non-interference under these conditions.

Our approach to these three tasks is described below and illustrated using the first bounded queue realization from the previous section.

4.1   Interference Contract

A functional specification, as given in Sect. 3.2, does not reveal the degree to which different parts of the abstract state are entangled in the implementation. The correspondence relation between concrete state and abstract state is part of the proof of correctness for the implementation, and modular verification precludes its use in reasoning about client code.

Reasoning about the independence of concurrent threads in client code, however, requires exposing more information. Our approach for describing this independence involves creating an intermediate model consisting of orthogonal components, and encapsulating the description of this intermediate model in a distinct specification, an *interference contract*. While this segmentation is all that is necessary for the example in this paper, in general, an augmentation may additionally supplement the abstract model with more elaboration in order to specify absence of interference among operations. In this case, the specification will also need to state the additional guarantees (ensures clauses) on the supplemental model for each operation, not just interference-related specifications as in the present example.

An interference contract for the bounded queue is given below.

---

interference contract LookupOffset **for** BoundedQueueTemplate

partition **for** Queue **is** (head, tail, offset)

operation Enqueue (**clears** e: Item, **updates** q: Queue)
   affects q.tail
   preserves q.offset

> **when** q = empty_string **affects** q.head
>
> **operation** SwapFirstEntry (**updates** e: Item, **updates** q: Queue)
>   **affects** q.head
>   **preserves** q.offset
> **end** LookupOffset

Names for different segments of the intermediate model are introduced with the partition keyword. These segments are independent of implementation particulars.

An interference contract includes the *effects* of each operation in terms of this partition. There are two kinds of possible effects: *affects* and *preserves*. The former reflects a possible perturbation (i.e., a write) while the latter reflects non-modifying access (i.e., a read). Standard RESOLVE parameter modes map to these two categories of effects. The partition, however, allows for a finer-granularity description of effects, which is particularly important when concurrent threads use the same variable as a parameter, for example the access of a shared data structure.

RESOLVE's clean semantics ensure that an operation is *oblivious* to (i.e. neither reads nor writes) any variable not explicitly included as a parameter. Similarly, an operation is oblivious any segment of a partition not explicitly mentioned in its effects. For example, SwapFirstEntry is oblivious to q.tail.

A *when* clause gives a condition that restricts the scope of effects. That is, the when predicate must hold initially for the stated effect to occur. For example, in order for Enqueue to affect q.head, the queue must be empty.

Notice that this partitioning of this state space is not the same as establishing the *independence* of these segments from the point of view of the correspondence relation. In this example, the independence of the Enqueue operation on front is conditioned by the queue being non-empty. These independence conditions are in addition to the usual preconditions of the corresponding operations from the template specification, so SwapFirstEntry must be oblivious to q.tail only when the queue is non-empty.

4.2   Modular Verification of Client Code

In order for a set of statements to be safely executed in parallel, each variable–or each segment in a variable's intermediate model–can be affected by at most one statement. Furthermore, if any segment is affected by some statement, all of the other statements must be oblivious to this segment.

For example, with the interference contract given above, SwapFirstEntry and Enqueue affect non-overlapping segments (q.head and q.tail, respectively). Furthermore, each is oblivious to the segment affected by the other, assuming the queue is non empty. Finally, the segment used by both (q.offset) is preserved by both. The following client code illustrates the parallel composition of these operations.

```
assume 0 < |q| < MAX_LENGTH
cobegin
  SwapFirstEntry(x, q)
  Enqueue(y, q)
end
```

First we note that the client code above can be executed concurrently only if there is no aliasing between objects x and y. This isolation is implied if the programming language is defined to have a clean semantics like RESOLVE or through disciplined programming in a language to avoid unintended aliasing. Under clean semantics, the effects of operations are restricted to their explicit parameters (or explicitly specified global variables) [4].

In addition to satisfying the usual preconditions for functional correctness, the verification of the client code includes establishing the independence conditions of the two operations. This verification is carried out entirely in the context of the client code, using only the abstract functional specification and interference contract of the bounded queue template.

The independence of the constituent statements of a cobegin block means that the statements can be executed in any concurrent or arbitrarily interleaved manner. The semantics of their execution is identical to that of their sequential composition.

4.3   Modular Verification of an Implementation

In order to map from concrete implementation state to abstract specification state, realizations provide a representation invariant (convention) and a correspondence function (or relation, more generally). Our approach for establishing operation independence is to augment this correspondence relation with a partitioning of the constituent concrete state space. That is, an implementation must provide a mapping from the concrete data structure involved in the implementation (e.g., contents, front, and length) to the partitioned model of the queue in the interference contract. Specifically, it must place each implementation structure for the queue realization into one of head, tail, and offset.

The restrictions imposed by the effect statements need to be proven for the implementation code of each operation, under the specified conditions. In order for an operation's implementation to meet the obliviousness requirement, all statements in its code must be oblivious to the corresponding parts of the data structure. When a statement does not mention a part of the data structure (e.g., front), it is trivially oblivious to that variable. (This observation also requires clean semantics.) Otherwise, a statement may use parts of the data structure from their obliviousness requirement only in operations which, themselves, are oblivious on the corresponding parts of the data structure. The underlying data structure itself might be built from other data abstractions. This is not a problem, because the lack of entanglement of one component can be layered on top of appropriately disentangled realization components.

---

realization ArrayWithLength **for** BoundedQueueTemplate
respects LookupOffset

type representation **for** Queue **is**
  (contents: **array** 0..MAX_LENGTH − 1 **of** Item,
   front: Integer,
   length: Integer)
exemplar q
  convention
    0 <= q.front < MAX_LENGTH **and**
    0 <= q.length <= MAX_LENGTH
  correspondence
    Conc.q = Iterated_Concatenation(i = q.front.. q.front + q.length + 1,
       q.contents(i **mod** MAX_LENGTH))
  interference correspondence
    head: q.contents.c[q.front]
    tail: q.length, q.contents.c except on {q.front}
    offset: q.front
end Queue

procedure Enqueue(**clears** e: Item; **updates** q: Queue)
  e :=: q.contents[q.front + q.length **mod** MAX_LENGTH]
  q.length := q.length + 1
  Clear(e)
end Enqueue

procedure SwapFirstEntry(**updates** e: Item; **updates** q: Queue)
  e :=: q.contents[q.front]
end SwapFirstEntry

end ArrayWithLength

The proof of Enqueue's obliviousness to q.head (when the queue is non-empty) is seen as follows. When the queue is non-empty, q.length >= 1. So the part of q.contents that is modified is distinct from q.contents[q.front]. Therefore, Enqueue is oblivious to q.head. SwapFirstEntry, on the other hand, is oblivious to q.tail. Firstly, the operation does not mention q.length. Secondly, only q.contents[q.front] is affected, so it is oblivious to the rest of the contents.

Notice that the partitioning of q.contents involves the interference contract for an array (i.e., q.contents.c). It is the partition at this nested level that is used in the realization's interference correspondence.

The proof of preserving q.offset amounts to a proof that no statement in the implementation affects q.front. This proof follows from the interference contracts of the operations used by Enqueue and SwapFirstEntry. In particular, the swapping of e and q.contents[q.front] preserves q.front.

5   Summary and Future Directions

This paper has presented a novel framework for modular verification of concurrent programs using data abstractions. Specifically, it has explained how multiple operations can be simultaneously invoked on an abstract data object if a set of interference conditions can be specified and verified using an augmentation to the abstract specification of the data abstraction. The proof process is strictly modularized. The paper has presented a concrete example to illustrate the ideas. Future directions include development of a formal proof system and automated verification.

Acknowledgments. This research is funded in part by NSF grants CCF-1161916 and DUE-1022941. Any opinions, findings, conclusions, or recommendations expressed here are those of the authors and do not necessarily reflect the views of the NSF.

References

1. Bagherzadeh, M., Rajan, H.: Panini: a concurrent programming model for solving pervasive and oblivious interference. In: Proceedings of the 14th International Conference on Modularity, MODULARITY 2015, pp. 93–108. ACM, New York (2015)
2. Harms, D.E., Weide, B.W.: Copying and swapping: influences on the design of reusable software components. IEEE Trans. Softw. Eng. **17**, 424–435 (1991)
3. Herlihy, M., Shavit, N.: The Art of Multiprocessor Programming. Morgan Kaufmann Publishers Inc., San Francisco (2008)
4. Kulczycki, G.W.: Direct reasoning. Ph.D. thesis, Clemson University, Clemson, SC, USA (2004). AAI3125470
5. Leino, K.R.M., Müller, P., Smans, J.: Verification of concurrent programs with chalice. In: Aldini, A., Barthe, G., Gorrieri, R. (eds.) FOSAD 2007/2008/2009. LNCS, vol. 5705, pp. 195–222. Springer, Heidelberg (2009). doi:10.1007/978-3-642-03829-7_7
6. Mostowski, W.: Dynamic frames based verification method for concurrent Java programs. In: Gurfinkel, A., Seshia, S.A. (eds.) VSTTE 2015. LNCS, vol. 9593, pp. 124–141. Springer, Heidelberg (2016). doi:10.1007/978-3-319-29613-5_8
7. Rodríguez, E., Dwyer, M., Flanagan, C., Hatcliff, J., Leavens, G.T.: Extending JML for modular specification and verification of multi-threaded programs. In: Black, A.P. (ed.) ECOOP 2005. LNCS, vol. 3586, pp. 551–576. Springer, Heidelberg (2005)
8. Sitaraman, M., Adcock, B., Avigad, J., Bronish, D., Bucci, P., Frazier, D., Friedman, H.M., Harton, H., Heym, W., Kirschenbaum, J., Krone, J., Smith, H., Weide, B.W.: Building a push-button resolve verifier: progress and challenges. Formal Aspects Comput. **23**(5), 607–626 (2011)
9. Smans, J., Jacobs, B., Piessens, F.: VeriCool: an automatic verifier for a concurrent object-oriented language. In: Barthe, G., Boer, F.S. (eds.) FMOODS 2008. LNCS, vol. 5051, pp. 220–239. Springer, Heidelberg (2008). doi:10.1007/978-3-540-68863-1_14

Accelerating the General Simplex Procedure
for Linear Real Arithmetic via GPUs

Steven T. Stewart[✉], Derek Rayside, Vijay Ganesh, and Krzysztof Czarnecki

University of Waterloo, Waterloo, Canada
steven.stewart@uwaterloo.ca

Abstract. This paper demonstrates the benefits of GPU parallelism for
a simplex-based decision procedure for conjunctions of linear constraints
over reals. This variant of the simplex method, called general simplex,
decides whether the set of constraints is satisfiable, and is intended to
be integrated into SMT solvers. We carried out comprehensive experiments over randomly generated instances for dense linear programming
problems on a mid-range consumer GPU (AMD Radeon 390X) using
floating point arithmetic. The GPU scheduled hundreds of thousands
of concurrent thread workgroups to process tableaus representing up to
8k variables and 8k constraints. We achieved speedup up to 25x over
a CPU-only implementation (quad-core AMD Kaveri 3.7 GHz) of the
same procedure. We compared this to a multithreaded OpenMP implementation that also achieved up to 1.8x speedup on the same inputs.
These results suggest that GPU processors may be further utilized in
the context of SMT and software verification tools.

1   Introduction

The landscape of processing hardware is increasingly heterogeneous. Transistor
density is no longer the primary constraint on hardware performance; instead,
the focus is on performance delivered per watt expended [3,16]. The transition to
many-core[1] processors, such as the GPU, and heterogeneous solutions is rapidly
moving forward. The next generation of software verification engines are likely
to take advantage of the massive parallelism of many-core processors.

In order to prepare such tools for this evolving hardware landscape, we
demonstrate a GPU-accelerated variant of the *general simplex* procedure [6,10].
Our initial prototype achieves up to 25x speedup over a CPU-only implementation using a mid-range GPU.

The accelerated GPU kernels demonstrated in this paper should be useful for
solvers employing mixed-floating point / rational strategies. In software verification, inexact solutions produced by floating-point arithmetic are generally not
acceptable. SMT solvers use rational arithmetic for linear real arithmetic (LRA),
though at the cost of extended precision arithmetic. As a result, exact solvers

---

[1] Many-core processors have orders of magnitude more processing elements than multi-
core processors [1,16].

© Springer International Publishing AG 2016
S. Blazy and M. Chechik (Eds.): VSTTE 2016, LNCS 9971, pp. 129–138, 2016.
DOI: 10.1007/978-3-319-48869-1_10

do not handle dense problem inputs with large coefficients very well. In recent years, it has been shown that an inexact, floating-point solver that produces an untrusted solution can be strategically used to guide an exact solver towards an accurate result [15].

2   Related Work

There are countless papers on solving linear programming (LP) problems using simplex, but only a handful are directly related to our work.

The use of alternative processing architectures for solving LP is not without precedence. Lalami et al. showed that the GPU can accelerate the simplex procedure. Their single- and multi-GPU CUDA implementations achieved an order of magnitude speedup over a CPU implementation [11,12]. Mittal et al. [14] suggested that advances in FPGA technology could be exploited to greatly accelerate simplex procedures. Our solver emerges from this same interest, but differs in that it is an implementation of *general simplex* for solving the decision problem rather than the optimization problem. The procedure for solving general simplex was introduced by Dutertre and de Moura [6] in 2006. Since then, general simplex has been integrated into SMT solvers such as Yices[2] and Z3[3].

Our work is related to the topic of combining inexact (floating-point arithmetic) and exact (extended precision arithmetic) solvers, such as those described by [7,15]. Monniaux [15] uses this approach to transform a "naïve and slow" solver into a competitive one.

SMT solvers rely on SAT-solving technology and there are a handful of papers that examine the use of GPUs for SAT-solving, a selection of which includes [2,5,8,9,13]. To date, no GPU-based SAT solver has demonstrated that it can be competitive with the state-of-the-art.

3   GPU Design Principles

In this paper, we focus on the programming model for GPUs using the OpenCL framework for writing parallel programs. The modern GPU offers a flexible programming model for writing thread-level or data-parallel code [16].

Whereas CPUs are designed to minimize latency, GPUs are designed for throughput. Like a SIMD computer, the GPU architecture is built upon a parallel array of processors, called *compute units* in the OpenCL nomenclature. Each compute unit, which is composed of many *processing elements*, is capable of concurrently executing hundreds of threads decomposed into *workgroups*. Threads within a workgroup can synchronize and access shared memory. When the host process launches a *kernel*, workgroups are distributed across the available compute units. Each thread in a workgroup has its own program counter and register

---

[2] http://yices.csl.sri.com/.
[3] http://research.microsoft.com/en-us/um/redmond/projects/z3/.

state, and – unlike a SIMD computer – threads within a workgroup are permitted to execute different instructions when they are required to follow divergent execution paths, offering the programmer greater flexibility.

The OpenCL programming model exposes more of the memory hierarchy than what is typical for CPU programmers, and memory access patterns can have a substantial impact on performance. Much of the performance gains of GPUs are achieved by effective use of programmable, on-chip local memory and registers, and by ensuring aligned and coalesced data access patterns that minimize relatively slow global memory transactions.

The GPU programmer's objective is to leverage as much parallelism as possible by keeping all compute units of the GPU busy. Achieving this involves somewhat complicated considerations of both execution behavior and how resources are distributed.

4   Problem Statement

In a linear programming problem, the goal is to find a solution to a set of linear constraints that maximizes (or minimizes) a linear objective function. A variant of this is called the feasibility problem, wherein the goal is to determine the existence or nonexistence of a feasible solution. The *general simplex* [6] procedure has properties that are advantageous for SMT solvers; thus, in this paper, we are interested in solving the feasibility problem using this procedure.

4.1   Problem Input

The feasibility problem is specified by a set of linear constraints without an objective function. A vector of decision variables $X = [x_1, x_2, \ldots, x_n]$ is assigned a vector of values, called an *assignment*, and each value is a nonnegative real number. An assignment is *feasible* if it respects all linear constraints represented by a vector $C = [c_1(X), \ldots, c_m(X)]$, representing the conjunction of constraints. This conjunction of constraints is a first-order formula, and a *feasible assignment* is said to be a *solution* to the formula.

4.2   The General Simplex Procedure for LRA

The general simplex procedure for LRA was designed to be efficient for SMT solvers, and is a variant of the simplex procedure developed by Danzig [4] in 1947. All constraints[4] must be expressed in general form: $a_1x_1 + \cdots + a_nx_n = 0$.

The problem is represented by a data structure called a tableau, which consists of m rows (for constraints) and n columns (for decision variables). The

---

[4] As described in [10], arbitrary weak linear constraints of the form $L \otimes R$, where $\otimes \in \{\leq, \geq, =\}$, can be translated to general form as follows for the ith constraint: (1) move all addends in R to the left-hand side to obtain $L' \otimes b$, where b is a constant; (2) introduce a new variable s_i and add the constraints $L' - s_i = 0$ and $s_i \otimes b$. The variables s are called *additional variables*.

entries in the tableau are the coefficients from the set of linear constraints. Each variable is subject to bounds (lower/upper), and the assignment of each variable must also be tracked.

The initial assignment to the variables begins at the origin $X = [0, \ldots, 0]$, and variables are partitioned into two sets: initially, decision variables belong to the set of *non-basic* variables N, and additional variables belong to the set of *basic* variables B. Respectively, these may be thought of as the independent and dependent variables, because the assignment of those in B are computed based on the those in N. Variables may switch membership between B and N when the procedure "pivots."

The procedure is fully specified in [6,10], and is intuitively described as follows. Suppose that the bounds of a basic variable x_i[5] are violated under the current assignment $\alpha(x_i)$, and call this a *broken* variable; in other words, $\alpha(x_i) < l_i$ or $\alpha(x_i) > u_i$, where l_i is a lower bound and u_i is an upper bound for variable x_i. Clearly, if a satisfying assignment were to exist, then the broken variable needs to be repaired; thus, a *suitable* non-basic variable is chosen whose current assignment can be "tweaked" such that the bounds violation of x_i is corrected. A suitable variable is a non-basic variable that has "room for tweaking." To achieve this, the current assignment of the suitable variable is either increased or decreased. If no suitable variable exists, then repair is not possible, no feasible solution exists, and the procedure reports "unsatisfiable"; otherwise, the broken variable is fixed, but this can lead to a bounds violation of another basic variable, which in turn must also be fixed. This iterative process continues until there are no further bounds violations, at which point the procedure reports "satisfiable" and returns the satisfying assignment, or until it reports "unsatisfiable" as described.

5   Implementation

We start by presenting a simple API of the solver, expressed in C++.

```
public:
  virtual void addConstraint(vector<T> &constr);
  virtual void setBounds(int idx, T lower, T upper);
  virtual vector<T> solution();
  virtual bool solve();
protected:
  virtual bool checkBounds(int &broken_idx);
  virtual bool findSuitable(int &broken_idx,
      int &suitable_idx);
  virtual void pivot(int pivot_row, int pivot_col);
  virtual void updateAssignment();
```

The four public methods enable an application to construct a problem instance, and the four protected methods are used internally by the solver. Some methods are templatized with the type T, indicating they may be instantiated with different types (*e.g.*, *float* or *double*). Constraints are built from variables of type

---

[5] Note that we are using x_i here to refer to any variable, whether it be a decision or an additional variable.

T and added by *addConstraint*. Variable bounds are set by *setBounds*, requiring a variable's index and lower/upper bounds. If the solver has found a solution, it can be obtained via *solution*.

The public *solve* method is a template method that specifies the solving procedure as part of an extensible abstract base class. It references the four protected virtual methods that must be implemented by a concrete class.

```
virtual bool solve {
  unsigned broken_idx, suitable_idx;
  while (!checkBounds(brokenIdx)) {
    if (!findSuitable(brokenIdx, suitableIdx))
      return false;
    pivot(brokenIdx, suitableIdx);
    updateAssignment();
  }
  return true;
}
```

The *checkBounds* method identifies a broken variable, saving its index in the output argument *brokenIdx*. If no broken variable is found, the procedure exits the while loop and returns true ("satisfiable"). The *findSuitable* method searches for a suitable non-basic variable. If one is found, its index is saved in *suitableIdx*; otherwise, false ("unsatisfiable") is returned.

The *pivot* method swaps the broken variable in B with the suitable variable in N. The row r of the table corresponding with the broken variable x_r is called the *pivot row*, and the column c of the table corresponding with the suitable variable x_c is called the *pivot column*. An element a_{rj} is said to belong to the pivot row, and an element a_{ic} is said to belong to the pivot column. The element a_{rc} at the intersection of the pivot row and pivot column is called the *pivot element*. All other elements a_{ij} where $i \neq r$ and $j \neq c$ are called *inner* elements. A call to *pivot* updates the tableau using the following expressions.

$$\text{(Inner element) } a'_{ij} = a_{ij} - (a_{ic} \cdot a_{rj})/a_{rc} \text{ where } i \neq r \text{ and } j \neq c$$
$$\text{(Pivot column) } a'_{ic} = a_{ic}/a_{ij}$$
$$\text{(Pivot row) } a'_{ir} = -a_{rj}/a_{ij}$$
$$\text{(Pivot element) } a'_{rc} = 1/a_{rc}$$

Finally, the *updateAssignment* method updates the current assignment of the basic variables after pivoting. The current assignment $\alpha(x_i)$ of a basic variable x_i is computed by the following summation.

$$x_i = \sum_{j=1}^{n} a_{ij} \cdot \alpha(x_j)$$

5.1   CPU-only

We present a concrete CPU implementation of the solver, listing its relevant data structures that include the tableau, assignments, and variable metadata.

```
private:
  T *tableau;        // the tableau manipulated by the solver
  T *assigns;        // the current assignment of each variable
  Variable vars;     // stores information about each variable
  set<Variable>
     basic;          // the current set of basic variables
  set<Variable>
     nonbasic;       // the current set of nonbasic variables

struct Variable {
  int idx;           // the unique index of the variable
  int tableau_idx;   // the row or column index of the tableau
                     //    associated with the variable
  T lower;           // the lower bound on the variable
  T upper;           // the upper bound on the variable
  T assignment;      // the current assignment of the variable
}
```

Each *Variable* has a unique index, a current mapping to a row or column index of the tableau, lower/upper bounds, and an assignment. The solver distinguishes between basic and nonbasic variables with two ordered sets (*basic* and *nonbasic*), which store *Variable* objects in the ascending order of their indices.

The public and protected methods required by *solve* have straightforward implementations: *checkBounds* iterates through the set *basic*, selecting the first broken variable it encounters; *findSuitable* iterates through nonbasic variables until a suitable one is found; *pivot* calls ancillary methods *update_inner*, *update_row*, and *update_column*, which respectively implement the expressions listed earlier for the pivot operation; *updateAssignment* performs a reduction operation across the rows of the tableau, updating the assignments using the summation expression listed earlier.

OpenMP. The *pivot* method presents an ample opportunity for parallelism. Each tableau element can be updated independently of the other. Loop constructs can be augmented with OpenMP preprocessor directives so that multiple CPU threads will carry out these independent operations. The simplest approach is to use the pragma *omp parallel for* to automatically parallelize a loop.

```
#pragma omp parallel for
  for (int i = 0; i < n; ++i) {
    ...
  }
```

5.2   CPU-GPU

The CPU-GPU variant extends the CPU solver, overriding *pivot* for GPU acceleration. In order to facilitate coalesced accesses to global memory, variable metadata are stored in contiguous arrays. Data structures used by *pivot* have both host and device OpenCL memory objects (*cl_mem*), as well as conventional host pointers for mapping OpenCL driver-allocated memory to the host process. There are two additional arrays used to map a tableau row and column index to corresponding variable indices (*rowToVar* and *colToVar*).

```
private:
  // host memory object, device memory object, followed by
  // pointer to the host memory of the data
  cl_mem h_tableau, d_tableau;
  cl_mem h_assigns, d_assigns;
  float *tableau, *assigns;
  cl_mem h_rowToVar, d_rowToVar;
  cl_mem h_colToVar, d_colToVar;
  int *rowToVar, *colToVar;
```

Pinned (or page-locked) memory transfers are preferred for high throughput. When the CL_MEM_ALLOC_HOST_PTR flag is specified, it is likely (though not guaranteed) that pinned memory will be used. The steps required to accomplished this are abbreviated as follows.

```
// Request the driver to allocate pinned host memory
cl_mem h_tableau = clCreateBuffer(...CL_MEM_ALLOC_HOST_PTR...);

// Map the pinned memory region to a host pointer
float *tableau = (float*) clEnqueueMapBuffer(...h_tableau...);

// Write some data to tableau
for (int i = 0; i < n; ++i) tableau[i] = ...

// Copy host data to device
clEnqueueWriteBuffer(...d_tableau_...);
```

The *pivot* method is nearly identical to its CPU parent, except that calls to *update_inner*, *update_row*, and *update_col* are replaced with corresponding calls to OpenCL kernel functions. Kernel calls are made using *clEnqueueNDRangeKernel* and require a launch configuration that specifies the magnitude and dimensionality of workgroups. Each GPU has an upper limit on the number of threads per workgroup, and the ideal number that maximizes device occupancy can only be determined by experimentation. As a default, we set this number to half of the maximum size of a workgroup for the device.

Each time *pivot* is called, the tableau is updated; thus, *findSuitable* is overridden so that the row of the tableau corresponding with the broken variable is copied back to the host. This ensures that the host has up-to-date data before searching for a suitable variable.

```
bool GpuSolver::findSuitable(int &broken_idx,
       int &suitable_idx) {
  // Copy updated row from device to host
  clEnqueueReadBuffer(...copy one row...);

  // Call parent method
  return CpuSolver::findSuitable(broken_idx, suitable_idx);
}
```

6 Experiments

Experiments were conducted on a quad-core AMD A10-7850K 3.7 GHz CPU and a mid-range GPU (AMD Radeon 390X).

In order to best identify opportunities for parallel acceleration, the CPU implementation was profiled using dense linear programming instances that were randomly generated with tableau sizes ranging from 1 million (1024×1024)

to 65 million elements (8192×8192). The percentage time of each method is depicted in Table 1. Our implementation uses a "lazy" version of *updateAssignment*, which dramatically reduced its percentage time from 37 % to a negligible cost, and the percentage time for *pivot* went from 60 % to 96 %. This boosted the potential gains available by parallelizing *pivot* on the GPU.

Table 1. Percentage time taken by each method in the CPU-only implementation.

Method	Contribution
checkBounds	0.4 %
findSuitable	0.1 %
pivot	96.0 %
(other)	3.6 %

The speedup measured for the general simplex procedure's *solve* method using OpenMP and the GPU is summarized in Table 2. Four conclusions are evident:

1. The benefits of parallelism increase with the size of the input.
2. There is never an advantage for using the serial CPU-only implementation, even for the smallest tableau ($1M = 1024 \times 1024$).
3. The CPU-GPU is superior to OpenMP. Overall speed increases for range from 3x for the smallest tableau studied ($1M = 1024 \times 1024$) to 25x for the largest ($65M = 8192 \times 8192$).
4. The pivot sub-procedure significantly benefits from parallelization.

Table 2. Speedup of the *solve* procedure.

Size	OpenMP	GPU
1M	1.2x	3x
4M	1.5x	8x
16M	1.8x	18x
64M	1.8x	25x

7   Conclusions and Future Work

Many-core processors, such as GPUs, can effectively accelerate the floating-point calculations of the *pivot* operations for an inexact LRA solver based on the general simplex procedure. These GPU kernels excel on dense problem inputs, demonstrating the potential of using GPUs for dense problems that current SMT solvers have difficulty solving.

For future work, the prototype solver needs to be extended to support additional features currently in use by state-of-the-art SMT solvers for LRA. In particular, it needs to support adding and removing of constraints (for backtracking), and the ability to propagate theory lemmas. The solver also needs to be tested with algorithms that combine inexact and exact solvers, such as those described by [7,15].

The potential for scaling up the performance and problem sizes for the GPU-accelerated solver is significant. Companies like AMD (Radeon and Firepro), NVIDIA (Geforce and Tesla), and Intel (Xeon Phi) continue to advance the hardware, and there are no apparent obstacles to scaling up the procedure to support multiple GPUs in a single machine with aggregate memory bandwidth in the order of TB/s. There is strong potential for using many-core processors in the context of SMT and software verification tools.

References

1. Asanovic, K., Bodik, R., Catanzaro, B.C., Gebis, J.J., Husbands, P., Keutzer, K., Patterson, D.A., Plishker, W.L., Shalf, J., Williams, S.W., Yelick, K.A.: The landscape of parallel computing research: a view from Berkeley. Technical report UCB/EECS-2006-183, Berkeley EECS, December 2006
2. Beckers, S., De Samblanx, G., De Smedt, F., Goedeme, T., Struyf, L., Vennekens, J.: Parallel hybrid SAT solving using OpenCL (2012)
3. Borkar, S., Chien, A.A.: The future of microprocessors. CACM **54**(5), 67–77 (2011). http://doi.acm.org/10.1145/1941487.1941507
4. Dantzig, G.B.: Linear Programming and Ext. Princeton University Press, Princeton (1963)
5. Deleau, H., Jaillet, C., Krajecki, M.: GPU4SAT: solving the SAT problem on GPU. In: PARA Workshop on Scientific & Parallel Computing (2008)
6. Dutertre, B., Moura, L.: A fast linear-arithmetic solver for DPLL(T). In: Ball, T., Jones, R.B. (eds.) CAV 2006. LNCS, vol. 4144, pp. 81–94. Springer, Heidelberg (2006)
7. Faure, G., Nieuwenhuis, R., Oliveras, A., Rodríguez-Carbonell, E.: SAT modulo the theory of linear arithmetic: exact, inexact and commercial solvers. In: Kleine Büning, H., Zhao, X. (eds.) SAT 2008. LNCS, vol. 4996, pp. 77–90. Springer, Heidelberg (2008)
8. Fujii, H., Fujimoto, N.: GPU Acceleration of BCP Procedure for SAT Algorithms (2012)
9. Gulati, K., Khatri, S.P.: Boolean satisfiability on a graphics processor, pp. 123–126 (2010)
10. Kroening, D., Strichman, O.: Decision Procedures: An Algorithmic Point of View. Springer (2008)
11. Lalami, M.E., Boyer, V., El-Baz, D.: Efficient implementation of the simplex method on a CPU-GPU system. In: IEEE International Symposium on Parallel and Distributed Processing Workshops and Ph.D. Forum, pp. 1999–2006 (2011)
12. Lalami, M.E., El-Baz, D., Boyer, V.: Multi GPU implementation of the simplex algorithm. In: 2011 IEEE International Conference on High Performance Computing and Communications, Banff, Canada, pp. 179–186, September 2011

13. Meyer, Q., Schonfeld, F., Stamminger, M., Wanka, R.: 3-SAT on CUDA: towards a massively parallel SAT solver. In: High Performance Computing and Simulation (HPCS), pp. 306–313. IEEE (2010)
14. Mittal, S., Vetter, J.: A Survey of CPU-GPU Heterogeneous Computing Techniques. ACM Comput. Surv. **47**, 1–35 (2015)
15. Monniaux, D.: On using floating-point computations to help an exact linear arithmetic decision procedure. In: Bouajjani, A., Maler, O. (eds.) CAV 2009. LNCS, vol. 5643, pp. 570–583. Springer, Heidelberg (2009)
16. Munshi, A., Benedict, R.G., Mattson, T.G., Fung, J., Ginsburg, D.: OpenCL Programming Guide. Addison-Wesley, Reading (2012)

JavaSMT: A Unified Interface
for SMT Solvers in Java

Egor George Karpenkov[1,2], Karlheinz Friedberger[3], and Dirk Beyer[3]

[1] Univ. Grenoble Alpes, VERIMAG, 38000 Grenoble, France
[2] CNRS, VERIMAG, 38000 Grenoble, France
[3] University of Passau, 94032 Passau, Germany

Abstract. Satisfiability Modulo Theory (SMT) solvers received a lot of attention in the research community in the last decade, and consequently their expressiveness and performance have significantly improved. In the areas of program analysis and model checking, many of the newly developed tools rely on SMT solving. The SMT-LIB initiative defines a common format for communication with an SMT solver. However, tool developers often prefer to use the solver API instead, because many features offered by SMT solvers such as interpolation, optimization, and formula introspection are not supported by SMT-LIB directly. Additionally, using SMT-LIB for communication incurs a performance overhead, because all the queries to the solver have to be serialized to strings. Yet using the API directly creates the problem of a solver lock-in, which makes evaluating a tool with different solvers very difficult. We present JavaSMT, a library that exposes a solver-independent API layer for SMT solving. Our library aims to close the gap between API-based and SMT-LIB-based communication, by offering a large set of features with minimal performance overhead. JavaSMT has been used internally in CPACHECKER since inception, and has been heavily tested in different verification algorithms. The library is available from its Github website https://github.com/sosy-lab/java-smt.

1 Introduction

During the last decade, SMT solvers have demonstrated an impressive increase in expressiveness (many supported theories) and efficiency (much larger scale of queries that can be answered within a small time-frame). As a consequence, many tools for software verification rely on an SMT solver as a back-end.

The SMT-LIB [3] initiative defines a common interface language for SMT solvers, much like SQL standardizes the interface to a relational database. However, from the perspective of a tool developer, using the textual SMT-LIB communication channel is often suboptimal. Firstly, it does not expose all the

The research leading to these results has received funding from the European Research Council under the European Union's Seventh Framework Programme (FP/2007-2013) / ERC Grant Agreement nr. 306595 "STATOR" and from the Free State of Bavaria.

© Springer International Publishing AG 2016
S. Blazy and M. Chechik (Eds.): VSTTE 2016, LNCS 9971, pp. 139–148, 2016.
DOI: 10.1007/978-3-319-48869-1_11

features that modern solvers offer: interpolation[1] multiple independent solvers, formula introspection, and optimization modulo theories are not included in SMT-LIB 2.0. It is also not possible to conditionally *store* formulas for future reuse and remove them when they are no longer needed. Secondly, such a textual communication can be very inefficient, because all queries to the solver have to be serialized to strings, and all of the solver output has to be parsed. For a tool that poses a large number of simple queries (such as in PDR [2]), parsing and serialization can become a performance bottleneck.

However, when using a solver API directly, users face the problem of "solver lock-in", which makes it difficult to evaluate different SMT solvers or to switch to a different SMT solver without rewriting a large chunk of the application.

We propose JavaSMT, a library that exposes a common API layer across several back-end solvers. It is written in Java and is available under the Apache 2.0 License on GitHub (https://github.com/sosy-lab/java-smt). JavaSMT communicates with solvers using their API, and imposes only a minimal amount of overhead. For the solvers that are implemented in Java the exposed API is used directly, and for the solvers in other languages we integrated JNI bindings.

Outlook. This paper refers to JavaSMT v1.01[2]. The contributions of this paper are structured as follows: First, we describe the features that JavaSMT exposes in Sect. 2. Second, we present the project structure and the requirements for adding a new solver into JavaSMT in Sect. 3. Third, Sect. 4 discusses the strategies for managing memory of the JNI bindings, and the associated performance problem. Finally, we present a case study based on the HOUDINI algorithm [4] in Sect. 5, and conclude by comparing JavaSMT to related projects and discussing possible future work in Sect. 6.

2   Features

JavaSMT currently provides access to five different SMT solvers: MATHSAT [1], OptiMathSAT [17], Z3 [14], SMTINTERPOL [12], and PRINCESS [16]. Table 1 lists the theories and features that are supported by these solvers.

Formula Representation. To keep the memory overhead low, JavaSMT does not store its own internal representation of the formulas, but keeps only one single pointer to each formula in the solver's memory, possibly with an additional pointer to the current solver context. Consequently, the memory footprint of JavaSMT is proportional to a small constant multiplied by the number of formulas that the client application needs a reference to, *regardless* of the size of the constructed formulas. This choice ensures high performance, but obstructs transferring formulas between different contexts for different operations, such as checking satisfiability with Z3 and performing interpolation with SMTINTERPOL. For such inter-solver translations we use SMT-LIB serialization.

---

[1] A proposal draft [11] exists since 2012.
[2] https://github.com/sosy-lab/java-smt/releases/tag/1.0.1.

Table 1. Theories and features supported by different solvers

	MathSAT	OptiMathSAT	Z3	SMTInterpol	Princess
Integer	+	+	+	+	+
Rational	+	+	+	+	-
Array	+	+	+	+	+
Bitvector	+	+	+	-	-
Float	+	+	-	-	-
Unsat Core	+	+	+	+	-
Partial Models	-	-	+	-	+
Assumptions	+	+	+	+	+
Quantifiers	-	-	+	-	+
Interpolation (Tree/Sequential)	+	+	+	+	+
Optimization	-	+	+	-	-
Incremental Solving	+	+	+	+	+
SMT-LIB2	+	+	+	+	+

Type Safety. Using and enforcing types is beneficial for a software library, because it guarantees the absence of errors that are caused by incorrect type usage *at compile time* and can increase the level of trust in the software. Improving such confidence is particularly important for tools for software verification, because the verdict of such tools is only reliable if all components operate correctly ("who verifies the software verifier").

JavaSMT uses the Java type system to differentiate between the different sorts of formulas (e.g., `BooleanFormula` and `IntegerFormula`) and guarantees that all operations respect the formula type. The typed interface avoids incorrect operations (such as adding integers to Booleans), which would not pass the compiler. Type safety also extends to model evaluation: for example, evaluating an `IntegerFormula` is guaranteed at compile time to return a `BigInteger`.

Formula Introspection. In many applications, formula introspection is a required feature. For instance, an analysis might wish to re-encode expensive non-linear operations as uninterpreted functions, or to find and rename all variables used in the formula.

In our experience with formula introspection and transformation code in CPACHECKER [6], we have discovered that writing *correct and robust* formula-traversing code can be very challenging, due to:

- cases missed by the client, e.g., an unexpected XOR,
- incorrect assumptions by the client, such as assuming that the input formula has no quantifiers,
- not performing memoization for recursive traversals, resulting in exponential blow-up on formulas represented as directed acyclic graphs, or
- performing recursive traversal using recursion, since it can result in stack-overflow exceptions on large formulas.

In order to decrease the likelihood of such bugs, we use the Visitor design pattern (cf. [9], Chap. 5) for formula traversal and transformation. Two visitor interfaces are exposed: BooleanFormulaVisitor and FormulaVisitor. The Boolean visitor requires implementations for Boolean primitives that can occur in the formulas (equality, implication, etc.) and matches all other formulas as atoms. It is useful for transformation of the Boolean structure of the formula, such as a conversion to negation normal form. The FormulaVisitor does not explicitly require matching each possible function, but provides an enumeration consisting of most common function declarations (addition, subtraction, comparison, etc.) and can be used to recursively traverse the entire formula, e.g., in order to find all used variables.

Our experience shows that such an approach leads to considerably safer code as compared to direct formula manipulation.

3 Project Architecture

The overall structure of the library is shown in Fig. 1. An interaction with the JavaSMT library starts with a SolverContextFactory, which is used to create a SolverContext object, encapsulating a context for a particular solver. All further interaction is performed through the SolverContext class, which exposes the features outlined in Sect. 2. Instances of SolverContext are *not* thread-safe, and should be accessed only from a single thread. However, separate contexts are independent from each other and can be safely used from different threads, provided that the underlying solver supports multithreading on different contexts.

An interface to every represented solver is implemented as a separate package with an entry class that implements the SolverContext API.

4 Memory Management

Different SMT solvers resort to different strategies for memory management. The solvers running in managed environments (e.g., SMTInterpol and Princess running on JVM) use the available garbage collector, while solvers exposing a C API have to expose the memory management API to a user. The underlying problem is that for a library that exposes its API through the native non-managed language, it is *impossible* to know whether a previously returned object is still referenced by the client application, or whether it can be deleted.

MATHSAT exposes a "manual" garbage-collection interface, which removes all formulas except those that are specifically requested to be kept. This requires an application to keep track of all created objects that can still be referenced.

Z3 uses a reference-counting approach, where an object is considered unreachable whenever its reference count reaches zero. While this interface can be effectively used from C++ to offer automatic memory management using RAII (incrementing references in constructors, and decrementing in destructors), using it in an *efficient* and correct way is surprisingly difficult from Java.

The official Z3 Java API is using Java finalizers [3] to decrement the references, explicitly performing locking on the queue of references that need to be decremented. Unfortunately, finalizers are known to have a very severe memory and performance penalty (cf. [10], Chap. 2.7). Thus we have developed our own Z3 JNI bindings with a memory strategy based on using `PhantomReference` and `ReferenceQueue`, provided by the JDK to get a more fine-grained control over the garbage collection.

We present the performance evaluation of three different memory managing strategies for Z3: (1) using the official Z3 API, which relies on finalizers, (2) using our phantom reference-based implementation, and (3) not closing resources at all. We have chosen a benchmark setup that runs a program analysis with local policy iteration [8] on the SV-COMP [5] data set. Obtained results are shown in Fig. 2. Unsurprisingly, the approach using finalizers has the worst performance by far, with performance penalty often eclipsing the analysis time, and a very large memory consumption. The no-GC approach minimizes both memory and time consumption. We attribute the high performance of the no-GC approach to the hash-consing used in Z3, which results in no additional memory consumption for ASTs that were previously already constructed.

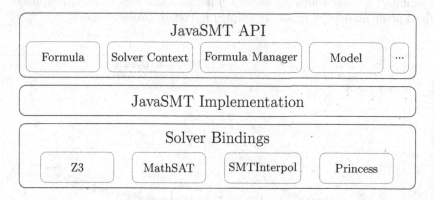

Fig. 1. JavaSMT Architecture

---

[3] Since the publication of this paper, Z3 bindings were updated by one of the authors of this paper to use a more efficient memory management strategy.

5   Case Study: Inductive Formula Weakening

To give a tour of the library, we present a usable implementation of the inductive-invariant synthesis algorithm HOUDINI [4]. In order to provide the context, we include a brief background that explains the algorithm and its motivation.

Background. We consider a program that manipulates a set X of variables. The program is defined by the initial condition $I(X)$ and the transition relation $\tau(X, X')$. Both I and τ are quantifier-free first-order formulas.

A lemma F is called inductive with respect to τ if it implies itself over the primed variables after the transition:

$$\forall X, X' : F(X) \wedge \tau(X, X') \implies F(X') \tag{1}$$

Inductiveness can be checked with a single query to an SMT solver. The lemma F is inductive with respect to τ iff the following formula (2) is unsatisfiable:

$$F(X) \wedge \tau(X, X') \wedge \neg F(X') \tag{2}$$

The HOUDINI algorithm finds a maximal inductive subset of a given set L of *candidate* lemmas which satisfies the initial condition $I(X)$. Firstly, it filters out all lemmas from L which are not implied by I. Then, it repeatedly checks $\bigwedge L$ for inductiveness using (2), and updates L to exclude the lemmas that give rise to counterexamples-to-induction. At the end the algorithm terminates with an inductive subset $L_I \subseteq L$.

Counterexamples-to-induction are derived from a *model* returned by an SMT solver in response to a query in (2) (such a model exists iff the conjunction of lemmas is not inductive). Given a model $\mathcal{M}$, the HOUDINI algorithm filters out all lemmas $l \in L$ for which $\mathcal{M} \models \neg l(X')$ holds. After such filtering is applied in a fixed-point manner, a (possibly empty) inductive subset remains.

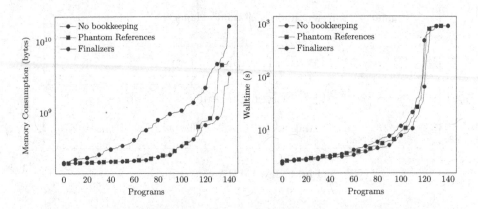

Fig. 2. Resource usage comparison across different memory management strategies for Z3

Implementation.

Initialization: To initialize JAVASMT, we pass the required classes using dependency injection, as shown in Listing 1. This code snippet generates a configuration from passed command-line arguments (configuration can choose a solver, and tweak any of its options), a logger instance, and initializes the solver context.

Formula Transformation: The HOUDINI algorithm gets a set of lemmas as an input. However, for checking inductiveness as shown in (2) we need *primed* versions of these lemmas, which we obtain by renaming all free variables using a transformation visitor as shown in Listing 2.

Instead of directly removing asserted lemmas from the solver, we use annotation with auxiliary *selector* variables. Each lemma l_i is converted to $l_i \lor s_i$, where s_i is a fresh Boolean variable. After such an annotation, the lemma l_i can be relaxed by asserting an assumption s_i. The code for input-lemma annotation is shown in Listing 3. Finally, the main HOUDINI loop, which performs lemma filtering until inductiveness, is shown in Listing 4.

```java
public class HoudiniApp {
    private final FormulaManager fmgr;
    private final BooleanFormulaManager bfmgr;
    private final SolverContext context;

    public HoudiniApp(String[] args) throws Exception {
        Configuration config = Configuration.fromCmdLineArguments(args);
        LogManager logger = BasicLogManager.create(config);
        ShutdownNotifier notifier = ShutdownManager.create().getNotifier();

        context = SolverContextFactory.createSolverContext(
            config, logger, notifier);
        fmgr = context.getFormulaManager();
        bfmgr = context.getFormulaManager().getBooleanFormulaManager();
    }
}
```

Listing 1: JAVASMT initialization

```java
private BooleanFormula prime(BooleanFormula input) {
    return fmgr.transformRecursively(input,
        new FormulaTransformationVisitor<Formula>() {
        @Override
        public Formula visitFreeVariable(Formula f, String name) {
            return fmgr.makeVariable(
                fmgr.getFormulaType(f), name + "'");
        }
    });
}
```

Listing 2: Transforming formulas with JAVASMT

```java
public List<BooleanFormula> houdini(
    List<BooleanFormula> lemmas, BooleanFormula transition)
    throws SolverException, InterruptedException {
  List<BooleanFormula> annotated = new ArrayList<>();
  List<BooleanFormula> annotatedPrimes = new ArrayList<>();
  Map<Integer, BooleanFormula> indexed = new HashMap<>();

  for (int i = 0; i < lemmas.size(); i++) {
    BooleanFormula lemma = lemmas.get(i);
    BooleanFormula primed = prime(lemma);

    annotated.add(bfmgr.or(getSelectorVar(i), lemma));
    annotatedPrimes.add(bfmgr.or(getSelectorVar(i), primed));
    indexed.put(i, lemma);
  }

  // ... Continuted Later ...
}

private BooleanFormula getSelectorVar(int idx) {
  return bfmgr.makeVariable("SEL_" + idx);
}
```

Listing 3: Annotating formulas with JavaSMT

```java
try (ProverEnvironment prover =
    context.newProverEnvironment(ProverOptions.GENERATE_MODELS)) {
  prover.addConstraint(transition);
  prover.addConstraint(bfmgr.and(annotated));
  prover.addConstraint(bfmgr.not(bfmgr.and(annotatedPrimes)));

  while (!prover.isUnsat()) {
    try (Model m = prover.getModel()) {
      for (int i = 0; i < annotatedPrimes.size(); i++) {
        BooleanFormula annotatedPrime = annotatedPrimes.get(i);
        if (!m.evaluate(annotatedPrime)) {
          prover.addConstraint(getSelectorVar(i));
          indexed.remove(i);
        }
      }
    }
  }
}
return new ArrayList<>(indexed.values());
```

Listing 4: HOUDINI main loop with JavaSMT

6   Related Work

JSMTLIB [7] is a solver-agnostic library for Java which uses SMT-LIB for communication with the solvers, and thus has the associated restrictions outlined in Sect. 1, including costly serialization overhead and a limitation to the features offered by SMT-LIB. In contrast, our work presents a solver-independent library for Java which connects directly to the solvers API.

The newly published JDART [13] tool bundles a JCONSTRAINTS library that offers a functionality similar to JAVASMT. However, JAVASMT has more features, communicates with solvers using their API, and provides an efficient memory-management strategy (JCONSTRAINTS uses the official Z3 Java API, which relies on finalizers). Additionally, our library provides several solvers that can be installed automatically and one simple configuration option to switch between them. For JCONSTRAINTS, the user has to manually include and configure all the solver's bindings and binaries. We have learned that these steps are complicated and error-prone, as the library might be used as part of a bigger software system. Thus, our solvers and their bindings do not require to setup any special environment.

The problem of creating such a library has also been tackled for Python in PYSMT [15]. In contrast to our work, PYSMT keeps the formula structure itself, while delegating the queries to the solvers. While this allows for creating formulas without any solvers installed, and for easier transfer of formulas between different contexts, it incurs a large memory overhead.

7   Conclusion

We have presented JAVASMT, a new library for efficient and safe communication with SMT solvers. The advantages of using such a library over communicating using SMT-LIB include performance, access to new features, and the ability to control which formulas remain in scope and which should be discarded. Some disadvantages exist as well — using JAVASMT means restricting to the supported solvers, and relying on JAVASMT developers to update the solvers in time. Our experience with using SMT solvers is that for applications that pose a few large, monolithic queries and need only standard features, the communication using SMT-LIB is optimal, while for tools that post many cheap, incremental queries, using the API via JAVASMT is the better solution. New editions of SMT-LIB could make missing features like interpolation available (proposed draft already exists [11]), but giving the user control over memory management for formulas (Sect. 4), or allowing efficient communication without string serialization and parsing may be far outside of the scope of SMT-LIB initiative. So for users requiring such features, an intermediate-layer library is always beneficial.

Acknowledgements. The authors thank P. Wendler for valuable discussions on design decisions and principles behind JAVASMT, and all JAVASMT contributors for their programming efforts.

References

1. Cimatti, A., Griggio, A., Schaafsma, B.J., Sebastiani, R.: The MATHSAT5 SMT Solver. In: Piterman, N., Smolka, S.A. (eds.) Tools and Algorithms for the Construction and Analysis of Systems. LNCS, vol. 7795, pp. 93–107. Springer, Heidelberg (2013)
2. Bradley, A.R.: SAT-based model checking without unrolling. In: Jhala, R., Schmidt, D. (eds.) VMCAI 2011. LNCS, vol. 6538, pp. 70–87. Springer, Heidelberg (2011)
3. Barrett, C., Fontaine, P., Tinelli, C.: The SMT-LIB Standard: Version 2.5. Technical report. Department of Computer Science, University of Iowa (2015). www.SMT-LIB.org
4. Flanagan, C., Leino, K.R.M.: HOUDINI, an annotation assistant for ESC/Java. In: Oliveira, J.N., Zave, P. (eds.) FME 2001. LNCS, vol. 2021, pp. 500–517. Springer, Heidelberg (2001)
5. Beyer, D.: Reliable and reproducible competition results with BENCHEXEC and witnesses (Report on SV-COMP 2016). In: Chechik, M., Raskin, J.-F. (eds.) TACAS 2016. LNCS, vol. 9636, pp. 887–904. Springer, Heidelberg (2016)
6. Beyer, D., Keremoglu, M.E.: CPACHECKER: A tool for configurable software verification. In: Gopalakrishnan, G., Qadeer, S. (eds.) CAV 2011. LNCS, vol. 6806, pp. 184–190. Springer, Heidelberg (2011)
7. Cok, D.R.: The JSMTLIB User Guide (2013). http://smtlib.github.io/jSMTLIB/jSMTLIBUserGuide.pdf. Accessed 10 Feb 2016
8. Karpenkov, E.G., Monniaux, D., Wendler, P.: Program analysis with local policy iteration. In: Jobstmann, B., Leino, K.R.M. (eds.) VMCAI 2016. LNCS, vol. 9583, pp. 127–146. Springer, Heidelberg (2016)
9. Gamma, E., Helm, R., Johnson, R., Vlissides, J.: Design Patterns: Elements of Reusable Object-Oriented Software. Addison-Wesley, Boston (1995)
10. Bloch, J.: Effective Java (The Java Series), 2nd edn. Prentice Hall, Upper Saddle River (2008)
11. Christ, J., Hoenicke, J.: Interpolation in SMTLIB 2.0 (2012). https://ultimate.informatik.uni-freiburg.de/smtinterpol/proposal.pdf. Accessed 10 Feb 2016
12. Christ, J., Hoenicke, J., Nutz, A.: SMTINTERPOL: An interpolating SMT solver. In: Donaldson, A., Parker, D. (eds.) SPIN 2012. LNCS, vol. 7385, pp. 248–254. Springer, Heidelberg (2012)
13. Luckow, K., Dimjašević, M., Giannakopoulou, D., Howar, F., Isberner, M., Kahsai, T., Rakamarić, Z., Raman, V.: JDART: A dynamic symbolic analysis framework. In: Chechik, M., Raskin, J.-F. (eds.) TACAS 2016. LNCS, vol. 9636, pp. 442–459. Springer, Heidelberg (2016)
14. de Moura, L., Bjørner, N.: Z3: An efficient SMT solver. In: Ramakrishnan, C.R., Rehof, J. (eds.) TACAS 2008. LNCS, vol. 4963, pp. 337–340. Springer, Heidelberg (2008)
15. Gario, M., Micheli, A.: PYSMT: A solver-agnostic library for fast prototyping of SMT-based algorithms. In: SMT 2015 (2015)
16. Rümmer, P.: E-matching with free variables. In: Bjørner, N., Voronkov, A. (eds.) LPAR 2012. LNCS, vol. 7180, pp. 359–374. Springer, Heidelberg (2012)
17. Sebastiani, R., Trentin, P.: OPTIMATHSAT: A tool for optimization modulo theories. In: Kröening, D., Păsăreanu, C.S. (eds.) CAV 2015. LNCS, vol. 9206, pp. 447–454. Springer, Heidelberg (2015)

Relational Program Reasoning Using Compiler IR

Moritz Kiefer, Vladimir Klebanov, and Mattias Ulbrich[✉]

Karlsruhe Institute of Technology, Karlsruhe, Germany
moritz.kiefer@student.kit.edu, {klebanov,ulbrich}@kit.edu

Abstract. Relational program reasoning is concerned with formally comparing pairs of executions of programs. Prominent examples of relational reasoning are program equivalence checking (which considers executions from different programs) and detecting illicit information flow (which considers two executions of the same program).

The abstract logical foundations of relational reasoning are, in the meantime, sufficiently well understood. In this paper, we address some of the challenges that remain to make the reasoning *practicable*. Two major ones are dealing with the feature richness of programming languages such as C and with the weakly structured control flow that many real-world programs exhibit.

A popular approach to control this complexity is to define the analyses on the level of an intermediate program representation (IR) such as one generated by modern compilers. In this paper we describe the ideas and insights behind IR-based relational verification. We present a program equivalence checker for C programs operating on LLVM IR and demonstrate its effectiveness by automatically verifying equivalence of functions from different implementations of the standard C library.

1 Introduction

Relational program reasoning. Over the last years, there has been a growing interest in *relational* verification of programs, which reasons about the relation between the behavior of two programs or program executions – instead of comparing a single program or program execution to a more abstract specification. The main advantage of relational verification over standard functional verification is that there is no need to write and maintain complex specifications. Furthermore, one can exploit the fact that changes are often local and only affect a small portion of a program. The effort for relational verification often only depends on the difference between the programs respectively program executions and not on the overall size and complexity of the program(s).

Relational verification can be used for various purposes. An example is *regression verification* resp. *equivalence checking*, where the behavior of two different versions of a program is compared under identical input. Another example is checking for absence of *illicit information flow*, a security property, in which executions of the same program are compared for different inputs. For concreteness'

© Springer International Publishing AG 2016
S. Blazy and M. Chechik (Eds.): VSTTE 2016, LNCS 9971, pp. 149–165, 2016.
DOI: 10.1007/978-3-319-48869-1_12

sake, we focus in this paper on regression verification/equivalence checking of C programs, though the presented techniques readily apply to other instances of relational reasoning.

Regression Verification. Regression verification is a formal verification approach intended to complement regression testing. The goal is to establish a formal proof of equivalence of two program versions (e.g., consecutive revisions during program evolution, or a program and a re-implementation). In its basic form, we are trying to prove that the two versions produce the same output for all inputs. In more sophisticated scenarios, we want to verify that the two versions are equivalent only on some inputs (*conditional equivalence*) or differ in a formally specified way (*relational equivalence*). Regression verification is not intended to replace testing, but when it is successful, it offers guaranteed coverage without requiring additional expenses to develop and maintain a test suite.

Challenges in Making Regression Verification Practicable. The abstract logical foundations of relational reasoning are, in the meantime, sufficiently well understood. For instance, in [8], we presented a method for regression verification that reduces the equivalence of two related C programs to Horn constraints over uninterpreted predicates. The reduction is automatic, just as the solvers (e.g., Z3 [15,18] or ELDARICA [23]) used to solve the constraints. Our current work follows the same principles.

Yet, the calculus in [8] only defined rules for the basic, well-structured programming language constructs: assignment, if statement, while loop and function call. The RÊVE tool implemented the calculus together with a simple self-developed program parser.

While the tool could automatically prove equivalence of many intricate arithmetic-intensive programs, its limited programming language coverage hampered its practical application. The underlying calculus could not deal with `break`, `continue`, or `return` statements in a loop body, loop conditions with side effects, `for` or `do-while` loops, let alone arbitrary `goto` statements.

Contributions. The main contribution of this paper is a method for automated relational program reasoning that is significantly more practical than [8] or other state-of-the-art approaches. In particular, the method supports programs with arbitrary unstructured control flow without losing automation. The gained versatility is due to a completely redesigned reduction calculus together with the use of the LLVM compiler framework [17] and its intermediate program representation (IR).

Furthermore, the calculus we present in this paper is fine-tuned for the inference of *relational* predicates and deviates from straightforward encodings in crucial points: (a) Loops are not always reduced to tail recursion (see Sect. 4.6), (b) mutual function summaries are separated into two predicates for pre- and postcondition (see Sect. 4.5), and (c) control flow synchronization points can be placed by the user manually to enable more flexible synchronization schemes.

We developed a tool implementing the approach, which can be tested online at http://formal.iti.kit.edu/improve/reve/. We have evaluated the tool by automatically proving equivalence of a number of string-manipulating functions from different implementations of the C standard library.

Main Idea of Our Method. First, we employ the LLVM compiler framework to compile the C source code to LLVM IR. This step reduces all control flow in a program to branches (jumps) and function calls. Next, we divide the (potentially cyclic) control flow graph of the program into linear segments. For the points at which these segments are connected, we introduce relational abstractions represented by uninterpreted predicate symbols (instead of concrete formulas). The same applies for pairs of corresponding function calls. Finally, we generate constraints over these predicate symbols linking the linear segments with the corresponding state abstractions. The produced constraints are in Horn normal form.

The generation of constraints is automatic; the user does not have to supply coupling predicates, loop invariants, or function summaries. The constraints are passed to a constraint solver for Horn clauses (such as Z3 [15,18] or ELDARICA [23]). The solver tries to find an instantiation of the uninterpreted abstraction predicates that would make the constraints true. If the solver succeeds in finding a solution, the programs are equivalent. Alternatively, the solver may show that no solution exists (i.e., disprove equivalence) or time out.

Advantages of Using LLVM IR. There are several advantages to working on LLVM IR instead of on the source code level. The translation to LLVM IR takes care of preprocessing (resolving typedefs, expanding macros, etc.) and also eliminates many ambiguities in the C language such as the size of types (which is important when reasoning about pointers). Building an analysis for IR programs is much simpler as the IR language has fewer instruction types and only two control flow constructs, namely branches (jumps) and function calls. Furthermore, LLVM provides a constantly growing number of simplifying and canonicalizing transformations (*passes*) on the IR level. If the differences in the two programs are merely of a syntactical nature, these simplifications can often eliminate them completely. Also, it was easy to incorporate our own passes specifically geared towards our use case.

Challenges Still Remaining. Of course, using a compiler IR does not solve all challenges. Some of them, such as interpreting integers as unbounded or the inability to deal with general bit operations or floating-point arithmetic remain due to the limitations of the underlying solvers. Furthermore, we, as is common, assume that all considered programs are terminating. Verifying this property is delegated to the existing termination checking technology, such as [7,9].

Listing 1. memchr(), dietlibc

```
1  #include <stddef.h>
2  extern int __mark(int);
3
4  void* memchr(const void *s,
5                int c,
6                size_t n) {
7   const unsigned char *pc =
8     (unsigned char *) s;
9   for (;n--;pc++) {
10    __mark(42);
11    if (*pc == c)
12      return ((void *) pc);
13  }
14  return 0;
15 }
```

Listing 2. memchr(), OpenBSD libc

```
1  #include <stddef.h>
2  extern int __mark(int);
3
4  void * memchr(const void *s,
5                int c,
6                size_t n) {
7   if (n != 0) {
8     const unsigned char *p = s;
9     do {
10      __mark(42);
11      if (*p++ == (unsigned char)c)
12        return ((void *)(p - 1));
13    } while (--n != 0);
14  }
15  return (NULL);
16 }
```

2   Illustration

We tested our approach on examples from the C standard library (or libc). The interfaces and semantics of the library functions are defined in the language standard, while several implementations exist. GNU libc [10] and OpenBSD libc [21] are two mature implementations of the library. The diet libc (or dietlibc) [27] is an implementation that is optimized for small size of the resulting binaries.

Consider the two implementations of the memchr() function shown in Listings 1 and 2. The function scans the initial n bytes of the memory area pointed to by s for the first instance of c. Both c and the bytes of the memory area pointed to by s are interpreted as unsigned char. The function returns a pointer to the matching byte or NULL if the character does not occur in the given memory area.

In contrast to full functional verification, we are not asking whether each implementation conforms with this (yet to be formalized) specification. Instead, we are interested to find out whether the two implementations behave the same. Whether this is the case is not immediately obvious due to the terse programming style, subtle pointer manipulation, and the different control flow constructs used.

While the dietlibc implementation on the left is relatively straightforward, the OpenBSD one on the right is more involved. The for loop on the left is replaced by a do-while loop wrapped in an if conditional on the right. This transformation known as *loop inversion* reduces the overall number of jumps by two (both in the branch where the loop is executed). The reduction increases performance by eliminating CPU pipeline stalls associated with jumps. The price of the transformation is the duplicate condition check increasing the size of the code. On the other hand, loop inversion makes further optimizations possible, such as eliminating the if statement if the value of the guard is known at compile time.

With one exception, the code shown is the original source code and can indeed be fed like that into our implementation LLRêve, which without further user interaction establishes the equivalence of the two implementations. The exception is the inclusion of the __mark() calls in the loop bodies. The calls identify *synchronization points* in the execution of two programs where the states of the two are most similar. The numerical arguments only serve to identify matching pairs of points. The user has to provide enough synchronization points to break all cycles in the control flow, otherwise the tool will abort with an error message. In [8], we used a simple heuristic to put default synchronization points automatically into loop bodies in their order of appearance, though this is not yet implemented in LLRÊVE.

Suppose that we are running the two implementations to look for the same character c in the same 100 byte chunk of memory. If we examine the values of variables at points in time when control flow reaches the _mark(42) calls for the first time, we obtain: for dietlibc $n = 99$, $pc = s$, and for OpenBSD $n = 100$, $p = s$. The second time: for dietlibc $n = 98$, $pc = s + 1$, and for OpenBSD $n = 99$, $p = s + 1$. The values of c, s, and the whole heap remain the same. At this point, one could suspect that the following formula is an invariant relating the executions of the two implementations at the above-mentioned points:[1]

$$(n_2 = n_1 + 1) \wedge (p_2 = pc_1) \wedge (c_2 = c_1) \wedge \forall i.\ heap_1[i] = heap_2[i] \ . \qquad (*)$$

That our suspicion is correct can be established by a simple inductive argument. Once we have done that, we can immediately derive that both programs produce the same return value upon termination.

We call an invariant like $(*)$ for two loops a *coupling (loop) invariant*. A similar construct relating two function calls is called a *mutual (function) summary* [13,14]. Together, they fall into the class of *coupling predicates*, inductive assertions allowing us to deduce the desired relation upon program termination. In [8], we have shown that coupling predicates witnessing equivalence of programs with `while` loops can be often automatically inferred by methods such as counterexample-guided abstraction refinement or property-directed reachability. In this paper, we present a method for doing this for programs with unstructured control flow.

3   Related Work

Our own previous work on relational verification of C programs [8] has already been discussed in the introduction.

Many code analysis and formal verification tools operate on LLVM IR, though none of them, to our knowledge, perform relational reasoning. Examples of non-relational verification tools building on LLVM IR are LLBMC [19] and Sea-Horn [12]. The SeaHorn tool is related to our efforts in particular, since it processes safety properties of LLVM IR programs into Horn clauses over integers. An interesting recent development is the SMACK [22] framework for rapid prototyping of verifiers, a translator from the LLVM IR into the Boogie intermediate verification language (IVL) [2].

---

[1] To distinguish identifiers from the two programs, we add subscripts indicating the program to which they belong. We may also concurrently use the original identifiers without a subscript as long as the relation is clear from the context.

The term regression verification for equivalence checking of similar programs was coined by Godlin and Strichman [11]. In their approach, matching recursive calls are abstracted by the same uninterpreted function. The equivalence of functions (that no longer contain recursion) is then checked by the CBMC model checker. The technique is implemented in the RVT tool and supports a subset of ANSI C.

Verdoolaege et al. [25, 26] have developed an automatic approach to prove equivalence of static affine programs. The approach focuses on programs with array-manipulating for loops and can automatically deal with complex loop transformations such as loop interchange, reversal, skewing, tiling, and others. It is implemented in the ISA tool for the static affine subset of ANSI C.

Mutual function summaries have been prominently put forth by Hawblitzel et al. in [13] and later developed in [14]. The concept is implemented in the equivalence checker SYMDIFF [16], where the user supplies the mutual summary. Loops are encoded as recursion. The tool uses Boogie as the intermediate language, and the verification conditions are discharged by the BOOGIE tool. A frontend for C programs is available.

The BCVERIFIER tool for proving backwards compatibility of Java class libraries by Welsch and Poetzsch-Heffter [28] has a similar pragmatics as SYMDIFF. The tool prominently features a language for defining synchronization points.

Balliu et al. [1] present a relational calculus and reasoning toolchain targeting information flow properties of unstructured machine code. Coupling loop invariants are supplied by the user.

Barthe et al. [3] present a calculus for reasoning about relations between programs that is based on pure program transformation. The calculus offers rules to merge two programs into a single *product program*. The merging process is guided by the user and facilitates proving relational properties with the help of any existing safety verification tool. We are not aware of an implementation of the transformation.

Beringer [4] defines a technique for deriving soundness arguments for relational program calculi from arguments for non-relational ones. In particular, one of the presented relational calculi contains a loop rule similar to ours. The rule targets so-called *dissonant* loops, i.e., loops not proceeding in lockstep.

Ulbrich [24] introduces a framework and implementation for relational verification on an unstructured intermediate verification language (similar to Boogie), mainly targeted at conducting refinement proofs. Synchronization points are defined and used similar to this work. However, the approach is limited to fully synchronized programs and requires user-provided coupling predicates.

4   The Method

4.1   From Source Code to LLVM IR

LLVM's intermediate representation is an abstract, RISC-like assembler language for a register machine with an unbounded number of registers. A program in LLVM-IR consists of type definitions, global variable declarations, and the program itself, which is represented as a set of functions, each consisting of a graph of basic blocks. Each basic block in turn is a list of instructions with acyclic control flow and a single exit point.

The branch instructions between basic blocks induce a graph on the basic blocks, called the *control flow graph* (CFG), in which edges are annotated with the condition under which the transition between the two basic blocks is taken. Programs in LLVM IR are in *static single assignment* (SSA) form, i.e., each (scalar) variable is assigned exactly once in the static program. Assignments to scalar variables can thus be treated as logical equivalences.

To obtain LLVM IR programs from C source code, we first compile the two programs separately using the Clang compiler. Next, we apply a number of standard and custom-built transformation passes that:

- eliminate load and store instructions (generated by LLVM) for stack-allocated variables in favor of register operations. While we do support the general load and store instructions, they increase deduction complexity.
- propagate constants and eliminate unreachable code.
- eliminate conditional branching between blocks in favor of conditional assignments (similar to the ternary operator ? in C). This step reduces the number of distinct paths through the program. As we are considering a product of all paths, this step is important.
- inline function calls where desired by the user.

4.2   Synchronization Points and Breaking Control Flow Cycles

If the compiled program contained loops or iteration formulated using goto statements, the resulting CFG is cyclic. Cycles are a challenge for deductive verification because the number of required iterations is, in general, not known beforehand.

We break up cycles in the control flow by defining *synchronization points*, at which we will abstract from the program state by means of predicates. The paths between synchronization points are then cycle-free and can be handled easily. Synchronization points are defined by labeling basic blocks of the CFG with unique numbers $n \in \mathbb{N}$. Additionally, the entry and the exit of a function are considered special synchronization points labeled with B and E. If every cycle in the CFG contains at least one synchronization point, the CFG can be considered as the set of all *linear paths* leading from one synchronization point directly to another. A linear path is a sequence of basic blocks together with the transition conditions between them. Formally, it is a triple $\langle n, \pi, m \rangle$ in which n and m

denote the beginning and end synchronization point of the segment and $\pi(x, x')$ is the two-state transition predicate between the synchronization points in which x are the variables before and x' after the transition. Since basic blocks are in SSA form, the transition predicate defined by a path is the conjunction of all traversed assignments (as equalities) and transition conditions. The treatment of function invocation is explained in Sect. 4.5.

4.3   Coupling and Coupling Predicates

Let in the following the two compared functions be called P and Q, and let x_p (resp. x_q) denote the local variables of P (resp. Q). Primed variables refer to post-states.

We assume that P and Q are related to each other, in particular that the control and data flow through the functions is similar. This means that we expect that there exist practicable *coupling predicates* describing the relation between corresponding states of P and Q. The synchronization points mark where the states are expected to be coupled. If a function were compared against itself, for instance, the coupling between two executions would be equality ranging over all variables and all heap locations. For the analysis of two different programs, more involved coupling predicates are, of course, necessary.

Formally, we introduce a coupling predicate $C_n(x_p, x_q)$ for every synchronization point index n. Note that these predicates have the variables of both programs as free variables. Two functions are considered coupled, if they yield *coupled traces* when fed with the same input values; coupled in the sense that the executions pass the same sequence of synchronization points in the CFG and that at each synchronization point, the corresponding coupling predicate is satisfied. See Fig. 1 for an illustration.

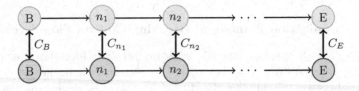

Fig. 1. Illustration of coupled control flow of two fully synchronized programs

The coupling predicates C_B and C_E for the function entry and exit are special in that they form the *relational specification* for the equivalence between P and Q. For pure equivalence, C_B encodes equality of the input values and state, and C_E of the result value and output state. Variations like conditional or relational equivalence can be realized by choosing different formulas for C_B and C_E.

4.4   Coupling Predicates for Cyclic Control Flow

In the following, we outline the set of constraints that we generate for programs with loops. If this set possesses a model, i.e., if there are formulas making the constraint true when substituted for the coupling predicate placeholders C_i, then the programs fulfill their relational specification.

The first constraint encodes that every path leading from a synchronization point to the next satisfies the coupling predicate at the target point. Let $\langle n, \pi, m \rangle$ be a linear path in the CFG of P and $\langle n, \rho, m \rangle$ one for the same synchronization points for Q. For each such pair of paths, we emit the constraint:

$$C_n(x_p, x_q) \wedge \pi(x_p, x'_p) \wedge \rho(x_q, x'_q) \to C_m(x'_p, x'_q) . \tag{1}$$

The above constraint only covers the case of *strictly synchronized* loops which are iterated equally often. Yet, often the number of loop iterations differs between revisions, e.g., if one loop iteration has been peeled in one of the programs. To accommodate that, we allow one program, say P, to loop at a synchronization point n more often than the other program.[2] Thus, P proceeds iterating the loop, while Q stutters in its present state. For each looping path $\langle n, \pi, n \rangle$ in P, we emit the constraint:

$$C_n(x_p, x_q) \wedge \pi(x_p, x'_p) \wedge \left(\bigwedge_{\substack{\langle n, \rho, n \rangle \\ \text{in } Q}} \forall x'_q. \, \neg\rho(x_q, x'_q) \right) \to C_n(x'_p, x_q) . \tag{2}$$

The second conjunct in the premise of the implication encodes that P iterates from n to n, while the third captures that no linear path leads from n to n in Q from initial value x_q. The coupling predicate in the conclusion employs the initial values x_q, since we assume that the state of Q stutters.

Emitting (2) to accommodate loops that are not strictly synchronized adds to the complexity of the overall constraint and may in practice prevent the solver from finding a solution. We thus provide the user with the option to disable emitting (2), if they are confident that strict synchronization is sufficient.

Finally, we have to encode that the control flow of P and Q remains synchronized in the sense that it must not be possible that P and Q reach different synchronization points m and k when started from a coupled state at n.[3] For each path $\langle n, \pi, m \rangle$ in P and $\langle n, \rho, k \rangle$ in Q with $m \neq k$, $n \neq m$, $n \neq k$, we emit the constraint:

$$C_n(x_p, x_q) \wedge \pi(x_p, x'_p) \wedge \rho(x_q, x'_q) \to \text{false} . \tag{3}$$

4.5   Coupling Predicates for Function Calls

Besides at synchronization points that abstract loops or iteration in general, coupling predicates are also employed to describe the effects of corresponding

---

[2] The situation is symmetric with the case for Q omitted here.

[3] This restriction is of minor practical importance but releases us from the need to create coupling predicates for arbitrary combinations of synchronization points.

function invocations in the two programs. To this end, matching pairs of function calls in the two CFGs are abstracted using mutual function summaries [13]. A heuristic used to match calls will be described later.

Mutual Function Summaries. Let f_p be a function called from the function P, x_p denote the formal parameters of f_p, and r_p stand for the (optional) result returned when calling f_p. Assume that there is an equally named function f_q defined in the program of Q. A mutual summary for f_p and f_q is a predicate $Sum_f(x_p, x_q, r_p, r_q)$ that relationally couples the result values to the function arguments. If the function accesses the heap, the heap appears as an additional argument and return value of the function.

In our experiments, we found that it is beneficiary to additionally model an explicit relational precondition $Pre_f(x_p, x_q)$ of f. Although it does not increase expressiveness, the solvers found more solutions with precondition predicates present. We conjecture that the positive effect is related to the fact that mutual summary solutions are usually of the shape $\phi(x_p, x_q) \rightarrow \psi(r_p, r_q)$, and that making the precondition explicit allows the solver to infer ϕ and ψ separately without the need to infer the implication.

For every pair of paths $\langle n, \pi, m \rangle \in P$ and $\langle n, \rho, m \rangle \in Q$ that contain a single call to f, we emit the following additional constraint:

$$C_n(x_p, x_q) \wedge \pi(x_p, x'_p) \wedge \rho(x_q, x'_q) \rightarrow Pre_f(x^*_p, x^*_q) \ . \tag{4}$$

in which x^*_p and x^*_q denote the SSA variables used as the argument for the function calls to f. The constraint demands that the relational precondition Pre_f must be met when the callsites of f are reached in P and Q.

For every such pair of paths, we can now make use of the mutual summary by assuming $Sum_f(x^*_p, x^*_q, r_p, r_q)$. This means that for constraints emitted by (1)–(3), the mutual summary of the callsite can be added to the premiss. The augmented version of constraint (1) reads, for instance,

$$C_n(x_p, x_q) \wedge \pi(x_p, x'_p) \wedge \rho(x_q, x'_q) \wedge Sum_f(x^*_p, x^*_q, r_p, r_q) \rightarrow C_m(x'_p, x'_q) \ , \tag{5}$$

with r_p and r_q the SSA variables that receive the result values of the calls.

The mutual summary also needs to be justified. For that purpose, constraints are recursively generated for f, with the entry coupling predicate $C_B = Pre_f$ and exit predicate $C_E = Sum_f$.

The generalization to more than one function invocation is canonical.

Example. To make the above clearer, let us look at the encoding of the program in Listing 3 when verified against itself. Let $C^f_B(n_1, n_2)$ and $C^f_E(r_1, r_2)$ be the given coupling predicates that have to hold at the entry and exit of f. When encoding the function f, we are allowed to use Sum_g at the callsite but have to show that Pre_g holds. Thus we get the following constraints:

```
1   int f(int n) {
2       return g(n-1);
3   }
4   int g (int n) {
5       return n+1;
6   }
```

Listing 3. f() calling g()

$$C^f_B(n_1, n_2) \wedge n^*_1 = n_1 - 1 \wedge n^*_2 = n_2 - 1 \rightarrow Pre_g(n^*_1, n^*_2)$$
$$C^f_B(n_1, n_2) \wedge n^*_1 = n_1 - 1 \wedge n^*_2 = n_2 - 1 \wedge Sum(n^*_1, n^*_2, r_1, r_2) \rightarrow C^f_E(r_1, r_2) \ .$$

To make sure that Pre_g and Sum_g are a faithful abstraction for g, we have a new constraint for g, which boils down to

$$Pre_g(n_1, n_2) \rightarrow Sum_g(n_1, n_2, n_1 + 1, n_2 + 1) \ .$$

At this point, the set of constraints is complete, and we can state the main result:

Theorem 1 (Soundness). *Let S be the set of constraints emitted by (1)–(5). If the universal closure of S is satisfiable, then P and Q terminate in states with x'_p and x'_q satisfying $C_E(x'_p, x'_q)$ when they are executed in states with x_p and x_q satisfying $C_B(x_p, x_q)$ and both terminate.*

Matching Function Calls. For treatment using mutual summaries, the function calls need to be combined into pairs of calls from both programs. Our goal is to match as many function calls between the two programs as possible. To this end, we look at any pair of possible paths from the two programs that start and end at the same synchronization points. For each path, we consider the sequence of invoked functions. To determine the optimal matching of function calls (i.e., covering as many calls as possible), an algorithm [20] for computing the longest common (not necessarily continuous) subsequence among the sequences is applied.

As an example, consider the functions in Fig. 2. There are no cycles in the control flow, so the only two synchronization points are the function entry and exit. In Program 1, there are two paths corresponding to $x > 0$ and $x \leq 0$ respectively. In Program 2, there is only a single path. That gives us two possible path pairs that we need to consider. The resulting longest matchings for the pairs are also shown in the figure. Matched calls are abstracted using mutual summaries, while unmatched calls have to be abstracted using conventional functional summaries.

```
int f(int x) {        int f(int x) {      g(int) ———— g(int)                 g(int)
  if (x > 0) {          x = g(x);         g(int) ———— g(int)                 g(int)
    x = g(x);           x = g(x);         h(int)                             g(int)
    x = g(x);           x = g(x);         h(int)              h(int) ———— h(int)
  }                     x = h(x);         g(int) ———— g(int)  h(int) ———— h(int)
  x = h(x);             x = h(x);         h(int)             g(int)
  x = h(x);             return x;         h(int)
  x = g(x);           }
  return x;
}

    Program 1            Program 2       Matching for x > 0   Matching for x ≤ 0
```

Fig. 2. Illustration of function call matching

An additional feature is that the user can request to inline a specific call or all calls to a function with an `inline` pragma. The feature is especially important

```
1  int f(int n) {
2      int i = 0;
3      while (i < n) {
4          i++;
5      }
6      int r = i;
7      return r;
8  }
```

$$\forall n.rel_{in}(n) \rightarrow inv(0, n)$$
$$\forall i, n.(i < n \land inv(i, n)) \rightarrow inv(i+1, n)$$
$$\forall i, n.(\neg(i < n) \land inv(i, n)) \rightarrow rel_{out}(i)$$

Listing 4. Function f

Fig. 3. Iterative encoding of f

if the callee function contains a loop that should be synchronized with a loop in the caller function of the other program. The pragma can also be used to inline some steps of a recursive call.

If a Function's Implementation is Not Available. A special case arises when there is a call from both programs to a function for which we do not have access to the sources. If such calls can be matched, we abstract the two calls using the canonical mutual summary $Sum_f : x_p = x_q \rightarrow r_p = r_q$ stating that equal inputs induce equal results. If a call cannot be matched, however, we have to use an uninterpreted functional summary, losing all information about the return value and the resulting heap. In most cases, this means that nothing can be proved.[4]

$$\forall n.rel_{in}(n) \rightarrow inv_{pre}(0, n) \land$$
$$(\forall r.inv(0, n, r) \rightarrow inv_f(n, r))$$
$$\forall i, n, r.(i < n \land inv_{pre}(i, n) \land inv(i+1, n, r)) \rightarrow inv(i, n, r)$$
$$\forall i, n.(\neg(i < n) \land inv_{pre}(i, n) \rightarrow inv(i, n, i)$$
$$\forall n, r.(rel_{in}(n) \land inv_f(n, r)) \rightarrow rel_{out}(r)$$

Fig. 4. Recursive encoding of f

4.6   Alternative Loop Treatment as Tail Recursion

When developing our method, we explored two different approaches to deal with iterative unstructured control flow.

The first one models a program as a collection of mutually recursive functions such that the function themselves do not have cyclic control flow. Loops must be translated to tail recursion. This aligns with the approach presented in [13]. It is attractive since it is conceptually simple allowing a unified handling of cyclic branching and function calls. However, our experiments have shown that for our purposes the encoding did not work as well as the one presented in Sect. 4.4 which

---

[4] Alternatively, it would also be possible to trade soundness for completeness and, e.g., assume that such a call does not change the heap.

handles loops using coupling predicates directly instead of by translation into tail recursion. A possible explanation for this observation could be that the number of arguments to the coupling predicates is smaller if (coupling) invariants are used. For these predicates, it suffices to use those variables as arguments which may be changed by the following code. The mutual summaries for tail recursion require more variables and the return values as arguments.

To illustrate the two styles of encoding, we explain how the program in Listing 4 is encoded. For simplicity of presentation, we encode a safety property of a *single* program. The point where the invariant *inv* has to hold is the loop header on Line 3. rel_{in} is a predicate that has to hold at the beginning of f and rel_{out} is the predicate that has to hold when f returns. In the recursive encoding (Fig. 4), *inv* has three arguments, the local variables i and n and the return value r. In the iterative case (Fig. 3), the return value is not an argument, so *inv* only has two arguments. The entry predicate inv_{pre} over the local variables i and n has to hold at every "call" to *inv*. The reasoning for having such a separate predicate has already been explained in Sect. 4.5.

In the end, a combination of the two encodings proved the most promising: We apply the iterative encoding to the function whose exit and entry predicates have been given as relational specification explained in Sect. 4.3. All other functions are modeled using the recursive encoding. Mutual summaries depend, by design, on the input parameters as well as the output parameters whereas the relational postcondition C_E usually only depends on the output parameters. Using an iterative encoding for the other functions would require passing the input parameters through every predicate to be able to refer to them when establishing the mutual summary at the exit point. The advantage of an iterative encoding of having fewer parameters in predicates is thereby less significant, and we employ the recursive encoding. A special case arises when the toplevel function itself recurses. In this case, we encode it twice: first using the iterative encoding, which then relies on the recursive encoding for the recursive calls.

4.7   Modeling the Heap

The heap is modeled directly as an SMT array and the LLVM load and store instructions are translated into the select and store functions in the SMT theory of arrays. We assume that all load and store operations are properly aligned; we do not support bit operations or, e.g., accessing the second byte of a 32 bit integer. Struct accesses are resolved into loads and stores at corresponding offsets. The logical handling of constraints with arrays requires quantifier reasoning and introduces additional complexity. We handle such constraints following the lines of [6].

5   Experiments

Our implementation of the approach consists of ca. 5.5 KLOC of C++, building on LLVM version 3.8.0.

In our experiments, we have proven equivalence across a sample of functions from three different libc implementations: dietlibc [27], glibc [10], and the OpenBSD libc [21]. Apart from the not yet automated placing of the synchronization marks, the proofs happen without user interaction. The runtimes of the proofs are summarized in Table 1. One of the more complex examples, the function memmove(), is shown in Fig. 5. It demonstrates the use of nested ifs, multiple loops with different loop structures (while/do-while) and goto statements.

Revisiting the memchr() example discussed in Sect. 2, the early implementation of memchr() in dietlibc is known to have contained a bug (Listing 5). In case of a found character, the return value is one greater than expected.

Unsurprisingly, this implementation cannot be proven equivalent to any of the other two, and LLRÊVE produces a counterexample. While counterexamples in the presence of heap operations in the program can be spurious (in the absence of heap operations, counterexamples are always genuine), in this case, the counterexample does demonstrate the problem.

Table 1. Performance with different solvers for the libc benchmarks

| | | Run time w/solver, seconds | |
Function	Source	ELDARICA	Z3/DUALITY
memccpy	d/o	0.733	0.499
memchr	d/o	0.623	0.328
memmem	d/o	1.545	3.634
memmove	d/o	4.195	4.219
memrchr	g/o	0.487	1.082
memset	d/o	0.263	1.211
sbrk	d/g	0.439	0.630
stpcpy	d/o	0.203	0.241
strchr	d/g	48.145	13.705
strcmp	g/o	0.545	0.985
strcspn	d/o	17.825	t/o
strncmp	g/o	1.046	4.556
strncmp	d/g	2.599	7.971
strncmp	d/o	0.602	1.742
strpbrk	d/o	3.419	3.237
strpbrk	d/g	1.029	2.083
strpbrk	g/o	1.734	3.453
swab	d/o	4.032	0.709

d = dietlibc, g = glibc, o = OpenBSD libc.
t/o = timeout after 300 s.
2 GHz i7-4750HQ CPU, 16 GB RAM

```
1   void* memchr(const void *s,
2                int c,
3                size_t n) {
4     const char* t=s;
5     int i;
6     for (i=n; i; --i)
7       if (*t++==c)
8         return (char*)t;
9     return 0;
10  }
```

Listing 5. Bug in memchr()

An interesting observation we made was that existentially quantified preconditions might potentially be necessary, such as requiring the existence of a null byte terminating a string. While techniques for solving existentially quantified Horn clauses exist [5], most solver implementations currently only support

```
1  void *memmove(void *dst,              1  void *memmove(void *dst0,
2               const void *src,          2               const void *src0,
3               size_t count) {           3               size_t length) {
4    char *a = dst;                       4    char *dst = dst0;
5    const char *b = src;                 5    const char *src = src0;
6                                         6    size_t t;
7                                         7    if (length == 0 || dst == src)
8                                         8      goto done;
9    if (src != dst) {                    9    if ((unsigned long)dst <
10                                        10        (unsigned long)src) {
11                                        11      t = length;
12      if (src > dst) {                  12      if (t) {
13        while (count--) {                13        do {
14          __mark(0);                     14          __mark(0);
15          *a++ = *b++;                   15          *dst++ = *src++;
16        }                                16        } while (--t);
17      } else {                          17      }
18        a += count - 1;                 18    } else {
19        b += count - 1;                 19      src += length;
20        while (count--) {                20      dst += length;
21          __mark(1);                     21      t = length;
22          *a-- = *b--;                   22      if (t) {
23        }                                23        do {
24      }                                  24          __mark(1);
25    }                                    25          *--dst = *--src;
26                                        26        } while (--t);
27                                        27      }
28    return dst;                         28    }
29  }                                     29  done:
                                          30    return (dst0);
                                          31  }
```

| (a) dietlibc | (b) OpenBSD libc |

Fig. 5. memmove()

universally quantified clauses. The libc implementations, however, were sufficiently similar so that such preconditions were not necessary.

6   Conclusion

We have shown how the automated relational reasoning approach presented in [8] can be taken in its applicability from a basic fragment to the full C language standard w.r.t. the control flow. In this work, LLVM played a crucial rule in reducing the complexity of a real-world language. We have successfully evaluated our approach on code actually used in production and were able to prove automatically that many string-manipulation functions from different implementations of libc are equivalent.

Acknowledgments. This work was partially supported by the German National Science Foundation (DFG) under the IMPROVE APS project within the priority program SPP 1593 "Design For Future – Managed Software Evolution".

References

1. Balliu, M., Dam, M., Guanciale, R.: Automating information flow analysis of low level code. In: Proceedings of the ACM SIGSAC Conference on Computer and Communications Security, CCS 2014, pp. 1080–1091. ACM (2014)
2. Barnett, M., Chang, B.-Y.E., DeLine, R., Jacobs, B., Leino, K.R.M.: Boogie: a modular reusable verifier for object-oriented programs. In: Boer, F.S., Bonsangue, M.M., Graf, S., Roever, W.-P. (eds.) FMCO 2005. LNCS, vol. 4111, pp. 364–387. Springer, Heidelberg (2006). doi:10.1007/11804192_17
3. Barthe, G., Crespo, J.M., Kunz, C.: Relational verification using product programs. In: Butler, M., Schulte, W. (eds.) FM 2011. LNCS, vol. 6664, pp. 200–214. Springer, Heidelberg (2011)
4. Beringer, L.: Relational decomposition. In: Eekelen, M., Geuvers, H., Schmaltz, J., Wiedijk, F. (eds.) ITP 2011. LNCS, vol. 6898, pp. 39–54. Springer, Heidelberg (2011)
5. Beyene, T.A., Popeea, C., Rybalchenko, A.: Solving existentially quantified horn clauses. In: Sharygina, N., Veith, H. (eds.) CAV 2013. LNCS, vol. 8044, pp. 869–882. Springer, Heidelberg (2013)
6. Bjørner, N., McMillan, K., Rybalchenko, A.: On solving universally quantified horn clauses. In: Logozzo, F., Fähndrich, M. (eds.) SAS 2013. LNCS, vol. 7935, pp. 105–125. Springer, Heidelberg (2013)
7. Falke, S., Kapur, D., Sinz, C.: Termination analysis of imperative programs using bitvector arithmetic. In: Joshi, R., Müller, P., Podelski, A. (eds.) VSTTE 2012. LNCS, vol. 7152, pp. 261–277. Springer, Heidelberg (2012). doi:10.1007/978-3-642-27705-4_21
8. Felsing, D., Grebing, S., Klebanov, V., Rümmer, P., Ulbrich, M.: Automating regression verification. In: Proceedings of the 29th ACM/IEEE International Conference on Automated Software Engineering, ASE 2014, pp. 349–360. ACM (2014)
9. Giesl, J., Thiemann, R., Schneider-Kamp, P., Falke, S.: Automated termination proofs with AProVE. In: Oostrom, V. (ed.) RTA 2004. LNCS, vol. 3091, pp. 210–220. Springer, Heidelberg (2004)
10. GNU C library (2016). https://www.gnu.org/software/libc/
11. Godlin, B., Strichman, O.: Regression verification. In: Proceedings of the 46th Annual Design Automation Conference, DAC 2009, pp. 466–471. ACM (2009)
12. Gurfinkel, A., Kahsai, T., Komuravelli, A., Navas, J.A.: The seahorn verification framework. In: Kroening, D., Păsăreanu, C.S. (eds.) CAV 2015. LNCS, vol. 9206, pp. 343–361. Springer, Heidelberg (2015)
13. Hawblitzel, C., Kawaguchi, M., Lahiri, S.K., Rebêlo, H.: Mutual summaries: unifying program comparison techniques. In: Proceedings, First International Workshop on Intermediate Verification Languages (BOOGIE) (2011). http://research.microsoft.com/en-us/um/people/moskal/boogie2011/boogie2011_pg40.pdf
14. Hawblitzel, C., Kawaguchi, M., Lahiri, S.K., Rebêlo, H.: Towards modularly comparing programs using automated theorem provers. In: Bonacina, M.P. (ed.) CADE 2013. LNCS (LNAI), vol. 7898, pp. 282–299. Springer, Heidelberg (2013)
15. Hoder, K., Bjørner, N.: Generalized property directed reachability. In: Cimatti, A., Sebastiani, R. (eds.) SAT 2012. LNCS, vol. 7317, pp. 157–171. Springer, Heidelberg (2012)
16. Lahiri, S.K., Hawblitzel, C., Kawaguchi, M., Rebêlo, H.: SYMDIFF: a language-agnostic semantic diff tool for imperative programs. In: Madhusudan, P., Seshia, S.A. (eds.) CAV 2012. LNCS, vol. 7358, pp. 712–717. Springer, Heidelberg (2012). doi:10.1007/978-3-642-31424-7_54

17. Lattner, C., Adve, V.: LLVM: a compilation framework for lifelong program analysis & transformation. In: Proceedings of the International Symposium on Code Generation and Optimization: Feedback-directed and Runtime Optimization, CGO 2004. IEEE Computer Society (2004)

18. McMillan, K., Rybalchenko, A.: Computing relational fixed points using interpolation. Technical Report MSR-TR-6, Microsoft Research (2013)

19. Merz, F., Falke, S., Sinz, C.: LLBMC: bounded model checking of C and C++ programs using a compiler IR. In: Joshi, R., Müller, P., Podelski, A. (eds.) VSTTE 2012. LNCS, vol. 7152, pp. 146–161. Springer, Heidelberg (2012)

20. Myers, E.W.: An O(ND) difference algorithm and its variations. Algorithmica 1(2), 251–266 (1986)

21. OpenBSD libc (2016). http://cvsweb.openbsd.org/cgi-bin/cvsweb/src/lib/libc/

22. Rakamarić, Z., Emmi, M.: SMACK: decoupling source language details from verifier implementations. In: Biere, A., Bloem, R. (eds.) CAV 2014. LNCS, vol. 8559, pp. 106–113. Springer, Heidelberg (2014). doi:10.1007/978-3-319-08867-9_7

23. Rümmer, P., Hojjat, H., Kuncak, V.: Disjunctive interpolants for horn-clause verification. In: Sharygina, N., Veith, H. (eds.) CAV 2013. LNCS, vol. 8044, pp. 347–363. Springer, Heidelberg (2013)

24. Ulbrich, M.: Dynamic logic for an intermediate language: verification, interaction and refinement. Ph.D. thesis, Karlsruhe Institute of Technology, June 2013. http://nbn-resolving.org/urn:nbn:de:swb:90-411691

25. Verdoolaege, S., Janssens, G., Bruynooghe, M.: Equivalence checking of static affine programs using widening to handle recurrences. ACM Trans. Program. Lang. Syst. 34(3), 11:1–11:35 (2012)

26. Verdoolaege, S., Palkovic, M., Bruynooghe, M., Janssens, G., Catthoor, F.: Experience with widening based equivalence checking in realistic multimedia systems. J. Electron. Test. 26(2), 279–292 (2010)

27. Felix von Leitner. diet libc (2016). https://www.fefe.de/dietlibc/

28. Welsch, Y., Poetzsch-Heffter, A.: Verifying backwards compatibility of object-oriented libraries using Boogie. In: Proceedings of the 14th Workshop on Formal Techniques for Java-like Programs, FTfJP 2012, pp. 35–41. ACM (2012)

Resolution in Solving Graph Problems

Kailiang Ji[✉]

LRI, Université Paris Sud, Orsay, France
kailiang.ji@lri.fr

Abstract. Resolution is a proof-search method on proving satisfiability problems. Various refinements have been proposed to improve the efficiency of this method. However, when we try to prove some graph properties, none of the refinements have an efficiency comparable with traditional graph traversal algorithms. In this paper we propose a way of solving some graph traversal problems with resolution. And we design some simplification rules to make the proof-search algorithm work more efficiently on such problems.

1 Introduction

Since the introduction of Resolution [11], many refinements have been proposed to increase the efficiency of this method, by avoiding redundancies. A first refinement, *hyper-resolution*, has been introduced by Robinson himself the same year as Resolution [10]. More recently *ordered resolution* [9,12], *(polarized) resolution modulo* (PRM) [5,6], and finally *ordered polarized resolution modulo* (OPRM) [1] introduced more restrictions. However, as we shall see, these kind of refinements are still redundant.

In order to address the question of the redundancy of proof search methods, we encode graph problems, e.g. accessibility or cycle detection, as Resolution problem, and we compare two ways to solve these problems: by using a proof-search method and by a direct graph traversal algorithm. If the proof-search method simulates graph traversal step by step, and in particular never visits twice the same part of the graph, we can say that it avoids redundancies. Otherwise, this helps us analyze and eliminate the redundancies of the method, by analyzing why the method visits twice the same part of the graph.

The two graph problems can be expressed by predicate formulae with class variables (monadic second-order logic) [4,7]. For instance, the cycle detection problem can be expressed as $\exists Y (s_1 \in Y \wedge \forall x(x \in Y \Rightarrow \exists x'(\mathsf{edge}(x, x') \wedge x' \in Y)))$. The satisfiability of this formula can be proved by reducing it to *effectively propositional* case [8], where the sub-formula $\forall x A$ is replaced by $A(s_1/x) \wedge \cdots \wedge A(s_n/x)$, and $\exists x A$ by $A(s_1/x) \vee \cdots \vee A(s_n/x)$, in which $s_1, ..., s_n$ are the constants for all the vertices of a graph. By representing the theory of the graph as a set of rewrite rules [7], these problems can be proved by some off-the-shelf automated

---

K. Ji—This work is supported by the ANR-NSFC project LOCALI(NSFC 61161130530 and ANR 11 IS02 002 01).

S. Blazy and M. Chechik (Eds.): VSTTE 2016, LNCS 9971, pp. 166–180, 2016.
DOI: 10.1007/978-3-319-48869-1_13

theorem provers, such as iProver Modulo [2]. As these problems can be expressed with temporal formulae [3], they can also be solved by model checking tools. In this paper, a propositional encoding of these two problems is given. To reduce the search space and avoid redundant resolution steps, we add a selection function and a new subsumption rule. This method works for encoding of several graph problems. Its generality remains to be investigated.

The paper is organized as follows. Section 2 describes the theorem proving system PRM. In Sect. 3, some basic definitions for the expressing of graph problems are presented. Sections 4 and 5 presents the encoding of cycle detection and accessibility respectively. In Sect. 6, some simplification rules are defined. Finally, an implementation result is presented.

2   Polarized Resolution Modulo

In Polarized Resolution Modulo (see Fig. 1), clauses are divided into two sets: one-way clauses (or theory clauses) and ordinary clauses. Each one-way clause has a selected literal and resolution is only permitted between two ordinary clauses, or a one-way clause and an ordinary clause, provided the resolved literal is the selected one (the one underlined later) in the one-way clause. In the rules of Fig. 1, P and Q are literals, C and D denote a set of literals. σ is a substitution function, which is equal to the maximal general unifier (mgu) of P and Q. $\mathcal{R}$ is a set of one-way clauses that are under consideration.

$$\textbf{Resolution } \frac{P \vee C \qquad Q^\perp \vee D}{\sigma(C \vee D)} \qquad \textbf{Factoring } \frac{P \vee Q \vee C}{\sigma(P, C)}$$

$$\textbf{Ext.Narr. } \frac{P \vee C}{\sigma(D \vee C)} \text{ if } \underline{Q^\perp} \vee D \text{ is a one-way clause of } \mathcal{R}$$

$$\textbf{Ext.Narr. } \frac{P^\perp \vee C}{\sigma(D \vee C)} \text{ if } \underline{Q} \vee D \text{ is a one-way clause of } \mathcal{R}$$

Fig. 1. Polarized resolution modulo

Proving the completeness of the rules in Fig. 1 requires to prove a cut elimination lemma [5,6] for Polarized Deduction Modulo, the deduction system with a set of rewrite rules, containing for each one-way clause $\underline{P^\perp} \vee C$ the rule $P \rightarrow^- C$ and for each one-way clause $\underline{P} \vee C$ the rule $P \rightarrow^+ C^\perp$.

Like in OPRM, in this paper we define a selection function to select literals in an ordinary clause which have the priority to be resolved and add the selection function to PRM.

Note that when applying a **Resolution** rule between an ordinary clause and a one-way clause, we are in fact using an **Extended Narrowing** rule on this ordinary clause. We write $\Gamma \mapsto_{\mathcal{R}} C$ if C can be derived from the set of clauses Γ by applying finitely many inference rules of PRM.

3   Basic Definitions

In this paper, we consider a propositional language which contains two atomic propositions B_i and W_i for each natural number. We denote a graph as $G = \langle V, E \rangle$, where V is a set of vertices enumerated by natural numbers, E is the set of directed edges in the graph. The sequence of vertices $l = s_0, ..., s_k$ is a *walk* if and only if $\forall 0 \le i < k$, $(s_i, s_{i+1}) \in E$. The walk l is *closed* if and only if $\exists 0 \le j \le k$ such that $s_k = s_j$. The walk l is *blocked* if and only if s_k has no successors. The method we proposed is inspired by graph traversal algorithms.

Definition 1 (Black literal, white literal). *Let G be a graph and $\{s_1, ..., s_n\}$ be the set of all the vertices in G. For any $1 \le i \le n$, the literal B_i is called a* black literal *and the literal W_i is called a* white literal.

Intuitively, the black literals denote the vertices that have already been visited, while the white literals denote the non-visited ones.

Definition 2 (Original clause, traversal clause, success clause). *Let G be a graph and $\{s_1, ..., s_n\}$ the set of vertices in G. For each graph traversal problem starting from s_i ($1 \le i \le n$), the clause of the form $B_i \lor W_1 \lor \cdots \lor W_n$ is called an* original clause *($\mathsf{OC}(s_i, G)$). A clause with only white and black literals is called a* traversal clause. *Let C be a traversal clause, if there is no i, such that both B_i and W_i are in C, then C is called a* success clause.

Among the three kinds of clauses, the original clause is related to the starting point of the graph traversal algorithm, the traversal clause is the current state of the traveling, and the success clause denotes that a solution is derived. Trivially, the original clauses and success clauses are also traversal clauses.

4   Closed-Walk Detection

In this section, we present a strategy of checking whether there exists a closed walk starting from a given vertex. For a graph, each edge is represented as a rewrite rule, and the initial situation is denoted by the original clause.

E-coloring rule. Let G be a graph and $V = \{s_1, ..., s_n\}$ be the set of vertices in G. For each pair of vertices $\langle s_i, s_j \rangle$ in V, if there exists an edge from s_i to s_j, then we formalize this edge as an *E-coloring rewrite rule*

$$W_i \hookrightarrow B_j.$$

The corresponding one-way clause of this rewrite rule is $W_i^{\perp} \lor B_j$ (called *E-coloring clause*). The set of all the E-coloring clauses for G is denoted as $\mathsf{EC}(G)$.

Resolution for closed-walk detection. Let G be a graph and s be a vertex of G, then the the problem of checking *whether, starting from s, there exists a closed walk* can be encoded as the set of clauses $\{OC(s,G)\} \cup EC(G)$. By applying resolution rules among these clauses, a success clause can be derived if and only if there exists a closed walk starting from s.

Example 1. Consider the following graph

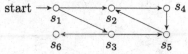

  We prove that there exists a closed walk starting from s_1. For this problem, the original clause is $B_1 \vee W_1 \vee W_2 \vee W_3 \vee W_4 \vee W_5 \vee W_6$ and the set of E-coloring clauses for this graph are

$$W_1^\perp \vee B_2, \quad W_1^\perp \vee B_3, \quad W_2^\perp \vee B_4, \quad W_3^\perp \vee B_5, \quad W_3^\perp \vee B_6, \quad W_4^\perp \vee B_5, \quad W_5^\perp \vee B_2.$$

The resolution steps are presented in the following tree from top to bottom

$$\frac{B_1 \vee W_1 \vee W_2 \vee W_3 \vee W_4 \vee W_5 \vee W_6 \quad W_1^\perp \vee B_2}{\dfrac{B_1 \vee B_2 \vee W_2 \vee W_3 \vee W_4 \vee W_5 \vee W_6 \quad W_2^\perp \vee B_4}{\dfrac{B_1 \vee B_2 \vee B_4 \vee W_3 \vee W_4 \vee W_5 \vee W_6 \quad W_4^\perp \vee B_5}{\dfrac{B_1 \vee B_2 \vee B_4 \vee W_3 \vee B_5 \vee W_5 \vee W_6 \quad W_5^\perp \vee B_2}{B_1 \vee B_2 \vee B_4 \vee W_3 \vee B_5 \vee W_6}}}}$$

The clause $B_1 \vee B_2 \vee B_4 \vee W_3 \vee B_5 \vee W_6$ is a success clause. Thus, there exists a closed walk starting from s_1.

Theorem 1. *Let G be a graph and s be a vertex of G. Starting from s, there exists a closed walk if and only if starting from $\{OC(s,G)\} \cup EC(G)$, a success clause can be derived.*

5 Blocked-Walk Detection

In this section, a method on testing whether, starting from a vertex, there exists a blocked walk or not is given. In this method, the set of edges starting from the same vertex are represented as a rewrite rule.

A-coloring rule. Let G be a graph and $V = \{s_1, ..., s_n\}$ the set of vertices in G. For each s_i in V, assume that starting from s_i, there are edges to $s_{i_1}, ..., s_{i_j}$, then we formalize such set of edges as an *A-coloring rewrite rule*

$$W_i \hookrightarrow B_{i_1} \vee \cdots \vee B_{i_j}.$$

The one-way clause of this rewrite rule is $W_i^\perp \vee B_{i_1} \vee \cdots \vee B_{i_j}$ (called *A-coloring clause*). The set of all the A-coloring clauses of G is denoted as $AC(G)$.

Resolution for blocked-walk detection. Let G be a graph and s be a vertex of G, then the problem of checking that *starting from s, whether there exists a blocked walk* can be encoded as the set of clauses $\{OC(s,G)\} \cup AC(G)$. By applying resolution rules among these clauses, a success clause can be derived if and only if *there is no blocked walk* starting from s.

Example 2. Consider the graph

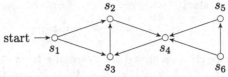

and check whether there exists a blocked walk starting from s_1. For this problem, the original clause is $B_1 \vee W_1 \vee W_2 \vee W_3 \vee W_4 \vee W_5 \vee W_6$ and the set of A-coloring clauses for this graph are

$$W_1^\perp \vee B_2 \vee B_3, \quad W_2^\perp \vee B_4, \quad W_3^\perp \vee B_2, \quad W_4^\perp \vee B_3, \quad W_5^\perp \vee B_4, \quad W_6^\perp \vee B_4.$$

The resolution steps are presented in the following tree top-down

$$\frac{B_1 \vee W_1 \vee W_2 \vee W_3 \vee W_4 \vee W_5 \vee W_6 \quad W_1^\perp \vee B_2 \vee B_3}{\dfrac{B_1 \vee B_2 \vee B_3 \vee W_2 \vee W_3 \vee W_4 \vee W_5 \vee W_6 \quad W_2^\perp \vee B_4}{\dfrac{B_1 \vee B_2 \vee B_3 \vee B_4 \vee W_3 \vee W_4 \vee W_5 \vee W_6 \quad W_3^\perp \vee B_2}{\dfrac{B_1 \vee B_2 \vee B_3 \vee B_4 \vee W_4 \vee W_5 \vee W_6 \quad W_4^\perp \vee B_3}{B_1 \vee B_2 \vee B_3 \vee B_4 \vee W_5 \vee W_6}}}}$$

The clause $B_1 \vee B_2 \vee B_3 \vee B_4 \vee W_5 \vee W_6$ is a success clause. Thus, there is no blocked walk starting from s_1.

Theorem 2. *Let G be a graph and s be a vertex of G. Starting from s, there is no blocked walk if and only if, starting from $\{OC(s,G)\} \cup AC(G)$, a success clause can be derived.*

6   Simplification Rules

Traditional automatic theorem proving methods are only practical for graphs of relatively small size. In this section, the reason why the resolution method is not as efficient as graph traversal algorithms is analyzed. Moreover, some strategies are designed to address such problems in proof-search algorithms.

6.1   Selection Function

First we show that the number of resolution steps strongly depend on the literals that are selected. More precisely, the number of literals that are selected will also affect the number of resolution steps. Then a selection function is given.

Example 3. For the graph

start $\longrightarrow \underset{s_1}{\circ} \xrightleftharpoons{\qquad} \underset{s_2}{\circ} \longrightarrow \underset{s_3}{\circ} \xrightleftharpoons{\qquad} \underset{s_4}{\circ}$

we prove the property: *starting from s_1, there exists a closed walk*. The original clause is $B_1 \vee W_1 \vee W_2 \vee W_3 \vee W_4$ and the E-coloring clauses of the graph are

$$\underline{W_1^\perp} \vee B_2, \quad \underline{W_2^\perp} \vee B_1, \quad \underline{W_2^\perp} \vee B_3, \quad \underline{W_3^\perp} \vee B_4, \quad \underline{W_4^\perp} \vee B_3.$$

Starting from the original clause, we can apply resolution as follows: First, apply resolution with E-coloring clause $\underline{W_1^\perp} \vee B_2$, which yields

$$B_1 \vee B_2 \vee W_2 \vee W_3 \vee W_4. \tag{1}$$

Then for (1), apply resolution with E-coloring clause $\underline{W_2^\perp} \vee B_1$, which yields

$$B_1 \vee B_2 \vee W_3 \vee W_4. \tag{2}$$

Clause (2) is a success clause. However, from (1), if we apply resolution with another E-coloring clause, more steps are needed to get a success clause.

The instinctive idea from Example 3 is similar to graph traversal algorithm. In a traversal clause, if there exists a pair of literals B_i and W_i, then the strategy of selecting W_i to have priority in applying resolution rules may have less resolution steps to get a success clause.

Definition 3 (Grey literal). *Let C be a traversal clause. For the pair of white literals and black literals $\langle W_i, B_i \rangle$, if both W_i and B_i are in C, then W_i is called a grey literal of C. The set of grey literals of C is defined as follows:*

$$\mathsf{grey}(C) = \{W_i \mid B_i \in C \,\&\, W_i \in C\}$$

Example 4. For the graph

start $\longrightarrow \underset{s_1}{\circ} \xrightarrow{\qquad \overset{s_2}{\circ} \qquad} \underset{s_3}{\circ} \longrightarrow \underset{s_4}{\circ}$

we prove the property: *starting from s_1, there is no blocked walk*. The original clause is $B_1 \vee W_1 \vee W_2 \vee W_3 \vee W_4$ and the A-coloring clauses of the graph are

$$\underline{W_1^\perp} \vee B_2 \vee B_3, \quad \underline{W_2^\perp} \vee B_3, \quad \underline{W_3^\perp} \vee B_4$$

For the original clause, apply resolution with A-coloring clause $\underline{W_1^\perp} \vee B_2 \vee B_3$, which yields

$$B_1 \vee B_2 \vee B_3 \vee W_2 \vee W_3 \vee W_4. \tag{3}$$

Then for (3), we can apply resolution rules with A-coloring clauses $\underline{W_2^\perp} \vee B_3$ and $\underline{W_3^\perp} \vee B_4$, and two new traversal clauses are generated:

$$B_1 \vee B_2 \vee B_3 \vee W_3 \vee W_4, \tag{4}$$

$$B_1 \vee B_2 \vee B_3 \vee B_4 \vee W_2 \vee W_4. \tag{5}$$

Then for (4), apply resolution rule with A-coloring clause $\underline{W_3^{\perp}} \vee B_4$, which yields

$$B_1 \vee B_2 \vee B_3 \vee B_4 \vee W_4, \tag{6}$$

and for this clause, we cannot apply resolution rules any more. For (5), we can apply resolution rule with A-coloring clause $\underline{W_2^{\perp}} \vee B_3$, and the clause generated is the same as (6). Thus, the clause (5) is redundant.

To avoid generating redundant clauses similar to Example 4, the following selection function is defined.

Definition 4 (Selection function). *For any traversal clause C, the selection function δ is defined as:*

$$\delta(C) = \begin{cases} \mathsf{single}(\mathsf{grey}(C)), & \mathsf{grey}(C) \neq \emptyset \\ C, & \textit{Otherwise} \end{cases}$$

in which single *is a random process to select only one literal from a set of literals.*

Notations. The *Polarized Resolution Modulo with δ* is written as PRM_{δ}. We write $\Gamma \rightarrow_{\mathcal{R}}^{\delta} C$ if the clause C can be derived from Γ in the system PRM_{δ}.

6.2   Elimination Rule

As we will see, selecting literals, which is at the base of Ordered Resolution, PRM, OPRM and this method are not sufficient enough, as we also have to restrict the method at the level of clauses.

Example 5. Reconsider the graph in Example 4, we prove the property: *starting from s_1, there exists a closed walk.* The original clause is $B_1 \vee W_1 \vee W_2 \vee W_3 \vee W_4$ and the E-coloring clauses of the graph are:

$$\underline{W_1^{\perp}} \vee B_2, \quad \underline{W_1^{\perp}} \vee B_3, \quad \underline{W_2^{\perp}} \vee B_3, \quad \underline{W_3^{\perp}} \vee B_4$$

For the original clause, apply resolution rules with $\underline{W_1^{\perp}} \vee B_2$ and $\underline{W_1^{\perp}} \vee B_3$, two new traversal clauses

$$B_1 \vee B_2 \vee W_2 \vee W_3 \vee W_4, \tag{7}$$

$$B_1 \vee B_3 \vee W_2 \vee W_3 \vee W_4 \tag{8}$$

are generated. For (7), apply resolution rule with $\underline{W_2^{\perp}} \vee B_3$, which yields

$$B_1 \vee B_2 \vee B_3 \vee W_3 \vee W_4. \tag{9}$$

Then for (9), apply resolution rule with $\underline{W_3^{\perp}} \vee B_4$, which yields

$$B_1 \vee B_2 \vee B_3 \vee B_4 \vee W_4. \tag{10}$$

Resolution rules cannot be applied on (10) any more. Then we can apply resolution rule between (8) and $W_3^{\perp} \vee B_4$, with

$$B_1 \vee B_3 \vee W_2 \vee B_4 \vee W_4 \tag{11}$$

generated, on which the resolution rules cannot be applied neither.

In Example 5, The clause (8) has the same grey literal as (9). Note that no success clause can be derived start from either (8) or (9).

Definition 5 (Path subsumption rule (PSR)). *Let M be a set of $A(E)$-coloring clauses and C be a traversal clause. If we have $C, M \rightarrow_{\mathcal{R}}^{\delta} C_1$ and $C, M \rightarrow_{\mathcal{R}}^{\delta} C_2$, in which $\mathsf{grey}(C_1) = \mathsf{grey}(C_2)$, the following rule*

$$\frac{C_1 \quad C_2}{C_i} \; \mathsf{grey}(C_1) = \mathsf{grey}(C_2), i = 1 \; or \; 2$$

can be applied to delete either C_1 or C_2, without breaking the final result.

After each step of applying resolution rules, if we apply PSR on the set of traversal clauses, the clause (8) in Example 5 will be deleted.

Theorem 3 (Completeness). PRM_{δ} *with PSR is complete.*

7 Implementation

In this section, we talk about the issues during the implementation, and then present the data of experiments.

7.1 Issues in Implementation

Success Clauses. In normal resolution based algorithms, the deduction will terminate if (i) an empty clause is generated, meaning the set of original clauses is **Unsat**isfiable or (ii) the resolution rule cannot be applied to derive any more new clauses, in this case the set of original clauses is **Sat**isfiable. However, for the problems in this paper, the derivation should stop when a success clause is derived, which is neither **Sat** nor **Unsat**. To implement our method in automated theorem provers, there may be two ways to deal with the success clauses. *The first way* is to give a set of rewrite rules, and make sure that every success clause can be rewritten into empty clause. For example, we can introduce class variables and treat the atomic propositions B_i and W_i as binary predicates, i.e., replace B_i with $B(s_i, Y)$ and W_i with $W(s_i, Y)$. Thus the success clause $B_1 \vee \cdots \vee B_i \vee W_{i+1} \vee \cdots \vee W_k$ is replaced by $B(s_1, Y) \vee \cdots \vee B(s_i, Y) \vee W(s_{i+1}, Y) \vee \cdots \vee W(s_k, Y)$. To deal with this kind of clause, the following rewrite rules are taken into account.

$B(x, add(y, Z)) \hookrightarrow x = y^{\perp} \wedge B(x, Z) \quad W(x, nil) \hookrightarrow \perp$
$W(x, add(y, Z)) \hookrightarrow x = y \vee W(x, Z) \quad x = x \hookrightarrow \top$
for each pair of different vertices s_i and s_j, $s_i = s_j \hookrightarrow \perp$

```
   Init      : original clause in U, coloring clauses in P
             G = ∅ // G is a set of sets of grey literals
   Output: Sat or Unsat
 1 while U ≠ ∅ do
 2  │  c = select(U);
 3  │  U = U \ c; // remove c from U
 4  │  if c is an empty clause or a success clause then
 5  │  │    return Unsat
 6  │  end
 7  │  g := δ(c); // δ is the literal selection function
 8  │  if g ∉ G then
 9  │  │    P = P ∪ {c}; // add c to P
10  │  │    G = G ∪ {g};
11  │  │    U = U + generate(c, P);
12  │  end
13 end
14 return Sat;
```

Algorithm 1. Proof Search Algorithm

This idea is a variation of the theory in [7]. *The second way* is to add a function to check whether a clause is a success clause or not to the proof-search procedure.

Path Subsumption Rule. To make it simple, an empty set G is given in the initial part of the proof-search algorithm, and for the selected traversal clause in U, if the selected grey literal of the traversal clause is in G, then the traversal clause is dead, otherwise, add the selected grey literal to G.

Algorithm. The proof-search algorithm with literal selection function and path subsumption rule is in Algorithm 1. In this algorithm, select(U) selects a clause from U, g is the selected grey literal in c and generate(c, P) produces all the clauses by applying an inference rule on c or between c and a clause in P.

7.2 Experimental Evaluation

In the following experiment, the procedure of identifying success clauses, the selection function, and the PSR are embedded into iProver Modulo. The data of the experiments on some randomly generated graphs are illustrated in Table 1.

Table 1. Closed-walk and blocked-walk detection

Graph				Result and time			
Prop	N(v)	N(e)	Num	Sat	Succ	PRM$_\delta$	PRM$_\delta$ + PSR
Closed walk	1.0×10^3	1.0×10^3	100	95	5	25 m 40 s	25 m 0 s
	1.0×10^3	1.5×10^3	100	50	50	1 h 06 m 40 s	1 h 02 m 46 s
	1.0×10^3	2.0×10^3	100	23	77	1 h 09 m 44 s	1 h 09 m 46 s
Blocked walk	1.0×10^3	2.0×10^3	100	100	0	17 m 48 s	
	1.0×10^3	3.0×10^3	100	100	0	1 h 06 m 28 s	
	1.0×10^3	1.0×10^4	100	0	100	24 h 50 m 43 s	

For the test cases of closed-walk detection, the total time on testing all the 100 graphs did not change much when we take PSR into account. By checking the running time of each graph, we found that *in most cases, PSR was inactive, as most of the vertices did not have the chance to be visited again.* However, *on some special graphs, the running time do reduces much.* On blocked walk detection, the running time grows while there are more edges on graphs, as the number of visited vertices increased.

8 Conclusion and Future Work

In this paper, two graph problems, closed-walk and blocked-walk detection, are considered. The problems are encoded with propositional formulae, and the edges are treated as rewrite rules. Moreover, a selection function and a subsumption rule are designed to address efficiency problems.

Safety and *liveness* are two basic model checking problems [3]. In a program, safety properties specify that "something bad never happens", while liveness assert that "something good will happen eventually". To prove the safety of a system, all the accessible states starting from the initial one should be traversed, which is a kind of blocked-walk detection problem. For liveness, we need to prove that on each infinite path starting from the initial state, there exists a "good" one. This problem can be treated as closed-walk detection. In the future, we will try to address some model checking problems by improving our strategy.

Acknowledgments. I am grateful to Gilles Dowek, for his careful reading and comments.

A Appendix

A.1 Correctness of the Encoding of Closed-Walk Detection Problem

To prove that this kind of encoding suit for all closed walk detection problems, a proof of the theorem below is given.

Theorem 4. *Let G be a graph and s be a vertex in G. Starting from s, there exists a closed walk if and only if starting from $\{\mathsf{OC}(s,G)\} \cup \mathsf{EC}(G)$, a success clause can be derived.*

Before proving this theorem, several notations and lemmas are needed, which will also be used in the following sections.

Notations. Let C_1, C_2, C_3 be clauses, Γ be a set of clauses:

- if C_3 is generated by applying resolution between C_1 and C_2, then write the resolution step as $C_1 \xrightarrow{C_2} C_3$; if the resolution is based on a selection function δ, then the resolution step is written as $C_1 \xrightarrow{C_2}_\delta C_3$.

– if C_2 is generated by applying resolution between C_1 and a clause in Γ, then write the resolution step as $C_1 \xrightarrow{\Gamma} C_2$; if the resolution is based on a selection function δ, then the resolution step is written as $C_1 \xrightarrow{\Gamma}_\delta C_2$.
– if C_1 is generated by one step of resolution on some clauses in Γ, then write the resolution step as $\Gamma \longrightarrow \Gamma, C_1$; if the resolution is based on a selection function δ, then the resolution step is written as $\Gamma \longrightarrow_\delta \Gamma, C_1$.

Lemma 1. *For any two traversal clauses, we cannot apply resolution rules between them.*

Proof. All the literals in traversal clauses are positive.   □

Lemma 2. *If resolution rules can be applied between a traversal clause and a coloring clause, then one and only one traversal clause can be derived.*

Proof. As all the literals in the traversal clause are positive and there is only one negative literal in the coloring clause, straightforwardly, only one traversal clause can be derived.   □

Proposition 1. *Let M be a set of coloring clauses, $C_1, \ldots, C_n$ be traversal clauses and S be a success clause. If $M, C_1, \ldots, C_n \to S$, then there exists $1 \le i \le n$, such that $M, C_i \to S$, and the length of the later derivation is at most equal to the former one.*

Proof. By induction on the size of the derivation $M, C_1, \ldots, C_n \to S$.

– If S is a member of $C_1, \ldots, C_n$, then there exists the derivation $M, S \to S$ without applying any resolution rules.
– If S is not a member of $C_1, \ldots, C_n$, then in each step of the derivation, by Lemma 1, the resolution rules can only be applied between a traversal clause and a coloring clause. Assume the derivation is $M, C_1, \ldots, C_n \longrightarrow M, C_1, \ldots, C_n, C' \to S$, in which, by Lemma 2, C' is a traversal clause. Then for the derivation $M, C_1, \ldots, C_n, C' \to S$, by induction hypothesis, $M, C' \to S$ or there exists $1 \le i \le n$ such that $M, C_i \to S$, with the steps of the derivation at most equal to $M, C_1, \ldots, C_n, C' \to S$. If $M, C_i \to S$, then the steps of the derivation are less than $M, C_1, \ldots, C_n \to S$, thus this derivation is as needed. If $M, C' \to S$, then by Lemma 1, there exists C_j in $C_1, \ldots, C_n$, such that $C_j \xrightarrow{M} C'$, thus the derivation $M, C_j \to S$, with the derivation steps at most equal to $M, C_1, \ldots, C_n \to S$, is as needed.   □

Proposition 2. *Let M be a set of coloring clauses, C be a traversal clause, and S be a success clause. If $M, C \to S(\pi_1)$[1], then there exists a derivation path $C(C_0) \xrightarrow{M} C_1 \xrightarrow{M} C_2 \cdots \xrightarrow{M} C_n(S)$.*

---

[1] We denote the derivation as π_1.

Proof. By induction on the size of the derivation π_1.

- If C is a success clause, then the derivation path can be built directly.
- Otherwise, by Lemma 1, in each step of the derivation, the resolution rules can only be applied between a traversal clause and a coloring clause. Assume the derivation is $M, C \longrightarrow M, C, C' \rightarrow S$, then for the derivation $M, C, C' \rightarrow S$, by Proposition 1, there exists a derivation $M, C \rightarrow S(\pi_2)^2$ or $M, C' \rightarrow S$, with the length less than π_1. For π_2, by induction hypothesis, there exists a derivation path $C(C_0) \xrightarrow{M} C_1 \cdots \xrightarrow{M} C_n(S)$, and this is just the derivation as needed. For $M, C' \rightarrow S$, by induction hypothesis, there exists a derivation path $C' \xrightarrow{M} C_1' \cdots \xrightarrow{M} C_m'(S)$. As $C \xrightarrow{M} C'$, the derivation path $C \xrightarrow{M} C' \xrightarrow{M} C_1' \cdots \xrightarrow{M} C_m'(S)$ is as needed. $\qquad\square$

Now it is ready to prove Theorem 4. The proof is as follows.

Proof of Theorem 4

- For the right direction, we assume that the path is

$$s_1(s_{k_1}) \rightarrow s_{k_2} \rightarrow \cdots \rightarrow s_{k_i} \rightleftarrows s_{k_{i+1}} \rightarrow \cdots \rightarrow s_{k_j}$$

By the method of generating E-coloring clauses of a graph, there exist E-coloring clauses:

$$W_{k_1}^\perp \vee B_{k_2}, \ \ W_{k_2}^\perp \vee B_{k_3}, \ \ \ldots, \ W_{k_{i-1}}^\perp \vee B_{k_i}, \ \ W_{k_i}^\perp \vee B_{k_{i+1}}, \ \ \ldots, \ W_{k_j}^\perp \vee B_{k_i}.$$

Then starting from the original clause $C_1 = B_1 \vee W_1 \vee \cdots \vee W_n$, the derivation

$$C_1 \xrightarrow{D_1} C_2 \xrightarrow{D_2} \cdots C_{i-1} \xrightarrow{D_{i-1}} C_i \xrightarrow{D_i} \cdots C_j \xrightarrow{D_j} C_{j+1}$$

can be built, in which C_{j+1} is a success clause and for each $1 \le m \le j$, D_m is the E-coloring clause $W_{k_m}^\perp \vee B_{k_{m+1}}$.
- For the left direction, by Proposition 2, starting from the original clause $C_1 = B_1 \vee W_1 \vee \cdots \vee W_n$, there exists a derivation path

$$C_1 \xrightarrow{D_1} C_2 \xrightarrow{D_2} \cdots C_{i-1} \xrightarrow{D_{i-1}} C_i \xrightarrow{D_i} \cdots C_j \xrightarrow{D_j} C_{j+1},$$

in which C_{j+1} is a success clause and for each $1 \le m \le j$, D_m is an E-coloring clause. As C_{j+1} is a success clause, for each black literal B_i in the clause C_{j+1}, there exists an E-coloring clause $W_i^\perp \vee B_{k_i}$ in $D_1, \ldots, D_j$. Thus for each black literal B_i in the clause C_{j+1}, there exists a vertex s_{k_i} such that there is an edge from s_i to s_{k_i}. As the number of black literals in C_{j+1} is finite, for each vertex s_i, if B_i is a member of C_{j+1}, then starting from s_i, there exists a path which contains a cycle. As the literal B_1 is in C_{j+1}, starting from s_1, there exists a path to a cycle. $\qquad\square$

---

[2] We denote the derivation as π_2.

A.2   Correctness of the Encoding of Block-Walk Detection Problem

Theorem 5. *Let G be a graph and s_1 be a vertex of G. Starting from s_1, there is no blocked walk if and only if, starting from $\{OC(s_1, G)\} \cup AC(G)$, a success clause can be derived.*

Before proving this theorem, a lemma is needed.

Lemma 3. *Let G be a graph and s_1 be a vertex of G. Starting from s_1, if all the reachable vertices are traversed in the order $s_1, s_2, \ldots, s_k$ and each reachable vertex has at least one successor, then starting from $\{OC(s_1, G)\} \cup AC(G)$, there exists a derivation path $C_1(OC(s_1, G)) \xrightarrow{D_1} C_2 \xrightarrow{D_2} \cdots C_k \xrightarrow{D_k} C_{k+1}$, in which C_{k+1} is a success clause and $\forall 1 \leq i \leq k$, D_i is an A-coloring clause of the form $\underline{W_i^\perp} \vee B_{i_1} \vee \cdots \vee B_{i_j}$.*

Proof. As $s_1, s_2 \ldots, s_k$ are all the reachable vertices starting from s_1, for a vertex s, if there exists an edge from one of the vertices in $s_1, s_2, \ldots, s_k$ to s, then s is a member of $s_1, s_2, \ldots, s_k$. Thus, after the derivation $C_1' \xrightarrow{D_1} C_2 \xrightarrow{D_2} \cdots C_j \xrightarrow{D_j} C_{j+1}$, for each black literal B_i, the white literal W_i is not in C_{j+1}, thus C_{j+1} is a success clause. $\square$

Now it is ready to prove Theorem 5. The proof is as follows.

Proof of Theorem 5

- For the right direction, assume that all the reachable vertices starting from s_1 are traversed in the order $s_1, s_2, \ldots, s_k$. For the resolution part, by Lemma 3, starting from the original clause, a success clause can be derived.
- For the left direction, by Proposition 2, starting from the original clause $C_1 = OC(s_1, G)$, there exists a derivation path

$$C_1 \xrightarrow{D_1} C_2 \xrightarrow{D_2} \cdots C_j \xrightarrow{D_j} C_{j+1},$$

in which C_{j+1} is a success clause and $\forall 1 \leq i \leq j$, D_i is an A-coloring clause with $W_{k_i}^\perp$ underlined. As there is no i such that both B_i and W_i are in C_{j+1}, for the vertices in $s_{k_1}, s_{k_2}, \ldots, s_{k_j}$, the successors of each vertex is a subset of $s_{k_1}, s_{k_2}, \ldots, s_{k_j}$. As the black literal B_1 is in the clause C_{j+1}, by the definition of success clause, the white literal W_1 is not in C_{j+1}, thus s_1 is a member of $s_{k_1}, s_{k_2}, \ldots, s_{k_j}$. Then recursively, for each vertex s, if s is reachable from s_1, then s is in $s_{k_1}, s_{k_2}, \ldots, s_{k_j}$. Thus starting from s_1, all the vertices reachable have successors. $\square$

A.3   Completeness of $PRM_\delta + PSR$

For the completeness of our method, we first prove that PRM_δ is complete, then we prove that PRM_δ remains complete when we apply PSR eagerly.

Proposition 3 (Completeness of PRM_δ). *Let M be a set of coloring clauses and $C_1, \ldots, C_n$ be traversal clauses. If $M, C_1, \ldots, C_n \to S$, in which the clause S is a success clause, then starting from $M, C_1, \ldots, C_n$, we can build a derivation by selecting the resolved literals with selection function δ in Definition 4 and get a success clause.*

Proof. By Propositions 1 and 2, there exists $1 \leq i \leq n$, such that $C_i(C_{i_0}) \xrightarrow{D_1} C_{i_1} \cdots \xrightarrow{D_n} C_{i_n}(S)$. As there are no white literals in any clauses of $D_1, \ldots, D_n$ and in each step of the resolution, the resolved literal in the traversal clause is a white literal, the order of white literals to be resolved in the derivation by applying Resolution rule with coloring clauses in $D_1, \ldots, D_n$ will not affect the result. Thus use selection function δ to select white literals to be resolved, until we get a traversal clause S' such that there are no grey literals in it. By the definition of success clause, S' is a success clause.   □

Lemma 4. *Let M be a set of coloring clauses and C be a traversal clause. Assume $C(H_0) \xrightarrow{D_1}_\delta H_1 \xrightarrow{D_2}_\delta \cdots H(H_i) \xrightarrow{D_i}_\delta \cdots \xrightarrow{D_n}_\delta H_n$ in which H_n is a success clause and for each $1 \leq j \leq n$, the coloring clause D_j is in M, and $M, C \to^\delta K$ such that $\mathsf{grey}(H) = \mathsf{grey}(K)$. If $K, D_1, \ldots, D_n \to^\delta K'$, and K' is not a success clause, then there exists a coloring clause D_k in $D_1, \ldots, D_n$, such that $K' \xrightarrow{D_k}_\delta K''$.*

Proof. As K' is not a success clause, assume that the literals B_i and W_i are in K'. As W_i cannot be introduced in each step of resolution between a traversal clause and a coloring clause, W_i is in C and K. As the literal B_i is in clause K', during the derivation of K', there must be some clauses which contains B_i:

- if the literal B_i is in K, as W_i is also in K, W_i is a grey literal of K. As $\mathsf{grey}(H) = \mathsf{grey}(K)$, the literal B_i is also in H, and as B_i cannot be selected during the derivation, it remains in the traversal clauses $H_{i+1}, \ldots, H_n$.
- if the literal B_i is introduced by applying Resolution rule with coloring clause D_j in $D_1, \ldots, D_n$, which is used in the derivation of H_n as well, so the literal B_i is also a member of H_n.

In both cases, the literal B_i is in H_n. As H_n is a success clause, the literal W_i is not a member of H_n. As W_i is in C, there exists a coloring clause D_k in $D_1, \ldots, D_n$ with the literal $W_i^\perp$ selected. Thus, $K' \xrightarrow{D_k}_\delta K''$.   □

Lemma 5. *Let M be a set of $A(E)$-coloring clauses and C be a traversal clause. If we have $M, C \to^\delta H$ and $M, C \to^\delta K$, such that $\mathsf{grey}(H) = \mathsf{grey}(K)$, then starting from M, H a success clause can be derived if and only if starting from M, K a success clause can be derived.*

Proof. Without loss of generality, prove that if starting from M, H we can get to a success clause, then starting from M, K, we can also get to a success clause. By Proposition 2, starting from C, there exists $H_0(C) \xrightarrow{M}_\delta H_1 \xrightarrow{M}_\delta \cdots H_i(H) \xrightarrow{M}_\delta \cdots \xrightarrow{M}_\delta H_n$, in which H_n is a success clause. More precisely,

$H_0(C) \xrightarrow{D_1}_\delta H_1 \xrightarrow{D_2}_\delta \cdots H_i(H) \xrightarrow{D_{i+1}}_\delta \cdots \xrightarrow{D_n}_\delta H_n$, where for each $1 \le j \le n$, the coloring clause D_j is in M. Then by Lemma 4, starting from M, K, we can always find a coloring clause in $D_1, \ldots, D_n$ to apply resolution with the new generated traversal clause, until we get a success clause. As the white literals in the generated traversal clauses decrease by each step of resolution, we will get a success clause at last. $\square$

Theorem 6. (Completeness). *PRM_δ with PSR is complete.*

Proof. By Lemma 5, each time after we apply PSR, the satisfiability is preserved. $\square$

References

1. Burel, G.: Embedding deduction modulo into a prover. In: Dawar, A., Veith, H. (eds.) CSL 2010. LNCS, vol. 6247, pp. 155–169. Springer, Heidelberg (2010). doi:10. 1007/978-3-642-15205-4_15
2. Burel, G.: Experimenting with deduction modulo. In: Bjørner, N., Sofronie-Stokkermans, V. (eds.) CADE 2011. LNCS (LNAI), vol. 6803, pp. 162–176. Springer, Heidelberg (2011). doi:10.1007/978-3-642-22438-6_14
3. Clarke Jr., E.M., Grumberg, O., Peled, D.A.: Model Checking. MIT Press, Cambridge (1999)
4. Courcelle, B.: The monadic second-order logic of graphs. I. Recognizable sets of finite graphs. Inf. Comput. **85**(1), 12–75 (1990)
5. Dowek, G.: Polarized resolution modulo. In: Calude, C.S., Sassone, V. (eds.) TCS 2010. IAICT, vol. 323, pp. 182–196. Springer, Heidelberg (2010). doi:10.1007/978-3-642-15240-5_14
6. Dowek, G., Hardin, T., Kirchner, C.: Theorem proving modulo. J. Autom. Reasoning **31**, 33–72 (2003)
7. Dowek, G., Jiang, Y.: Axiomatizing Truth in a Finite Model (2013). https://hal.inria.fr/hal-00919469/document
8. Navarro-Pérez, J.A.: Encoding and solving problems in effectively propositional logic. Ph.D. thesis, The University of Manchester (2007)
9. Reiter, R.: Two results on ordering for resolution with merging and linear format. J. ACM (JACM) **18**(4), 630–646 (1971)
10. Robinson, J.A.: Automatic deduction with hyper-resolution. J. Symbolic Logic **39**(1), 189–190 (1974)
11. Robinson, J.A.: A machine-oriented logic based on the resolution principle. J. ACM (JACM) **12**(1), 23–41 (1965)
12. Slagle, J.R., Norton, L.M.: Experiment with an automatic theorem-prover having partial ordering inference rules. Commun. ACM **16**(11), 682–688 (1973)

SMT-based Software Model Checking: An Experimental Comparison of Four Algorithms

Dirk Beyer and Matthias Dangl

University of Passau, Passau, Germany

Abstract. After many years of successful development of new algorithms for software model checking, there is a need to consolidate the knowledge about the different algorithms and approaches. This paper gives a coarse overview in terms of effectiveness and efficiency of four algorithms. We compare the following different "schools of thought" of algorithms: bounded model checking, k-induction, predicate abstraction, and lazy abstraction with interpolants. Those algorithms are well-known and successful in software verification. They have in common that they are based on SMT solving as the back-end technology, using the theories of uninterpreted functions, bit vectors, and floats as underlying theory. All four algorithms are implemented in the verification framework CPACHECKER. Thus, we can present an evaluation that really compares only the core algorithms, and keeps the design variables such as parser front end, SMT solver, used theory in SMT formulas, etc. constant. We evaluate the algorithms on a large set of verification tasks, and discuss the conclusions.

Keywords: Software verification · Program analysis · Bounded model checking · k-induction · IMPACT · Lazy abstraction · SMT solving

1 Introduction

In recent years, advances in automatic methods for software verification have lead to increased efforts towards applying software verification to industrial systems, in particular operating-systems code [3,5,13,30]. Predicate abstraction [24] with counterexample-guided abstraction refinement (CEGAR) [18] and lazy abstraction [27], lazy abstraction with interpolants [33], and k-induction with auxiliary-invariants [8,22] are some of the concepts introduced to scale verification technology from simple toy problems to real-world software. In the 5th International Competition of Software Verification (SV-COMP'16) [7], ten out of the 13 candidates participating in category *Overall* used some of these techniques, and out of the remaining three, two are bounded model checkers [15]. Considering this apparent success, we revisit an earlier work that presented a unifying algorithm for lazy predicate abstraction (BLAST-like) and lazy abstraction with interpolants (IMPACT-like), and showed that both techniques perform similarly [14]. We conduct a comparative evaluation of bounded model checking, k-induction, lazy

© Springer International Publishing AG 2016
S. Blazy and M. Chechik (Eds.): VSTTE 2016, LNCS 9971, pp. 181–198, 2016.
DOI: 10.1007/978-3-319-48869-1_14

predicate abstraction, and lazy abstraction with interpolants, observe that the previously drawn conclusions about the two lazy-abstraction techniques still hold today, and show that k-induction has the potential to outperform the other two techniques. We restrict our presentation to safety properties; however, the techniques that we present can be used also for checking liveness [38].

Availability of Data and Tools. All presented approaches are implemented in the open-source verification framework CPACHECKER [10], which is available under the Apache 2.0 license. All experiments are based on publicly available benchmark verification tasks from the last competition on software verification [7]. To ensure technical accuracy, we used the open-source benchmarking framework BENCHEXEC[1] [12] to conduct our experiments. Tables with our detailed experimental results are available on the supplementary web page[2].

Related Work. Unfortunately, there is not much work available in rigorous comparison of algorithms. General overviews over methods for reasoning [6] and of approaches for software model checking [28] exist, but no systematic comparison of the algorithms in a common formal setting. This paper tries to give an abreast comparison of the effectiveness and efficiency of the algorithms.

Figure 1 tries to categorize the main approaches for software model checking that are based on SMT technology; we use this structure also to give pointers to other implementations of the approaches.

Bounded Model Checking. Many software bugs can be found by a bounded search through the state space of the program. Bounded model checking [15] for software encodes all program paths that result from a bounded unrolling of the program in an SMT formula that is satisfiable if the formula encodes a feasible program path from the program entry to a violation of the specification. Several implementations were demonstrated to be successful in improving software quality by revealing shallow program bugs, for example CBMC [19], ESBMC [20], LLBMC [39], and SMACK [35]. The characteristics to quickly verify a large portion of the state space without the need of computing expensive abstractions made the technique a basis component in many verification tools (cf. Table 4 in the report for SV-COMP 2016 [7]).

Unbounded — No Abstraction. The idea of bounded model checking (to encode large portions of a program as SMT formula) can be used also for unbounded verification by using an induction argument [40], i.e., a safe inductive invariant needs to be implied by all paths from the program entry to the loop head and by all paths starting from the assumed invariant (induction hypothesis) at the loop head through the loop body. The remaining problem, which is a main focus area of research on k-induction, is to compute a sufficient safe inductive invariant. The approach of k-induction is implemented in CBMC [19], CPACHECKER [8], ESBMC [36], PKIND [29], and 2LS [37]. The approach of k-induction with continuously-refining invariant generation [8] was independently reproduced later in 2LS [17].

Unbounded — With Abstraction. A completely different approach is to compute an over-approximation of the state-space, using insights from data-flow analysis [1,31,34].

---

[1] https://github.com/sosy-lab/benchexec
[2] https://www.sosy-lab.org/~dbeyer/k-ind-compare/

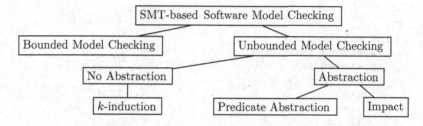

Fig. 1. Classification of algorithms

The idea of state-space abstraction is often combined with the idea of counterexample-guided abstraction refinement (CEGAR) [18] and lazy abstraction refinement [27]. Several verifiers implement a predicate abstraction [24]: SLAM [4], BLAST [9], and CPACHECKER [10]. A safe invariant is computed by iteratively refining the abstract states by discovering new predicates during each CEGAR step. Interpolation [21,32] is a successful method to obtain useful predicates from error paths. ULTIMATE AUTOMIZER [26] combines predicate abstraction with an automaton-based approach.

Instead of using predicate abstraction, it is possible to construct the abstract state space directly from interpolants using the IMPACT algorithm [33].

Combinations. Of course, the best features of all approaches should be combined into new, "hybrid" methods, such as implemented in CPACHECKER [41], SEAHORN [25], and UFO [2].

2 Algorithms

In the following, we will give a unifying overview over four widely-used algorithms for software model checking: bounded model checking (BMC), k-induction, predicate abstraction, and the IMPACT algorithm.

As shown in Fig. 1, all four algorithms are SMT-based model checking algorithms: They rely on encoding program paths as SMT formulas.

Preliminaries. We restrict the presentation to a simple imperative programming language, where all operations are either assignments or assume operations, and all variables range over integers.[3] We use control-flow automata (CFA) to represent programs. A *control-flow automaton* consists of a set L of program locations (modeling the program counter), the initial program location $l_2 \in L$ (modeling the program entry), a target program location $l_E \in L$ (modeling the specification violation), and a set of control-flow edges (modeling the operation that is executed during the flow of control from one program location to another).

Example. Figure 2 shows an example C program and the corresponding CFA. We will use this example to illustrate the algorithms. The displayed C program contains two variables x and y, which are both initialized to 0. In the loop of lines 4–10,

---

[3] Our implementations are based on CPACHECKER [10], which supports C programs.

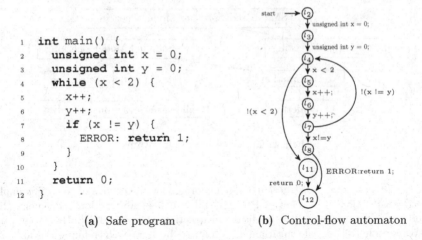

```
1    int main() {
2      unsigned int x = 0;
3      unsigned int y = 0;
4      while (x < 2) {
5        x++;
6        y++;
7        if (x != y) {
8          ERROR: return 1;
9        }
10     }
11     return 0;
12   }
```

(a) Safe program   (b) Control-flow automaton

Fig. 2. An example C program (a) and its CFA (b)

both variables are incremented as long as x is lower than 2. The CFA nodes corresponding to this loop are l_4, l_5, l_6, and l_7, with l_4 being the loop head. At the end of the loop body in line 7, x and y are checked for equality. If the variables are not equal, control flows to the error location l_8 in line 8.

ABE: An SMT-formula-based program analysis. For the algorithms presented in this paper, it is frequently required to represent the reachability of a program state as a precise or over-approximated set of program paths that are encoded as SMT formulas. A configurable program analysis (CPA) for this purpose has been formally defined in previous work [11]. Adjustable-block encoding (ABE) is a forward-reachability analysis that unrolls the control-flow automaton (CFA) into an abstract reachability graph (ARG) while keeping track of arbitrarily-definable (adjustable) blocks. An abstract state in the ARG is defined as a triple consisting of a program location, an abstract-state formula, which represents an abstract over-approximation of the reachability of the block entry, and a concrete path formula, which for any state within a block represents the set of concrete paths from the block entry to the location of this state. This mechanism can be used to control if and when to apply abstraction by configuring the definition of block(s). Two of the algorithms we present, BMC and k-induction, do not use abstraction, while the other two, predicate abstraction and IMPACT, do. In the former case, the abstract-state formula is always *true* and has no effect. For consistency, however, we display the abstract-state formula in all our graphical representations.

Another feature required by the presented algorithms is the configuration of a limit for unrolling the control-flow automaton into an ARG, because a complete unrolling is not always desirable or even feasible. In addition to the configurability of the definition of blocks, we therefore introduce such a limit on unrolling the CFA as another parameter to configure the SMT-formula-based program analysis ABE. In the following, we will describe the presented algorithms informally and discuss their usage of configurable ABE program analysis as a convenient way to construct, manage, and apply SMT formulas.

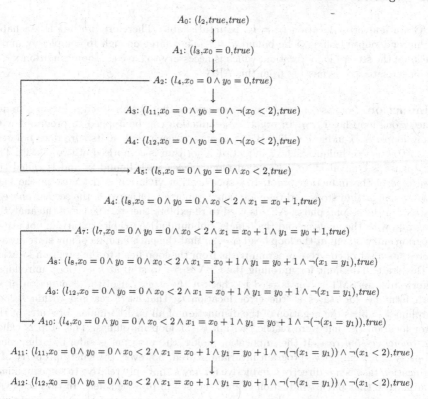

Fig. 3. ARG fragment for applying BMC to the example of Fig. 2

Bounded Model Checking. In BMC, the state space of the analyzed program is explored without using abstraction by unrolling loops up to a given bound k. In this setting, ABE is configured so that there is only one single block of unbounded size starting at the program entry. This way, there is never any abstraction computation. The limit for unrolling the CFA with ABE in the context of BMC is given by the loop-unrolling bound k.

Due to the single ABE block that contains the whole program, the path formula of any state always represents a set of concrete program paths from the program entry to the program location of this state. After unrolling a loop up to bound k, the state-space exploration stops. Then, the disjunction of the path formulas of all states in the explored state space at error location l_E is checked for satisfiability using an SMT solver. If the formula is satisfiable, the program contains a real specification violation. If the formula is unsatisfiable, there is no specification violation in the program within the first k loop unrollings. Unless an upper bound lower than or equal to k for a loop is known, a specification violation beyond the first k loop iterations may or may not exist. Due to this limitation, BMC is usually not able to prove that a program satisfies its specification.

If we apply BMC with $k = 1$ to the example in Fig. 2, unrolling the CFA yields the ARG depicted in Fig. 3. The path formula of the ARG state A_8, which is the only

ARG state at error location $l_E = l_8$, is unsatisfiable. Therefore, no bug is reachable within one loop unrolling. The bound $k = 1$ is not large enough to completely unroll the loop; the second loop iteration, which is necessary to have the loop condition $x < 2$ no longer satisfied, is missing from this ARG.

k-Induction. For ease of presentation, we assume that the analyzed program contains exactly one loop head l_{LH}. In practice, k-induction can be applied to programs with many loops [8]. k-induction, like BMC, is an approach that at its core does not rely on abstraction techniques. The k-induction algorithm is comprised of two phases. The first phase is equivalent to a bounded model check with bound k, and is called the *base case* of the induction proof. If a specification violation is detected in the base case, the algorithm stops and the violation is reported. Otherwise, the second phase is started. In the second phase, ABE is used to re-explore the state space of the analyzed program, with the analysis and the (single, unbounded) ABE block starting not at the program entry l_2, but at the loop head l_{LH}, so that the path formula of any state always represents a set of concrete program paths from the loop head to the program location of this state. The limit for unrolling the CFA is set to stop at $k + 1$ loop unrollings. Afterwards, an SMT solver is used to check if the negation of the disjunction of all path formulas for states at the error location l_E that were reached within k loop unrollings, implies the negation of the disjunction of all path formulas for states at the error location l_E that were reached within $k + 1$ loop unrollings. This step is called the *inductive-step case*. If the implication holds, the program is safe, i.e., the safety property is a k-inductive program invariant. Often, however, the safety property of a verification task is not directly k-inductive for any k, but only relative to some auxiliary invariant, so that plain k-induction cannot succeed in proving safety. In these cases, it is necessary to employ an auxiliary-invariant generator and inject these invariants into the k-induction procedure to strengthen the hypothesis of the inductive-step case.

If we apply k-induction with $k = 1$ to the example in Fig. 2, the first phase, which is equivalent to BMC, yields the same ARG as in Fig. 3. Figure 4 shows the ARG of the second phase, which is constructed by unrolling the CFA starting at loop head $l_{LH} = l_4$ and using loop bound $k = 1$. The negation of the disjunction of the path formulas of the ARG states A_5 and A_{10} at the error location $l_E = l_8$, which were reached within at most one loop iteration, implies the negation of the disjunction of the path formulas of the ARG states A_5, A_{10}, and A_{18} at the error location $l_E = l_8$, which were reached within at most $k + 1 = 2$ loop iterations, which in combination with the base case (BMC) from the first phase proves that the program is safe. This inductive proof is strong enough to prove safety even if we replace the loop condition in line 4 of the sample program by a nondeterministic value.

Predicate Abstraction. Predicate abstraction with counterexample-guided abstraction refinement (CEGAR) directly applies ABE within the CEGAR loop. The abstraction-state formula of an abstract state over-approximates the reachable concrete states using a boolean combination of predicates over program variables from a given set of predicates (the *precision* π). This abstraction is computed by an SMT solver. Using CEGAR, it is possible to apply lazy abstraction, starting out with an empty initial precision. When the analysis encounters an abstract state at the error location l_E, the concrete program path leading to this state is reconstructed and checked for feasibility using an SMT solver. If the concrete error path is feasible, the algorithm reports the error and terminates. Otherwise, the precision is refined (usually by employing an

Fig. 4. ARG fragment for the inductive-step case of k-induction applied to the example of Fig. 2

SMT solver to compute Craig interpolants [21] for the locations on the error path) and the analysis is restarted. Due to the refined precision, it is guaranteed that the previously identified infeasible error paths are not encountered again.

For this technique, the blocks can be arbitrarily defined; in our experimental evaluation we define a block to end at a loop head. To enable CEGAR, the unrolling of the CFA must be configured to stop if the state-space exploration hits a state at the error location l_E.

If we apply predicate abstraction to the example in Fig. 2 using a precision $\pi : \{x = y\}$ and defining all blocks to end at the loop head l_4, we obtain the ARG depicted in Fig. 5: The first block consists of the locations l_2 and l_3. If the ABE analysis hits location l_4, which is a loop head, the path formula $x_0 = 0 \land y_0 = 0$ is abstracted using the set of predicates π. Precision π contains only the predicate $x = y$, which is implied by the path formula and becomes the new abstraction formula, while the path formula for the new block beginning at l_4 is reset to *true*. From that point onwards,

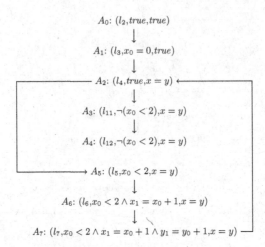

Fig. 5. ARG for predicate abstraction applied to the example of Fig. 2

there are two possible paths: one directly to the end of the program the loop if **x** is greater than or equal to 2, and another one into the loop if **x** is less than 2. The path avoiding the loop is trivially safe, because from l_{11} or l_{12} there is no control-flow path back to the error location. The path through the loop increments both variables before encountering the assertion. Using the abstraction formula encoding the reachability of the block entry in combination with the path formula, it is easy to conclude that the assertion is true, so that the only feasible successor is at the loop head l_4, which causes the previous block to end. The abstraction computation yields again the abstraction formula $x = y$ at l_4, which is already covered by the ARG state A_2. Therefore, unrolling the CFA into the ARG completed without encountering the error location $l_E = l_8$. The algorithm thus concludes that the program is safe.

Impact. Lazy abstraction with interpolants, more commonly known as the IMPACT algorithm due to its first implementation in the tool IMPACT, also uses ABE to create an unwinding of the CFA similar to predicate abstraction. Impact, however, does not base its abstractions on an explicit precision. Initializing all new abstract-state formulas to *true*, the algorithm repeatedly applies the following three steps until no further changes can be made:

(1) *Expand(s)*: If the state s has no successors yet (s is currently a leaf node in the ARG) and is not marked as *covered*, the successor states of s are created with *true* as their initial abstract-state formula.
(2) *Refine(s)*: If s is an abstract state at the error location l_E with an abstract-state formula different from *false*, inductive Craig interpolants for the path from the root of the ARG to this state s are computed using an SMT solver. Each abstract state at an ABE block entry along this path is marked as *not covered*, and its abstract-state formula is strengthened by conjoining it with the corresponding interpolant, guaranteeing that if the state s is unreachable, the formula of s becomes *false*.

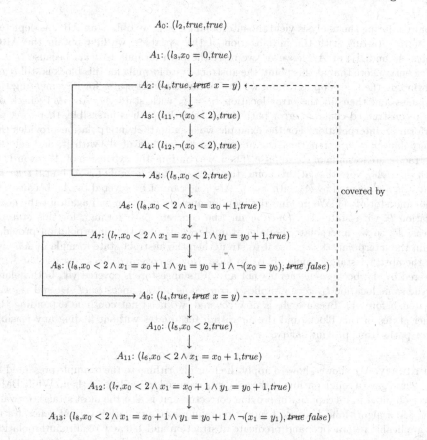

A_0: (l_2,*true*,*true*)

A_1: (l_3,$x_0 = 0$,*true*)

A_2: (l_4,*true*, ~~*true*~~ $x = y$)

A_3: (l_{11},$\neg(x_0 < 2)$,*true*)

A_4: (l_{12},$\neg(x_0 < 2)$,*true*)

A_5: (l_5,$x_0 < 2$,*true*)

covered by

A_6: (l_8,$x_0 < 2 \wedge x_1 = x_0 + 1$,*true*)

A_7: (l_7,$x_0 < 2 \wedge x_1 = x_0 + 1 \wedge y_1 = y_0 + 1$,*true*)

A_8: (l_8,$x_0 < 2 \wedge x_1 = x_0 + 1 \wedge y_1 = y_0 + 1 \wedge \neg(x_0 = y_0)$, ~~*true*~~ *false*)

A_9: (l_4,*true*, ~~*true*~~ $x = y$)

A_{10}: (l_5,$x_0 < 2$,*true*)

A_{11}: (l_6,$x_0 < 2 \wedge x_1 = x_0 + 1$,*true*)

A_{12}: (l_7,$x_0 < 2 \wedge x_1 = x_0 + 1 \wedge y_1 = y_0 + 1$,*true*)

A_{13}: (l_8,$x_0 < 2 \wedge x_1 = x_0 + 1 \wedge y_1 = y_0 + 1 \wedge \neg(x_1 = y_1)$, ~~*true*~~ *false*)

Fig. 6. Final ARG for applying the IMPACT algorithm to the example of Fig. 2

(3) *Cover*(s_1, s_2): A state s_1 gets marked as *covered* by another state s_2 if neither s_2 nor any of its ancestors are covered, both states belong to the same program location, the abstract-state formula of s_2 is implied by the formula of s_1, s_1 is not an ancestor of s_2, and s_2 was created before s_1.

As in predicate abstraction, the ABE blocks can be arbitrarily defined; again, we define a block to end at a loop head in our experimental evaluation of the IMPACT algorithm. Since this algorithm is also based on CEGAR, the unrolling of the CFA must again be configured to stop when the state-space exploration hits a state at the error location l_E, so that interpolation can be used to compute the abstractions.

The original presentation of the IMPACT algorithm [33] also includes a description of an optimization called *forced covering*, which improves the performance significantly but is not relevant for understanding the fundamental idea of the algorithm and exceeds the scope of our summary.

If we apply the IMPACT algorithm to the example program from Fig. 2 defining blocks to end at the loop head l_4 and assuming that both interpolations that are required during the analysis yield the interpolant $x = y$, we obtain an ARG as depicted in Fig. 6: Starting with the initialization of the variables, we first obtain the ARG states A_0 and A_1; at A_2, however, we reset the path formula to *true*, because l_4 is a block entry. Note that at this point, the abstract-state formula for this block is still *true*. Unwinding the first loop iteration, we first obtain abstract states for incrementing the variables and then hit the error location $l_E = l_8$ with state A_8. An SMT check on the reconstructed concrete error path shows that the path is infeasible, therefore, we perform an interpolation. For the example we assume that interpolation provides the interpolant $x = y$, strengthen the abstract-state formula of A_2 with it, and set the abstract-state formula of A_8 to *false*. Then, we continue the expansion of A_7 towards l_4 with state A_9. Note that at this point, the abstract-state formula for A_9 is still *true*, so that it is not covered by A_2 with $x = y$. Also, A_2 cannot be covered by A_9, because A_2 is an ancestor of A_9. We unwind the loop for another iteration and again hit the error location l_8 with state A_{13}. Once again, the concrete path formula for this state is infeasible, so we interpolate. For the example we assume that interpolation provides again the interpolant $x = y$, use it to strengthen the abstract-state formula of A_9, and set the abstract-state formula of A_{13} to *false*. Now, a coverage check reveals that A_9 is covered by A_2, because neither A_9 nor any of its ancestors is covered yet, both belong to the same location l_4, $x = y$ implies $x = y$, A_9 is not an ancestor of A_2, and A_2 was created before A_9. Because A_9 is now covered, we need not continue expanding the other states in this block, and the algorithm terminates without finding any feasible error paths, thus proving safety.

Summary. We showed how to apply the four algorithms to the example presented in Fig. 2 and gave a rough outline of the concepts required to implement them. While BMC is very limited in its capacity of proving correctness, it is also the most straightforward of the four algorithms, because k-induction requires an auxiliary-invariant generator to be applicable in practice, and predicate abstraction and IMPACT require interpolation techniques. While invariant generator and interpolation engine are usually treated as a black box in the description of these algorithms, the efficiency and effectiveness of the techniques depends on the quality of these modules.

3   Evaluation

We evaluate bounded model checking, k-induction, predicate abstraction, and IMPACT, on a large set of verification tasks and compare the approaches.

Benchmark Set. As benchmark set we use the verification tasks from the 2016 Competition on Software Verification (SV-COMP'16) [7]. We took all 4 779 verification tasks from all categories except *ArraysMemSafety*, *HeapMemSafety*, *Overflows*, *Recursive*, *Termination*, and *Concurrency*, which are not supported by our implementations of the approaches. A total of 1 320 tasks in the benchmark set contain a known specification violation, while the rest of the tasks is assumed to be free of violations.

Experimental Setup. Our experiments were conducted on machines with two 2.6 GHz 8-Core CPUs (Intel Xeon E5-2650 v2) with 135 GB of RAM. The operating system was Ubuntu 16.04 (64 bit), using Linux 4.4 and OpenJDK 1.8. Each verification task was limited to two CPU cores, a CPU run time of 15 min and a memory

Table 1. Experimental results of the approaches for all 4 779 verification tasks, 1 320 of which contain bugs, while the other 3 459 are considered to be safe

Algorithm	BMC	k-induction	Predicate abstraction	Impact
Correct results	1024	2482	2325	2306
Correct proofs	649	2116	2007	1967
Correct alarms	375	366	318	339
False alarms	1	1	0	0
Timeouts	2786	2047	1646	1607
Out of memory	180	98	75	104
Other inconclusive	788	151	733	762
Times for correct results				
Total CPU time (h)	8.3	54	32	32
Avg. CPU time (s)	29	79	49	50
Times for correct proofs				
Total CPU time (h)	4.3	44	26	27
Avg. CPU time (s)	24	75	47	50
Times for correct alarms				
Total CPU time (h)	4.0	10	5.4	4.8
Avg. CPU time (s)	38	100	61	51

usage of 15 GB. We used version `cpachecker-1.6.8-vstte16` of CPACHECKER, with MATHSAT5 as SMT solver. We configured CPACHECKER to use the SMT theories over uninterpreted functions, bit vectors, and floats. To evaluate the algorithms, we used ABE for IMPACT and predicate abstraction [14]. For IMPACT we also activated the forced-covering optimization [33], and for k-induction we use continuously-refined invariants from an invariant generator that employs an abstract domain based on intervals [8]. For bounded model checking we use a configuration with forward-condition checking [23].

Experimental Validity. We implemented all evaluated algorithms using the same software-verification framework, CPACHECKER. This allows us to compare the actual algorithms instead of comparing different tools with different front ends and different utilities, thus eliminating influences on the results caused by such implementation differences unrelated to the actual algorithms.

Results. Table 1 shows the number of correctly solved verification tasks for each of the algorithms, as well as the time that was spent on producing these results. None of the algorithms reported incorrect proofs[4], there was one false alarm for bounded model checking, and one false alarm for k-induction. When an algorithm exceeds its time or memory limit, it is terminated inconclusively. Other inconclusive results are caused

---

[4] For BMC, real proofs are accomplished by successful forward-condition checks, which prove that no further unrolling is required to exhaustively explore the state space.

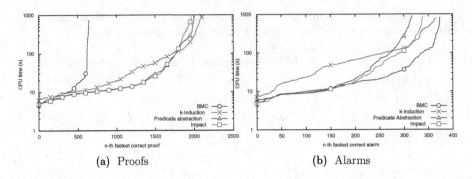

(a) Proofs   (b) Alarms

Fig. 7. Quantile plots for all correct proofs and alarms

by crashes, for example if an algorithm encounters an unsupported feature, such as recursion or large arrays. For k-induction, there is sometimes a chance that while other techniques must give up due to such an unsupported feature, waiting for the invariant generator to generate a strong invariant will help avoid the necessity of handling the problem, which is why k-induction has fewer crashes but instead more timeouts than the other algorithms. The quantile plots in Fig. 7 shows the accumulated number of successfully solved tasks within a given amount of CPU time. A data point (x, y) of a graph means that for the respective configuration, x is the number of correctly solved tasks with a run time of less than or equal to y seconds. As expected, bounded model checking produces both the fewest correct proofs and the most correct alarms, confirming BMC's reputation as a technique that is well-suited for finding bugs. Having the fewest amount of solved tasks, BMC also accumulates the lowest total CPU time for correct results. Its average CPU time is on par with the abstraction techniques, because even though the approach is less powerful than the other algorithms, it still is expensive, because it has to completely unroll loops. On average, BMC spends 3.0 s on formula creation, 4.7 s on SMT-checking the forward condition, and 13 s on SMT-checking the feasibility of error paths. The slowest technique by far is k-induction with continuously-refined invariant generation, which is the only technique that effectively uses both available cores by running the auxiliary-invariant generation in parallel to the k-induction procedure, thus almost spending twice as much CPU time as the other techniques. Like BMC, k-induction also does not use abstraction and spends additional time on building the step-case formula and generating auxiliary invariants, but can often prove safety by induction without unrolling loops. Considering that over the whole benchmark set, k-induction generates the highest number of correct results, the additional effort appears to be mostly well spent. On average, k-induction spends 4.4 s on formula creation in the base case, 4.2 s on SMT-checking the forward condition, 4.8 s on SMT-checking the feasibility of error paths, 22 s on creating the step-case formula, 21 s on SMT-checking inductivity, and 11 s on generating auxiliary invariants, which shows that much more effort is required in the inductive-step case than in the base case. Predicate abstraction and the IMPACT algorithm both perform very similarly for finding proofs, which matches the observations from earlier work [14]. An interesting difference is that the IMPACT algorithm finds more bugs. We attribute this observation to the fact that abstraction in the IMPACT algorithm is lazier than with predicate abstraction, which allows IMPACT larger parts of the state space in a shorter amount of time than predicate abstraction, causing IMPACT to find bugs sooner. For verification

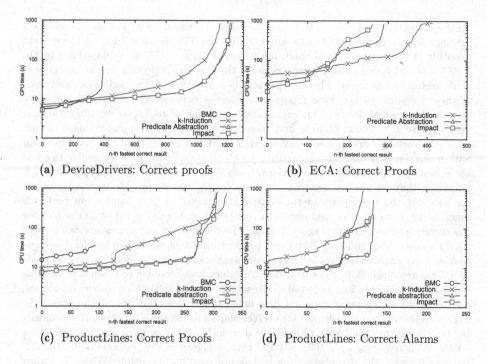

(a) DeviceDrivers: Correct proofs   **(b)** ECA: Correct Proofs

(c) ProductLines: Correct Proofs   **(d)** ProductLines: Correct Alarms

Fig. 8. Quantile plots for some of the categories

tasks without specification violations, however, the more eager predicate-abstraction technique pays off, because it requires fewer recomputations. Although in total, both abstraction techniques have to spend the same effort, this effort is distributed differently across the various steps: While, on average, predicate abstraction spends more time on computing abstractions (21 s) than the IMPACT algorithm (7.5 s), the latter requires the relatively expensive forced-covering step (13 s on average).

Although the plot in Fig. 7a suggests that k-induction with continuously-refined invariants outperforms the other techniques in general for finding proofs, a closer look at the results in individual categories, some of which are displayed in Fig. 8, reveals that how well an algorithm performs strongly depends on the type of verification task, but also reconfirms the observation of Fig. 7b that BMC consistently performs well for finding bugs. For example, on the safe tasks of the category on Linux device drivers in Fig. 8a, k-induction performs much worse than predicate abstraction and IMPACT. These device drivers are often C programs with many lines of code, containing pointer arithmetics and complex data structures. The interval-based auxiliary-invariant generator that we used for k-induction is not a good fit for such kinds of problems, and a lot of effort is wasted, while the abstraction techniques are often able to quickly determine that many operations on pointers and complex data structures are irrelevant to the safety property. We did not include the plot for the correct alarms in the category on device drivers, because each of the algorithms only solves about 20 tasks, and although k-induction and BMC are slower than the abstraction techniques, which matches the previous observations on the correct proofs, there is not enough data among the correct alarms to draw any conclusions. The quantile plot for the correct proofs in the category of event condition action systems (ECA) is displayed in Fig. 8b. BMC is not included in this figure, because there is no single task in the category it could unroll exhaustively. These tasks usually only consist of a single loop, but each of these loops contains very complex branching structures over many different integer variables, which leads to an exponential explosion of paths, so unrolling them is very expensive in terms of time and memory. Also, because in many tasks, almost all of the variables are in some way relevant to the reachability of the error location within this complex branching structure, the abstraction techniques are unable to come up with useful abstractions, and perform badly. The interval-based auxiliary-invariant generator that we use for k-induction, however, appears to provide invariants useful for handling the complexity of the control structures, so that k-induction performs much better than all other techniques in this category. We did not include the plot for the correct alarms in this category, because the abstraction techniques are not able to detect a single bug, and only BMC and k-induction detect one single bug for the same task, namely `Problem10_label46_false-unreach-call.c`. Figure 8c shows the quantile plot for correct proofs in the category on product lines. Similar to the proofs over all categories depicted in Fig. 7a, k-induction solves more tasks than the other techniques, but is becomes even more apparent how much slower than the other techniques it is. Figure 8d shows the quantile plot for correct alarms in the same category. It is interesting to observe that the IMPACT algorithm distinctly outperforms predicate abstraction on the tasks requiring over 100 s of CPU time, whereas in the previous plots, the differences between the two abstraction techniques were hardly visible. While, as shown in Fig. 8c, both techniques report almost the same amount of correct proofs (305 for predicate abstraction, 308 for IMPACT), IMPACT detects 130 bugs, whereas predicate abstraction detects only 121. This seems to indicate that the state space spanned by the different product-line features can be explored more quickly by lazy abstraction of IMPACT than with the more eager predicate abstraction.

Individual Examples. The previous discussion showed that while overall, the algorithms perform rather similar (apart from BMC being inappropriate for finding proofs, which is expected), each of them has some strengths due to which it outperforms the other algorithms on certain programs. In the following, we will list some examples from our benchmark set that were each solved by one of the algorithms, but not by the others, and give a short explanation of the reasons.

BMC. For example, only BMC can find bugs in the verification tasks `cs_lazy_false-unreach-call.i` and `rangesum40_false-unreach-call.i`. Surprisingly, by exhaustively unrolling a loop, BMC is the only of our four techniques that is able to prove safety for the tasks `sep20_true-unreach-call.i` and `cs_stateful_true-unreach-call.i`. All four of these tasks have in common that they contain bounded loops and arrays. The bounded loops are a good fit for BMC and enable it to prove correctness, while the arrays make it hard in practice for predicate abstraction and IMPACT to find good abstractions by interpolation. k-induction, which in theory is at least as powerful as BMC, spends too much time trying to generate auxiliary invariants and exceeds the CPU time limit before solving these tasks.

k-induction. k-induction is the only of our four techniques to prove the correctness of all of the safe tasks in the (non-simplified) `ssh` subset of our benchmark set, while none of the other three techniques can solve any of them. These tasks encode state machines, i.e., loops over switch statements with many cases, which in turn modify the variable that is considered by the switch statement. These loops are unbounded, so that BMC cannot exhaustively unroll them, and the loop invariants that are required to prove correctness of these tasks need to consider the different cases and their interaction across consecutive loop iterations, which is beyond the scope of the abstraction techniques but very easy for k-induction (cf. [8] for a detailed discussion of a similar example).

Predicate Abstraction. `toy_true-unreach-call_false-termination.cil.c` is a task that is only solved by predicate abstraction but by none of our other implementations. It consists of an unbounded loop that contains complex branching structure over integer variables, most of which only ever take the values 0, 1 or 2. Interpolation quickly discovers the abstraction predicates over these variables required to solve the task, but in this example, predicate abstraction profits from eagerly computing a sufficiently precise abstraction early after only 9 refinements while the lazy refinement technique used by IMPACT exceeds the time limit after 129 refinements, and the invariant generator used by k-induction fails to find the required auxiliary invariants before reaching the time limit.

IMPACT. The task `Problem05_label50_true-unreach-call.c` from the ECA subset of our benchmark set is only solved by IMPACT: BMC fails on this task due to the unbounded loop, and the invariant generator used by k-induction does not come up with any meaningful auxiliary invariants before exceeding the time limit. Predicate abstraction exceeds the time limit after only three refinements, and up to that point, over 80 % of its time is spent on eagerly computing abstractions. The lazy abstraction performed by IMPACT, however, allows it to progress quickly, and the algorithm finishes after 7 refinements.

4   Conclusion

This paper presents an overview over four state-of-the-art algorithms for SMT-based software model checking. First, we give a short explanation of each algorithm and illustrate the effect on how the state-space exploration looks like. Second, we provide the results of a thorough experimental study on a large number of verification tasks, in order to show the effect and performance of the different approaches, including a detailed discussion of particular verification tasks that can be solved by one algorithm while all others fail. In conclusion, there is no clear winner: there are disadvantages and advantages for each approach. We hope that our experimental overview is useful to understand the difference of the algorithms and the potential application areas.

Future Work. In our comparison, one well-known algorithm is missing: PDR (property-driven reachability) [16]. We plan to formalize this algorithm in our framework and implement it in CPACHECKER as well.

References

1. Aho, A.V., Sethi, R., Ullman, J.D.: Compilers: Principles, Techniques, and Tools. Addison-Wesley, Boston (1986)
2. Albarghouthi, A., Li, Y., Gurfinkel, A., Chechik, M.: UFO: A framework for abstraction- and interpolation-based software verification. In: Madhusudan, P., Seshia, S.A. (eds.) CAV 2012. LNCS, vol. 7358, pp. 672–678. Springer, Heidelberg (2012)
3. Ball, T., Cook, B., Levin, V., Rajamani, S.K.: SLAM and static driver verifier: Technology transfer of formal methods inside microsoft. In: Boiten, E.A., Derrick, J., Smith, G. (eds.) IFM 2004. LNCS, vol. 2999, pp. 1–20. Springer, Heidelberg (2004)
4. Ball, T., Levin, V., Rajamani, S.K.: A decade of software model checking with SLAM. Commun. ACM 54(7), 68–76 (2011)
5. Ball, T., Rajamani, S.K.: The SLAM project: Debugging system software via static analysis. In: POPL 2002, pp. 1–3. ACM (2002)
6. Beckert, B., Hähnle, R.: Reasoning and verification: State of the art and current trends. IEEE Intell. Syst. 29(1), 20–29 (2014)
7. Beyer, D.: Reliable and reproducible competition results with BENCHEXEC and witnesses (report on SV-COMP 2016). In: Chechik, M., Raskin, J.-F. (eds.) TACAS 2016. LNCS, vol. 9636, pp. 887–904. Springer, Heidelberg (2016)
8. Beyer, D., Dangl, M., Wendler, P.: Boosting k-induction with continuously-refined invariants. In: Kröning, D., Păsăreanu, C.S. (eds.) CAV 2015. LNCS, vol. 9206, pp. 622–640. Springer, Heidelberg (2015)
9. Beyer, D., Henzinger, T.A., Jhala, R., Majumdar, R.: The software model checker BLAST. Int. J. Softw. Tools Technol. Transf. 9(5–6), 505–525 (2007)
10. Beyer, D., Keremoglu, M.E.: CPACHECKER: A tool for configurable software verification. In: Gopalakrishnan, G., Qadeer, S. (eds.) CAV 2011. LNCS, vol. 6806, pp. 184–190. Springer, Heidelberg (2011)
11. Beyer, D., Keremoglu, M.E., Wendler, P.: Predicate abstraction with adjustable-block encoding. In: FMCAD 2010, pp. 189–197 (2010)
12. Beyer, D., Löwe, S., Wendler, P.: Benchmarking and resource measurement. In: Fischer, B., Geldenhuys, J. (eds.) SPIN 2015. LNCS, vol. 9232, pp. 160–178. Springer, Heidelberg (2015)
13. Beyer, D., Petrenko, A.K.: Linux driver verification. In: Margaria, T., Steffen, B. (eds.) ISoLA 2012. LNCS, vol. 7610, pp. 1–6. Springer, Heidelberg (2012)
14. Beyer, D., Wendler, P.: Algorithms for software model checking: Predicate abstraction vs. IMPACT. In: FMCAD 2012, pp. 106–113 (2012)
15. Biere, A., Cimatti, A., Clarke, E., Zhu, Y.: Symbolic model checking without BDDs. In: Cleaveland, W.R. (ed.) TACAS 1999. LNCS, vol. 1579, pp. 193–207. Springer, Heidelberg (1999)
16. Bradley, A.R.: SAT-based model checking without unrolling. In: Jhala, R., Schmidt, D. (eds.) VMCAI 2011. LNCS, vol. 6538, pp. 70–87. Springer, Heidelberg (2011)
17. Brain, M., Joshi, S., Kröning, D., Schrammel, P.: Safety verification and refutation by k-invariants and k-induction. In: Blazy, S., Jensen, T. (eds.) SAS 2015. LNCS, vol. 9291, pp. 145–161. Springer, Heidelberg (2015)
18. Clarke, E.M., Grumberg, O., Jha, S., Lu, Y., Veith, H.: Counterexample-guided abstraction refinement for symbolic model checking. J. ACM 50(5), 752–794 (2003)

19. Clarke, E., Kröning, D., Lerda, F.: A tool for checking ANSI-C programs. In: Jensen, K., Podelski, A. (eds.) TACAS 2004. LNCS, vol. 2988, pp. 168–176. Springer, Heidelberg (2004)
20. Cordeiro, L., Morse, J., Nicole, D., Fischer, B.: Context-bounded model checking with ESBMC 1.17 (competition contribution). In: Flanagan, C., König, B. (eds.) TACAS 2012. LNCS, vol. 7214, pp. 534–537. Springer, Heidelberg (2012)
21. Craig, W.: Linear reasoning. A new form of the Herbrand-Gentzen theorem. J. Symb. Log. **22**(3), 250–268 (1957)
22. Donaldson, A.F., Haller, L., Kröning, D., Rümmer, P.: Software verification using k-induction. In: Yahav, E. (ed.) SAS 2011. LNCS, vol. 6887, pp. 351–368. Springer, Heidelberg (2011)
23. Gadelha, M.Y.R., Ismail, H.I., Cordeiro, L.C.: Handling loops in bounded model checking of C programs via k-induction. STTT, 1–18 (2015)
24. Graf, S., Saïdi, H.: Construction of abstract state graphs with PVS. In: Grumberg, O. (ed.) CAV 1997. LNCS, vol. 1254, pp. 72–83. Springer, Heidelberg (1997)
25. Gurfinkel, A., Kahsai, T., Navas, J.A.: SEAHORN: A framework for verifying C programs (competition contribution). In: Baier, C., Tinelli, C. (eds.) TACAS 2015. LNCS, vol. 9035, pp. 447–450. Springer, Heidelberg (2015)
26. Heizmann, M., Dietsch, D., Greitschus, M., Leike, J., Musa, B., Schätzle, C., Podelski, A.: ULTIMATE AUTOMIZER with two-track proofs (competition contribution). In: Chechik, M., Raskin, J.-F. (eds.) TACAS 2016. LNCS, vol. 9636, pp. 950–953. Springer, Heidelberg (2016)
27. Henzinger, T.A., Jhala, R., Majumdar, R., Sutre, G.: Lazy abstraction. In: POPL 2002, pp. 58–70. ACM (2002)
28. Jhala, R., Majumdar, R.: Software model checking. ACM Comput. Surv. **41**(4), 21:1–21:54 (2009)
29. Kahsai, T., Tinelli, C.: PKIND: A parallel k-induction based model checker. In: PDMC 2011. EPTCS, vol. 72, pp. 55–62 (2011)
30. Khoroshilov, A., Mutilin, V., Petrenko, A., Zakharov, V.: Establishing linux driver verification process. In: Pnueli, A., Virbitskaite, I., Voronkov, A. (eds.) PSI 2009. LNCS, vol. 5947, pp. 165–176. Springer, Heidelberg (2010)
31. Kildall, G.A.: A unified approach to global program optimization. In: POPL 1973, pp. 194–206. ACM (1973)
32. McMillan, K.L.: Interpolation and SAT-based model checking. In: Hunt, W.A., Somenzi, F. (eds.) CAV 2003. LNCS, vol. 2725, pp. 1–13. Springer, Heidelberg (2003)
33. McMillan, K.L.: Lazy abstraction with interpolants. In: Ball, T., Jones, R.B. (eds.) CAV 2006. LNCS, vol. 4144, pp. 123–136. Springer, Heidelberg (2006)
34. Nielson, F., Nielson, H.R., Hankin, C.: Principles of Program Analysis. Springer, Heidelberg (1999)
35. Rakamarić, Z., Emmi, M.: SMACK: Decoupling source language details from verifier implementations. In: Biere, A., Bloem, R. (eds.) CAV 2014. LNCS, vol. 8559, pp. 106–113. Springer, Heidelberg (2014)
36. Rocha, H., Ismail, H.I., Cordeiro, L.C., Barreto, R.S.: Model checking embedded C software using k-induction and invariants. In: SBESC 2015. IEEE (2015)
37. Schrammel, P., Kröning, D.: 2LS for program analysis. In: Chechik, M., Raskin, J.-F. (eds.) TACAS 2016. LNCS, vol. 9636, pp. 905–907. Springer, Heidelberg (2016)
38. Schuppan, V., Biere, A.: Liveness checking as safety checking for infinite state spaces. Electr. Notes Theor. Comput. Sci. **149**(1), 79–96 (2006)

39. Sinz, C., Merz, F., Falke, S.: LLBMC: A bounded model checker for LLVM's interme-
    diate representation (competition contribution). In: Flanagan, C., König, B. (eds.)
    TACAS 2012. LNCS, vol. 7214, pp. 542–544. Springer, Heidelberg (2012)
40. Wahl, T.: The k-induction principle (2013). http://www.ccs.neu.edu/home/wahl/
    Publications/k-induction.pdf
41. Wendler, P.: CPAChecker with sequential combination of explicit-state analysis
    and predicate analysis. In: Piterman, N., Smolka, S.A. (eds.) TACAS 2013. LNCS,
    vol. 7795, pp. 613–615. Springer, Heidelberg (2013)

Author Index

Printed in the United States
By Bookmasters